D1101619

LAST OF THE
MEDICINE MEN

LAST OF THE
MEDICINE MEN

BENEDICT ALLEN

To my Godson, Hugh

Acknowledgements
Ten per cent of my income from this book goes to the Little Stars dance troupe of the Kyzyl School for the Deaf, by way of thanks to those communities around the world who have contributed to this project.

For specialist knowledge in Siberut, my thanks to Reimar Schefold, Gerard Persoon, and Aurelius Yan; in Tuva, Piers Vitebsky, Misha Maltsev, Mongush Kenin-Lopsan, S.I. Vajnstejn, Dina Oyan, Aldynai, Rollanda and Sayana; in Haiti, Chantal Regnault, Lois Wilcken, Leah Gordon, Aboudja, Fabrice, and Edele; and in Mexico, Silviano Camberos, Susana Valadez and Marciano de la Cruz. Thanks also to John Hesling, for guidance and support, likewise to Charlotte Lochhead, Sally Potter, Christine King, Linda Blakemore and David Cottingham; also Catherine Marsh, Bob Long, Salim Salam, Ruhi Hamid, Caroline Gucklhorn, Becky Atkinson, Estien McKenzie, Edward Capes, Glenn Chappell, Alia Syed, and in the field, Wayne Derrick, Nick Reeks, Michael Yorke, Richard Stanley, Immo Horn, Chinna Boapeah, Dennis Madden and Bill Rudolph. Finally, to Hi-Tec, whose footwear still hasn't let me down, and to Louise Thorogood, Colin Allen, Suzie Allen, Katie, Paul, Luc and Rowan Pestille for their support through two years.

This book is published to accompany the television series
Last of the Medicine Men, first broadcast on BBC 2 in 2000
Executive producer: Bob Long · Producer: Salim Salam

Published by BBC Worldwide Limited, Woodlands, 80 Wood Lane, London W12 0TT
First published in 2000

Copyright © Benedict Allen 2000. The moral right of the author has been asserted

ISBN 0 563 55121 6

Commissioning editor: Sally Potter · Project editor: Charlotte Lochhead
Text editor: Christine King · Designer: Linda Blakemore

Photographs by Steve Watkins for Indonesia (except section page 3, below) and Haiti (except section page 6). All other photographs by Benedict Allen.
Maps by All Terrain Mapping

Set in Berling by Ferdinand Pageworks
Printed and bound in Great Britain by Butler & Tannner Ltd, Frome and London
Jacket and plate sections printed by Lawrence Allen Ltd, Weston-super-Mare

CONTENTS

INTRODUCTION

For almost twenty years, on and off, I've had the rare privilege of living alone for months at a time with remote peoples all around the globe. My aim was simple: to learn from each community, to lay myself open to its way of life and the traditions that underlie it. I wasn't interested in travel as such, but I was a writer with a burning desire to explore other ways of viewing the world. My simple, if rather too heroic, philosophy was if that meant sitting in the steaming New Guinea forest for six months at a stretch, or being scarred in an initiation ceremony, so be it – I felt I should have the courage of my convictions as some sort of modern-day explorer. However, underlying this there was something else. For all its emphasis on 'progress', its undeniable material wealth, I felt that my own society was failing to provide the answers for a fulfilling, contented life. I felt that there must be better ways of doing things. And I knew that I wasn't alone in thinking this.

Though we may congratulate ourselves on having more or less explored the world, we in the West somehow seem to be less and less confident in ourselves. As our rapacious culture engulfs others, indeed, seemingly threatens the very fabric of the planet, many, just like me, are wondering about the price of our progress, and even wonder if the West's scientific, rationalizing culture has helped us 'progress' at all. It's as if, caught up in a hectic whirl of consumerism, and forced onward by commercial pressures, we have lost our way. No wonder then that there's increasing interest in other cultures that seem to allow harmony with nature, cultures that might hint at a better way forward. We are now all aware of the last of the Amazon Indians who, unlike exploiters from outside, use their forest without destroying it. They seem to live now much as all our ancestors once did, so might perhaps show what has been left behind in the march of 'progress'. In a sharply ironic twist to the history of exploration, though it is we in the West who charted the world – the lands occupied by 'primitive tribes' – in this light it may be we, not they, who are the true primitives.

At the hub of many of these exotic communities are colourful characters once largely dismissed as mumbo-jumbo merchants who preyed on the superstitious. In my travels I found, time and time again, that it was difficult to ignore local 'spirit-men'. Charismatic and mysterious, they would demonstrate their formidable herbal knowledge or, more rarely, the spirit world that they interpreted for their people. I remember how Pablito, a Matses Indian of the Peruvian Amazon, used to go on his spiritual quests after a child blew a green snuff called nú-nú up his nose. In Australia's Gibson Desert, a middle-aged aborigine called Wili talked of his power as coming to him through crystals, one red, one white, from the Dreamtime, a sacred dimension that empowered time and life itself. Up in the Andes a *curandero* tried, with spectacular lack of success, to enlighten me with a dose of the hallucinogenic – or spiritually charged – cactus San Pedro; and in Borneo, the *manang* went into a trance, walking and paddling his way through a thickly forested spirit world to negotiate with the spirits living there and save the life of an old lady.

All around the world it was the same – among the Maasai of the Savannah, Himba of the Namib, Gabbra of the Chalbi, or for that matter the Warao of Orinoco mangroves, or the Hmong of the northern Thai hills. In traditional societies there is this central figure charged with the responsibility of interpreting and healing problems in the community. Increasingly now, with growing respect in the West for the cultures that nurture them, such figures are depicted as wise men, who maintain a harmony with the land, a harmony with God or the gods, and have much to teach us – or do they? Mightn't they be fantasy figures? To paraphrase G. K. Chesterton, when people give up believing in God, they don't believe in nothing – they believe in anything.

It was only a matter of time, I felt, before I dedicated myself exclusively to these mysterious characters. I would find out how they served their people, and by implication see if they might, potentially, serve us. Two years ago, the chance at last came to embark on the project, and this book, and a TV series, is the result.

One obstacle was soon apparent – what to call these spiritual specialists. 'Witchdoctor' was a word associated with Africa, and furthermore conjured up a crude picture of people with bones through their noses. 'Faith healer' clearly wasn't right either – if you're living in the forests of innermost Sumatra, it isn't a question of having 'faith' or not in your spirits. They are everywhere, and there is nothing to be done without them.

Then what about the term 'shaman'? It's been said that shamanism is more a technique than philosophy and organization, and is therefore not a religion *per se*, but it seems to have been practised in one form or other by all our hunter–gatherer ancestors. It is therefore perhaps the bedrock of all religions. The classic definition of a shaman, given by anthropologist Mircea Eliade, is that he 'specializes in a trance during which his soul is believed to leave his body and ascend to the sky or descend to the underworld'. This, however, would exclude many of the characters I'd encountered: in Africa, for instance, really only a few relict hunter–gatherer peoples, notably in the Kalahari, go on these trance-journeys.

Traditionally, the shaman-figure seems to have been associated with peoples who were still nomadic, operating in tight tribal units as we all once did, in a daily struggle with the ever-threatening environmental forces. While every adult member of the clan generally played a part in the communal tasks of everyday life, the shaman character was the one specialist, the earliest professional – alongside the midwife and prostitute: the person everyone could turn to, who was responsible for maintaining an awareness of the resources around, and could communicate with the spirit world on which everything depended. The shaman still exists in this original form in the remote world; now, as in our ancestors' day, he uses hallucinogens, dance, the drum, fasting, to help him on his journey into that spirit dimension.

In the end, I opted to call these mercurial characters simply 'medicine men' – whatever else they did, their main activity was to heal rifts between the physical world and the spiritual. Generally, though, I've tried to use the name that they themselves go by: the *kereis* of Siberut, the *khams* of Tuva, the *oungan* of Haiti, the *marakate* of Mexico. I've tried to avoid the word 'tribe' because in this context the word unnecessarily separates these people from the rest of us, and likewise 'magic' because of its fanciful associations, ones which we don't attribute to, for example, the power of prayer. I have also been wary of using the words 'natural' and 'nature' because in most of these societies the workings of man and things 'natural' are inseparable.

This is a record of my experiences, notes from the frontier, rather than an attempt to review a vast subject – which centres on religion, but touches pharmacy, history, sociology, psychiatry, anthropology, ecology and every other facet of life that the medicine man serves. I decided that my most useful contribution would be to go out there and give a clear and honest account of what I felt I saw with my own eyes.

The big challenge was: how would I ever get inside medicine men's heads? They are special even among their own, usually isolated and therefore guarded, community, part of an elite group to which initiates gain access only after months or years. They continue to learn through life. And in sharing their knowledge, they make themselves vulnerable – the powers they possess can be used against them as well as for them. It is like giving someone a loaded gun. Therefore I couldn't even guarantee that the *kereis*, or anyone else, would open up much to me. And even if they did, how would I understand what they meant? You can't see beliefs.

However far I succeeded in my quest, there were great rewards. The lives of these remote people seemed simple, but their esoteric knowledge, their pantheons, had a bewildering complexity. Some medicine men stunned me with their apparent foresight, wisdom, cures. Others – though these were generally individuals not accountable to a community – seemed downright frauds. One way or another, though, they all commanded respect – both because of a fear of their spiritual power, and because of their knowledge of healing, for example through herbs. (We shouldn't forget that even nowadays, some 60 per cent of our own drugs are wholly or partly natural in origin.) Above all, though, is their insight into the human mind.

We may have mapped our planet and solar system, and understand even the universe in outline; but there is another frontier that we have done little to push back, and it is the future of exploration today: it is the world within us, not the world beyond. Our minds are little understood – why we dream, how we remember, how mere belief in something can in itself be enough to physically strengthen and heal. But the workings of the mind are the speciality of the medicine men; this is their world, and sometimes it seemed to me that there was no mystery there for them at all.

INDONESIA
SPIRIT HEALERS OF THE RAINFOREST

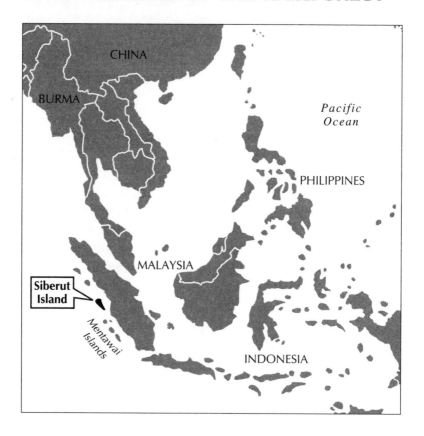

CHAPTER ONE

'If the wood spirits were here, then I would be afraid to talk about them.
They would say, "Listen to him explaining about the sacred things!"
But they are not here so I can talk to you. And the ancestor spirits,
if they were here, I could say to them, "Please, here are my children,
they want to know the way, the meaning of things and to understand." '
Amam Maom, kerei

My exploration of the medicine man's world would begin,
I decided, with a journey to the island of Siberut. I had
been there once before, and remembered two extraordinary
men I'd met – only a short encounter but something about them
must have profoundly impressed me because I could recall
them vividly, even after thirteen years.

To Siberut, then. The island in itself made a good starting
point. The largest of the Mentawai chain, running to the west of
Sumatra, it had with the help of an oceanic trench remained
isolated from the rest of the Indonesian archipelago for half a
million years. Siberut's remote location, together with the tem-
peramental nature of the Indian Ocean, had enabled its people's
culture and forest to survive, to a remarkable degree, the ravages
of the outside world.

I set out in a wooden boat with hand-carved portholes on a
sea-crossing that would take at least the full night – indeed, we
had turned back to the Sumatran mainland once already, having
begun to sink. There was ample time to reflect on my first visit
of all those years ago.

Still clear in my memory was Seggulubek, a little settlement
spread out along a sandy path – women carrying sugarcane from
forest gardens, boys and girls with bright, dark eyes, beach crabs,
coconuts rolling in the surf. But one memory stood out from all
others. Late one night there'd been a banging on the tin door of

my room. Drunks? Rabble-rousers? Whoever they were, I decided that it would not be a good idea to let them in.

At first light, I opened the door cautiously and found two men in bark loincloths squatting at my feet. Both men were in the middle of sorting some arrows. They hastily put them back in their quivers, and stood up. I stepped back; whatever I was expecting, it wasn't this. They had long hair that was tied in a red band, and both wore bead crowns decorated with hibiscus flowers. Around their necks hung sepire bead necklaces; little bells dangled from them. Tattoo lines curled up their faces, down their throats and descended down their chests and legs. Other tattoos rose up, in garters, hoops. Then I saw their eyes were friendly, even gentle – in fact, mischievous charm was radiating from both men. They beamed at me, revealing teeth stained by prolific smoking. It was not clear what they wanted – they did not speak Indonesian – but hung around as if they just wanted to sit and be with me. I gave them cigarettes and they jokingly examined my pockets for more.

With the language barrier, there wasn't much we could do together but sit and smile. I later learned from the villagers, who were clearly appalled, even scared, by them, that they came from Sakkudei, in the remote forest. They were 'backward'. They lived as most people had, until the Indonesian government came along. Not that the Mentawai people had been untouched until then – their culture was on a losing wicket when the very first godfearing outsiders began taking an interest in the islands in the sixteenth century. Spice traders and pirates were replaced by Dutch colonialists, and then, on Independence in 1950, the East Indies became Indonesia, with a centralized government in Java. In an attempt to unite this huge and disparate archipelago, composed of 13,700 islands and 300 ethnic groups, President Sukarno introduced the Pancasila, a doctrine for the Republic's citizens – central to this being a belief in One God. This aimed to isolate the communists – theoretically atheists – and usefully would also help pressurize those in need of civilizing to hurry up and advance. These were generally the animists, that is, those such as the

Mentawai, and other 'medicine men cultures' which attributed souls and spirits to objects around us.

Now, without goodbyes, the two forest men were suddenly gone; they walked back into their world. And now I saw they had, without saying a word I could understand, changed my view of the island. Seggulubek had been a paradise, the verdant forest just a little bit ordered to man's liking, yet still alongside it, unthreatening to it. But now I saw that this charming settlement was the outside world, a vanguard, a beginning of the end. And those two men were from the old, forest world that was about to be lost for good.

All these years later, travelling again to Siberut through the night, I knew the two men were *kereis*, who had the duty of dealing with the spirits and souls which were all about us. The Mentawai traditionally believed that everything had a soul – the trees, the pebbles in the river. And these souls, and the wood, earth, sea and ancestor spirits, all the invisible beings which shared our world must be shown respect – just as we show respect to members of our family. If you killed a monkey without apologizing to its soul, you might be attacked by an aggrieved monkey spirit. This was an integrated universe, a disruption of the spirit world causing a disruption in ours. And it was the job of the *kerei* to maintain the harmony, to ensure that no spirit or soul was upset – not easy, when you live off the plants and animals of the forest.

Nor could it have been easy to continue your job when your rituals were banned – along with tattooing, the wearing of loincloths and other traditional elements of your culture. While various government schemes to log the forests of Siberut had been thwarted, following international outrage, that hadn't stopped Siberut's culture being clear-felled. Aurelius Yan, who originated from Siberut and was coming along to help me on this trip, told me his home village of Saibi had been 'modernized' along government lines. Not only did this have the desired effect of putting Backward People Into Civilized Houses – these built according to the Javanese idea of a model village – but neatly it also hindered all the traditional, now prohibited, rituals, because the new houses weren't big enough for clan gatherings.

And yet, according to Yan, still somehow surviving among these people were the individuals I'd come to see: the *kereis*, those chosen by the spirits to act as their messengers. Or had Yan been away too long? He now lived in Amsterdam, and claimed the *kereis* would want only brass bells as presents – they used these to call their spirits. Wasn't that a touch romantic? I suspected that Nike trainers or a Sony Walkman would be nearer the mark.

Our party – my BBC producer John Hesling travelling with Yan and me – arrived off Siberut at daybreak on 14 March 1999, the sun rising from a marbled mauve sea to light the mist unwinding from the island's forest. It was reassuring to see the forest – as if the island itself was still breathing. The main settlement, Muara Siberut, had spread out along the shore, but was still not dominating the coast, only clinging on. As on my earlier visit, there were men knee-deep out in the mud with the white egrets, sweeping the shallow waters with huge fishing nets extending from each arm. The nets flapped slowly like the wings of alighted butterflies, and terns swept the sky.

Yan's brother Anjel came alongside in a motorized canoe and we made for the silt harbour. Coming ashore, I could see that where once there'd been only wood and tin houses, a here-to-stay mosque had mushroomed. The muddy ditches were now cement troughs, and coral was no longer flourishing offshore under the turquoise bay water but could be observed lying dead, underfoot, where it had been crunched into paths.

A road pierced the forest – unusable to cars, of which there were apparently still scarcely any on the island – and the local people, accustomed to walking along forest tracks, made their way along the spacious highway single file.

We bought provisions and were soon on our way to Taileleu, down in the south, where Yan had arranged for me to meet an old *kerei* called Amam Maom. Apparently, he no longer wore the long uncut hair of a *kerei*, this having been proscribed by officials long ago, but his belief in his role was undiminished.

We took a short cut through the mangroves – mudskippers flipping and blinking around the roots, crabs twitching and manoeuvring – then we curved out to sea. Huge rollers played with our boat as we followed the forested shore, till we were at last adjacent to Taileleu, some huts just visible behind a line of palms. We jumped ashore, and hauled the boat up on to the beach a little. A coral track led inland, so I went ahead, trying to remember what it was like on my last visit, when my boat had stopped here to pick up rattan. There'd been a sandy track, palm-thatched houses…

But not now. There was a cement path and corrugated iron roofs. And before long there was a little shop with a satellite dish. There were youths hanging around a table-tennis table. Further up the track there were rows of plank houses, some with neat flowerbeds, others with a lick of paint. I walked a little further. Men and women in T-shirts were coming and going, carrying fish and sugarcane; there were clothes hanging on lines, and smelling of fake-lemon detergent. 'Money from all the lobsters,' Yan explained. 'They're rich now.' They wouldn't be for long. Soon the lobsters would have gone the way of the crocodiles (once protected by taboos but now shot out of existence), and rattan (also previously subject to certain taboos, now being extracted from the island, roots and all), and fishing (now being cleaned up by factory ships).

I kept walking, hoping for something left from the old days. On my first visit, I remembered glimpsing an old *uma*, one of the family houses around which life once revolved. It had been more than a large thatched building, it had been a social unit, and also a spiritual one – it seemed that, traditionally, even buildings had souls, and the wellbeing of the clan was dependent on the *uma*'s soul being content.

So far, I wasn't doing well – a chainsaw was eating through a nearby tree, and some youths were kicking a ball about. However, the houses were getting further apart and between them I had glimpses of the forest. I could now hear the hissing of the tree insects; it was as if the forest was getting stronger, was regaining its voice.

Now the houses around me had the traditional sago-palm roofs, and twice I saw in the shadows old ladies who weren't wearing T-shirts but necklaces of beads. Their teeth had been filed to points in the customary way and across their dry, wrinkled skin were tattoos just as I remembered, hoops rising to their shoulders, bars, bands, straps encompassing their wrists. They weren't *kereis* – who were anyway always men – but old-timers adorned the way everyone used to be. None the less, here among the chainsaws and radios, they seemed like nuns, living their lives on a more spiritual plane.

It wasn't until the next day, having installed ourselves in an unused house, that we set eyes on Amam Maom himself. I was standing by the nearby creek, filming the women slipping their canoes into the water for a day's fishing, when an old man walked up with a paddle in his hand, and stopped in front of me. He wore a T-shirt embossed with the name of an American sports team, baggy shorts and a very wide-brimmed pink hat. He stood there in this hat, right in the way of my filming, and grinned.

'*Selamat pagi*,' I said, wishing him good morning, and hoping he would get out of the way soon.

'*Pagi*,' he said. But he didn't move. He took off his hat, so I could see him better, and I realized that I was meant to guess who he was.

It can't be, I thought. Where is his *kerei* bead necklace? His flowers? I looked again into the shadow cast by the pink hat. 'Amam Maom?'

He grinned even harder, and said he was sorry, but now he had to go off into the sago forests with his wife.

'When will you be back?' I asked as he walked off.

'*Nanti, nanti*,' he said vaguely over his shoulder. Later, later.

We had a slow day, filming the freshwater crabs, and old men on expeditions to gather roofing palms and women to gather fish. All this time I wondered about Amam Maom. What did this pink-hatted man believe in now? I wondered if he even owned a *kerei* bead crown of the sort I remembered from over a decade ago.

That night, Yan led us with a paraffin lamp through Taileleu and finally over a slippery log bridge to Amam Maom's house. He lived with his son, Maom – the Mentawai take the name of their first born, so 'Amam Maom' simply means Father of Maom – though his son ran a busy shop adjacent to his house and didn't look likely himself to want to communicate with the spirits.

I hadn't been able to picture where an ancient *kerei* might live, but I certainly didn't expect a plush suburban house with a TV blaring into the darkness from it, and around the screen assembled perhaps fifty village children. Their goggling eyes were lit by the blue light; they seemed as mesmerized as the moths that flitted around the clearing.

Amam Maom himself was up on the veranda. He might wear baggy shorts instead of a loincloth, but he seemed oblivious to the approaching twenty-first century, the TV his son was using to lure children to his little shop. He was fixing a fishing net with his wife, a gentle-faced woman who sat with her knees neatly tucked under her. Over their heads was suspended a stuffed bird; across one rafter were images of a spread-eagled monkey, across another, a monkey walking.

As we came up the steps, the old couple put down the net, and the children rushed to offer their stools. For a moment, their attention was away from the Hong Kong movie and on us, this delegation of foreigners from nowhere. Receiving us, his special guests, I noticed Amam Maom's chest visibly puffed up a little with pride. And, just as Yan had predicted, he was thrilled to receive a gift of brass bells – he wasn't waiting for his Nike trainers.

After the opening pleasantries, conducted through Yan, who was interpreting the Mentawai for me, we asked Amam Maom to begin by telling us about himself. 'I was married long ago,' he said, 'when I was still free.'

I turned to Yan. 'Free?'

Yan said that he meant he was free because he still wasn't a *kerei* – a *kerei*'s life was circumscribed by taboos which kept him spiritually pure and strong. 'He says that there are so many things he can't eat any more. It's very hard for him.'

'Eels,' he said to Yan, 'tell him I can't eat eels!'

At this point, we were interrupted by the arrival of two men who wanted to know why we were here. 'They are afraid a bit,' Yan explained. 'They think you are from the government...'

Amam Maom wasn't the slightest worried what they thought – perhaps he was too old to care. He sat blinking at us, waiting for the next question. He seemed to be enjoying himself; we, the foreigners, had come around the world to speak to *him*, not the old village head.

'Why are you not interviewing the old *kepala desa?*' one of the men interrupted again. 'He is so very wise,' he said.

'So very rich,' added the other.

There were a lot of reasons why we weren't interviewing the old *kepala desa*. Just one of them was that he was a trader and no doubt more than happy that a predecessor had moved the village from the forested interior, in accordance with official policy. Just how badly conceived the new settlements are by virtually any other measure – religious, environmental, health, cultural, democratic – is spelt out by the researcher, Wanda Avé, one of the few people to have seriously studied the Mentawai. Traditionally, villages were inland – away from tidal waves, nearer the forests that provided their staple food, sago, building materials and meat. Because Mentawai society was egalitarian, labour could be split equally between the men, who focused on the forest itself as a resource, and the women, who specialized in the use of the rivers of the interior. They had a non-hierarchical leadership, which better reflected local needs, their large clan houses – as opposed to the small government-approved houses – ensured closer social support and cohesion, and sago was healthier, more efficient, less time-consuming and in just about every other way better than the food of the Civilized, rice.

The two men at Amam Maom's house only meant well – and they had a point. After all, now the children could go to school, wear uniforms and have (at a cost) access to western medicine. But in the end the men went away confused by our lack of interest in their advancement, just as village heads worldwide are baffled by the growing western disenchantment with

Progress. To many westerners, having lost what they are trying to get away from, Progress simply doesn't seem as good an idea as it once did.

We turned back to Amam Maom. I asked him if he enjoyed being a *kerei*.

'I feel special,' he said. 'And if I'm doing a two-day ritual to chase out a bad spirit, or bring in a good one, I get given six things. I get a chicken, a chick, a bell for my neck, a sago tree… a… I can't remember, but six things. It's very nice.'

'So it's good being a *kerei*.'

'It's hard work. You wouldn't believe how much hard work it is. And I'm quite old, you know.'

We had some discussion about this and decided in the end that he was probably older than sixty, and probably – though not necessarily – younger than eighty.

'And you like this new settlement of Taileleu?'

'Actually,' he said, 'no. I prefer to live out there in the forest and the spirits like it as well. It keeps my soul happy, and so I do not get sick.' He added, 'But that telly is quite an interesting thing.'

'So there's not much that appeals to you here…'

'Some things don't appeal to me at all.' Reading between the lines, one of these unappealing things was the *kepala desa*. 'He checks to see if this house is too dirty. If so, he knows I've lingered too long at my forest house. Then he says, "You are not quite listening to the government, so I will have to send you to Muara Siberut." By this he means I might have to go there to cut long grass in the sun, or help build the Pointless Road – the one from the harbour. Sometimes it is better just to pay him to avoid that.'

'And your son, he visits you in the forest often?'

'Twice,' said Amam Maom.

'Twice a month?'

'Twice. Twice so far.'

I looked over beyond the TV to Maom, who was dishing out sweeties in the little shop. It wasn't as bad as it looked, because apparently Maom did allow his father to heal his children when they were sick, but still it must be hard for Amam Maom. I suspected *kereis* would one day be like vicars often were in my culture, doing the prayers for the rest of us, who only go to church once a year.

Yan and I walked back through the darkness and fireflies over the slippery bridge and to our house, and I thought of how old men were sent to work like slaves cutting grass. Passing tourists probably thought that these slow, bent-over figures were peasants, and of little consequence. But once, as *kereis*, they would have been seen as the key to life itself.

We were woken the next morning by a hollow knocking sound: 'tock-tock, tock-tock'. It was a double beat, like the rhythm of a heart, quavering through the trees. Our neighbours were beating a *duddukat*, a set of three or four hollowed-out logs, celebrating having killed a wild pig. We learned that it had been trying to seduce one of their domesticated herd, and had been killed with a single poisoned arrow. The men enthusiastically cut the pig up, stuffing chunks into bamboo tubes for baking over the fire, and an hour later everyone was flat on their backs, bloated, having somehow consumed it all.

Amam Maom offered to take us to his forest house, but first wanted to finish a chore somewhere nearby where he kept some pigs. We took him in our canoe through sago forests and nipa palm, passing fishing women paddling their canoes, their heads under round palm-leaf hats, and moored opposite a little hut on stilts. We clambered up the grey riverbank mud, to be greeted both by Amam Maom's sister, who lived here to keep an eye on things, and a herd of pigs. The pigs got over-excited seeing Amam Maom, and followed us to the house, looking up at us expectantly. They looked as if they were used to getting a little treat.

However, Amam Maom got straight down to work. He might have been sixty years old (or he might have been eighty) but he was soon hacking away at the forest, extracting poles with which to reinforce his house. 'I'm so busy, it's like having a thousand insects chasing me from dawn to dusk,' he said, whirling his parang about. 'And I'm a *kerei* as well!'

Sometimes Amam Maom had a moment to point out the medicinal herbs that were growing among the weeds, surviving despite the ever-questing pigs. 'Can't eat that one,' he said, jabbing at a plant with long, paddle-like leaves and a fruit like a red hand-grenade. 'It's *totonan* – a sour food, taboo. And this,' he said, plucking a pair of soft green leaves, 'is *aile'ppet*.' He deftly tucked them into his necklace, and threw away two leaves that were already there, but now wilting. 'It is to make your body cool. This is what your soul likes, to be cool.'

What this meant to him, I couldn't begin to understand. 'You learned these herbs in some sort of *kerei* initiation ceremony?' I asked. With Yan's help, I'd already written a list of thirty herbs – and I'd only been here for a couple of days.

'Well,' Amam Maom said, 'even young boys learn herbs, as they work in the forest. Girls spend their time fishing and cooking, so they know less. But I learnt most when I was initiated, yes. And I've initiated twenty-four *kereis* myself!' He turned to Yan and laughed. 'Make sure he writes that down properly: twenty-four!'

Then it was back to work, tying up some sago-palm roofing. As we watched, Yan said quietly, 'He doesn't want to talk about it, but he told me to say that many medicines he is taught in dreams, the time your soul travels away from the body and meets the ancestors, as well as by the souls of other living *kerei* and laymen. This knowledge is very secret: you have been given this knowledge personally by an ancestor or spirit.' I understood that the Mentawai saw dreaming as potentially dangerous. When your soul journeyed away from your body, and experienced the spiritual dimension, where food was plentiful and life easy, it might decide not to come back.

While we watched Amam Maom beavering away surrounded by the hopeful pigs, his sister meanwhile flinging coconut to the perpetually neurotic chickens, Yan told us a story that the spirits of the forest are owed special consideration because once, long ago, the people of primeval times split into two groups, both sharing the same hidden world of the Beyond. One group became the people thought of as the first ancestors, who, with their descendants, live in their own invisible *umas*. As well as these, the *ukkui* or ancestor spirits, there are the second group, the forest spirits or *sai ka leleu*, some of whom resemble pixies and elves. The problem was that we humans couldn't see these spirits and so found it difficult to communicate with them. And this was where the *kereis* came in: they were given the gift of being able to see the spirits, so that they could interpret their needs. These needs were complicated and made more so by the fact that the spirits lived in the forest that the Mentawai depended on for food and herbs. Every time you hunted an animal or harvested the trees you were in danger of causing the ancestors upset.

The more I began to hear about Amam Maom's perception of the world, the more I realized I needed to get away to the forest. It was clearly more than just a physical resource – somewhere you got your timber, and at your forest house kept your pigs. It was a spiritual resource, the home of the entities that kept you healthy, kept you alive.

The following day, we had a chance to go at least a little way into the forest. Amam Maom's grandchildren had slight fevers, and he wanted to gather some medicines. We walked out of Taileleu and upslope, following a stream. Amam Maom – ahead, plodding along, his feet splayed – every now and then, without even leaving the path, reached out to the greenery. He plucked leaves from spindly saplings, leaves from darker shrubs with plastic-looking leaves, or peeled away a plant that had been working like ivy up a tree trunk. Each he slipped into his shoulder basket.

Gradually, the sound of the village fell away. The brook tinkling along beside us, cool clear water from somewhere up ahead, we went deeper and deeper into the forest, the place where the spirits lived.

'*Baja*,' I said to Amam Maom – I'd finally learnt to address him with the appropriate title of respect – 'how would you describe a *kerei*? Is he a sort of priest?'

'I had a friend who was a Protestant priest,' he replied. 'Then he got sick, and like me decided he had been chosen to become a *kerei*. After eighteen years! And I asked him a little later, what are the main differences between being a preacher in church and being a *kerei*. He said, "In general, there is no difference at all!"'

Of course he was joking. A *kerei* may be a priest, but his was certainly not the Christian philosophy – that man was a steward of nature, looking after the plants and animals for God. 'Have dominion over the fish of the sea, and over the fowls of the air and over every living thing that moveth upon the earth,' says Genesis 1:28. To Amam Maom, the animals, the plants, even the rocks had souls, and his well-being relied on his respect for these things around him, each with their own desires and emotions.

Amam Maom collected another dozen species – ferns, creepers, ground plants – then he suddenly stopped, turned and said, 'Really, I'm a *doktor*. Though I do not wear a white coat, or mask, or stethoscope.'

If he was a doctor, flowers were his uniform. Like anyone who was Mentawai, he found it normal to place a hibiscus flower in his hair, or a leaf in his necklace. He did not, like a doctor, wear a white coat to suggest purity, a distance from microbes – he wore a piece of the forest that he depended on.

At last Amam Maom had the final ingredient – it resembled a pennywort, a tender-looking lover of damp rocks – and we came back downslope. Beside a stream Amam Maom took out the leaves and washed them, one by one. He arranged them in four bundles, then grated them on the thorny stem of a *gigiup* palm and packed them into banana leaves. Then off we went back to his house, where his grandchildren were set down on the veranda. The little boy and girl, who didn't seem very ill at all, obediently followed their mother's order to stay put.

They would now be restored to health, literally, because the Mentawai believed illnesses came about because the souls of the sick have left their bodies, and needed to be encouraged back with sweet songs, flowers and food.

The herbs that Amam Maom had gathered were brought forward and they were now also talked to, and asked to help in the process of making the children well. Chickens, too, were caught, and addressed so their souls would understand their role in the ritual. The children were then given the plant medicine to swallow and gently massaged with the herbs, which were said to have cooling properties that would make their bodies attractive for their souls to return to.

Next, Amam Maom prepared his special handbell for summoning the spirits; his family, however, chatted away as if this were a birthday party. During a church service back home, you'd at least try to talk in a whisper. But Amam Maom's wife, though having a traditional role of assistant to the *kerei*, kept yawning, and Maom, Amam Maom's son, kept zapping a misbehaving dog with blunted arrows. Here, there was no divide between spiritual occasion and normal life, the sacred and the profane. The spirits were always with you, and so the occasion was no different from any other in this respect.

Amam Maom now went to the front of the veranda, brushing away any bad spirits with sweeping broom movements, then placed on the floorboards a plate decorated with flowers and heaped with generous helpings of boiled egg and rice. Having left this inducement to the missing souls, he began ringing the bell and singing a refrain in the special *kerei* language which is said to be pleasing to them.

'Soul, please help us,' he sang. 'While the cock crows, please come to us and answer our call. Please hurry to be here with us. Hurry… Here, see the meal we have prepared for you, friend. We have made a delicious meal for you and have it here on a plate. Please, please come to us. Don't stay out there on your own, we are scared without you here. Here is your meal. Come to see your flowers and the cool plants we have for you. Please come back, soul, don't be afraid… Come here on to the *bekeu* flower.'

Gradually the souls were being drawn back to the children, to where they traditionally resided in the front of the head.

Before we knew it, the ritual was over – but, as the sickness might be a sign of some imbalance in the whole *uma*, the whole clan, a divination was done on the chickens' intestines to make sure all was now well. After crouching over them for a while, Amam Maom stood up. 'The veins are running straight and clear,' he said, and handed the bowl to his wife, smiling. Straight and clear was good, it seemed.

It was an interesting ceremony, but more interesting perhaps is how it's survived to this day – despite decades of disapproval from the authorities and not to mention a sceptical son, who spent much of the ritual watching a low-grade soap opera on TV or shooting at the dog. So why have the *kerei* rituals survived? Because, it seems, though the outside world has tried to stop the native healers, it hasn't come up with an alternative.

There are only two doctors on the island: that's one doctor for every 10,000 people. People still go to the *kereis* – if only because they have to. They die otherwise. And though Taileleu does sometimes get a visit from a doctor – he likes coming here, because Taileleu is rich and it's a chance to sell his own private stock of lucrative medicines – it's once in a blue moon.

The next day we set off properly at last into the home of the spirits, the forest, Amam Maom wearing a T-shirt emblazoned with the motto of some Singaporean school: 'Conquer thyself.' He had said this would be just a 'little walk'. In fact it was half a day by canoe and then another half-day hike on foot. John and I were in totally inappropriate footwear – I was wearing flip-flops.

This was beautiful forest – not virgin, as foreigners often describe it, but a forest tended like a garden for its timber, fruit, medicine and animals. Squirrels clattered through the canopy, and when we broke out of the trees and waded the rivers, king-fishers looped over the water ahead of us.

'How tranquil, how beautiful to live here,' I felt like saying, as Amam Maom walked along ahead. But already I could see that this forest, so picturesque to outsiders' eyes, is not the par-adise I once thought. People wore flowers in their hair and dec-orated themselves with tattoos not to be attractive for those around them, but to keep their souls content. The world of the spirits being more attractive than our world, the fear was that their souls might be tempted to leave. Likewise, when someone died, people adorned themselves to encourage their souls not to leave with that of the deceased. Yes, the Mentawai were living 'in harmony' with the forest, but it wasn't a tranquil, easy-going harmony, it was a danger-loaded one. And if you didn't maintain it, you, your pigs and everyone living in your *uma* would die.

On through the trees, down and up mud gullies, showered all the way by the sounds of competing birds and busy insects. Plants stacked all around us, thrusting for the daylight, fighting it out. To me they were wonderful living things which made up a competitive ecosystem. But to Amam Maom, even the water and stones were part of the living system. In a way I had yet to hear him express for himself, he believed that each and everything radiates a *bajou*, an energy that must be respected. In the Mentawai world, even your bow might not shoot straight if you neglect this, the life source of its soul.

CHAPTER TWO

'We can live in the forest for months and for years and there is everything here that we need. If we get a fever there is medicine there for it. If we get stomach sickness there is medicine here. If we get dizzy we have medicine, a swelling we have medicine. Even if we have an accident with our bush knife and cut ourselves we can treat it with medicine from the forest.'
Amam Maom, kerei

Finally, there we were at the forest house. We could see it up on the riverbank, a wood building thatched in sago palm and sitting above a spread of grey mud. To avoid the quagmire, and the pigs loitering there, you had to totter along a narrow footbridge that led to the veranda. As we did this, a dog ran forward – 'He is called "Lost",' said a girl of about twelve, standing shyly on the veranda. 'And he eats bananas.'

Apart from the girl, Sarti, who was Amam Maom's daughter, there was only a hunchback called Bojuok living here. He was now busy seeing to the pigs' supper, chopping up sago logs and throwing them down into the mud.

The house was like a mini version of a traditional *uma*. In the veranda roof were hung hand-drums – each with python skins – miscellaneous cigarettes not quite finished, and bits and pieces of Amam Maom's *kerei* regalia, including a *leilei*. Worn on the back, it was a sheaf made from a sugar palm leaf, decorated with chicken feathers and containing a secret talisman from his *kerei* teacher – and probably his own long hair if he managed to salvage it. Also here, a palm-skin quiver of arrows, and an array of monkey skulls belonging to the Mentawai macaque, the pig-tailed langur and the long-tailed joja – only the gibbon missing of the four indigenous primates. These were each carefully decorated with paint and rattan, and, being the remains of monkeys that had ended up in the cooking pot, were considered a beautiful place for their souls to be.

I soon realized that Amam Maom was more relaxed out here, away from Taileleu's culture. However, he wasn't fully out of its reach – he said he usually travelled back to the village for the weekly church service, otherwise he got what he called a 'talk from the priest'.

'You go to church?' I asked. 'And you pray and so on?'

'I pray, of course I pray…'

He didn't choose to expand on this, but I got the feeling his devoted attendance on the Sabbath was more to do with a strategy for keeping in favour with the outside world than the Christian God. He had told me he'd been a Muslim for six months, but he gave that up because he found he couldn't eat pork; next he was a Baha'i – until the religion was banned; next a Protestant, but stopped that one because they said *kereis* were evil, which I could see would be a problem. So then he became a Catholic, feeling more at home with a religion that recently had begun to accommodate – even respect – indigenous beliefs.

Later that evening, as we finished supper, Amam Maom began to talk about the healing ceremony. And now, for the first time, he talked not as someone providing facts, but someone teaching. He had chosen to open up to us.

I sat beside him with the others – his wife with her hair down, smoking tobacco rolled in a banana-leaf, with Sarti beside her, and Bojuok as always still shovelling down food – and just listened. Even though he spoke in Mentawai, a language I didn't understand, his words carried authority. You'd believe in him as your doctor, you'd feel he could heal.

I've put down here exactly what he said, as translated by Yan. These were his words, this was his world:

'*Soibo, kauant nuitco'ka bat lalepmai taagai bara oringen…*'

'Sometimes you look inside a house and you can tell that the house is not safe and there may be a lot of sickness coming. We *kereis* look to see if there are spirits of sickness there. If I see any then maybe the family has broken a taboo like eating an old egg or an eel at the wrong time. I ask the *bakat katsaila* [family altar].

He might tell us that the family has eaten this or done that.

'I talk with other *kereis* about what the signs mean and what is the right thing to do, so that we can drive the evil spirits away and purify the house, and give offerings. When they have told me what they think, I can judge how good they are as *kereis* and how much experience they have – sometimes *kerei* initiations today last only four days and nights! People my age took eight days and nights! But there's one thing that still doesn't vary: however long it takes, the *kerei* won't stop dancing around and around in the ritual until he has been given the power to see spirits.

'Anyway, the family will say to me, "Come, Amam Maom, dance for us… this is your duty as a *kerei*. Call the souls of the household and the ancestors. And after they have arrived, dance for them. There is no other way. This is the only way. Please go to the bamboo tree and call the souls."

'So I call the souls – as you have seen me do. And after the soul has come back to the *uma*, it sees the food and quickly jumps into it. We sing, "Spring quickly, soul, see your body, return to your friend and believe in your body again. Please come." This is what we do and it is very serious. You must do it perfectly, as, once you have started, you cannot go back to the beginning.

'If the patient is better, if the family members are happy, if the person is already stronger and he is walking about, then we can stop calling. Then I talk to the soul of the chicken which is to be killed and ask it what is happening – if the soul of the sick person has returned and if he is better. This is what we *kereis* sing about. We give leaves as offerings and we ask the soul to tell us what to do. The next day we collect herbs again to clean the sick man's hands from evil spirits, and to strengthen his soul and make sure the sickness has been driven away.

'We make his body healthy and we also need to keep his body the right temperature. For this we use the *pelekak* plant and also the *silula, polaga, kopuk*, the yellow flower of *mattai lagak*, also the *matdaraingat* plant, the *kateleuleugat simaingo, simabulaum, simasinging*, and the *kerei* flower.'

The next day we visitors woke up at five o'clock, the hour called *patoknia*, 'still dark', by the Mentawai islanders. Amam Maom would have already been up for an hour; his mornings began at *lui lui bilou*, 'voice of the gibbon', when he would light a fire, often by using a flint. By daybreak – *mosarabak* or 'opening' – he would be well into his day, drying out a new bark bowstring, preparing coconut for the chickens, or carving an ideal knife blade out of wood so that his son could take it to Muara Siberut and make an exact copy.

What woke us that morning was the sound of coconuts having their husks chopped off. As we lay in our sleeping bags, the husks were grated for the chickens, and then the pigs started to get excited as sections of sago trunk were lobbed down to them. They snapped and chomped at the sago and then scampered away, threatened by the next pig queuing behind.

Apparently the pigs gnashed their way through a tree a week – that's a lot of trees, fifty or so a year. Amam Maom wasn't about to lose the chance of having this extra labour force, and led us out to work in the sago forests before we'd even finished our coffee. Accompanied by his wife, we went to the place where he'd been storing some sago trunks in a pool. Unlike rice, sago can sit like this for a year without degrading – though there were little fingermarks in the pith, where monkeys had been trying their best to get at it.

One by one we rolled these barrels downriver, through the low, dry-season water. Sarti rolled the tree trunk sections as lightly as if they were empty dustbins. Despite both being over six feet tall and fit, John and I very soon had crippling back pain and had to hand over the rest of the job to the twelve-year-old. Such was her isolation at the forest house, Sarti had never seen a white person face to face – I gathered we were a disappointment.

Later, while we recovered with a cup of tea, Sarti was off again to do another task – putting the chickens and chicks in baskets, safe for the night from snakes and monitor lizards. When she came back I asked her if she wanted to go to school. 'I have tried it already,' she said, as if talking about a new dish of food. 'And actually I don't like it.'

'So you like it here?'

'Yes, in fact I like everything here. I like rolling sago logs, fishing for prawns, fishing for little fish. I like the quietness.'

'Don't you get lonely here? Don't you want to be with other young people in Taileleu?'

'No, no. It's true that I don't have many young friends, but I visit my best friend Taparerekatogok – that means "Don't Ask" Flower.' She remembered something, and added hastily, 'And of course I get on well with my mother.' Her mother looked up, and smiled at her daughter. 'Yesterday,' continued Sarti, 'we ate prawns we caught together with our hand-held scoop nets. That is the sort of thing I like to do.'

It was poignant to watch Sarti – so content with her lot, and utterly dependent on a world that we outsiders are determined to destroy. The latest news was that Muslims were introducing sarongs for women, the government introducing riverbank-destroying buffalo. Would Sarti do better to go to school? Hardly. To equip them for their future, the children in Taileleu were being taught the vocabulary of cities – alleyways, concrete, mopeds. They learnt that they were not 'maju' – 'developed' – the key word of President Suharto's vision for Indonesia's future; they were at the bottom of a hierarchy, and at the other end were the fat cats living in Jakarta. They should abandon their forest ways that work, and adopt those that didn't.

In short, after completing their schooling, the pupils of Siberut no longer fitted in here, and yet were unfit for the Outside World as well – it was still out of their reach.

Amam Maom was all too aware of the implications of 'progress' for his traditional way of life. It seemed to me that he knew we were giving him the chance to lay down his record, his epitaph. This was a last chance to pass his story on. His son showed no interest, but we were here to listen.

Later, we walked into the forest, and he fished around for a particular leaf or twig, sat on the ground, and told us about it. He spoke through Yan, who listened acutely, his body straining with the importance he saw in his task. Scientists such as Wanda Avé have done valuable work, but only one anthropologist,

Reimar Schefold, has studied the rituals of the *kereis* in great detail and over an extended period of time. We recorded each word Amam Maom spoke, knowing they might never be heard by the world again.

'*Ki ki ki ne lakgeknia dap lakgek leiti... sangberi leiti... taipulaplap na le saba, pepekdak ta marot lakgeknia, komenta tmara...*' he began...

'We scrape off this medicine, and put it on the injury. It is a good medicine for worms, all types of worms. It is also good for python bites, but for other poison snakes like the *pepekdak*, you need different types of herbs. Snakes like the red tail need a different medicine, which we also have. And if that medicine doesn't work, then we try something else like the bark of *tummu*, or *jalai teile*.

'To reduce the pain we use those herbs which we find on the banks of streams. We need several different herbs to make the medicine, *tummu* bark, *loina sabeuga*, *som*, *tai malaulau*... together with the *buluk pot*.'

This encyclopaedic knowledge of the forest flowed from Amam Maom for a while. Then he talked about the bulldozers that might one day come.

'They will destroy the trees, the plants, the animals and the water. I went with some other Mentawai to Bogor to meet with the Minister of the Environment, to tell him why the plants are essential for our lives here.'

He produced a tender shoot from the leaf litter near his feet.

'Look at this small plant. We use the young leaves of it for medicine. The stem we use for a healing bath ritual, and we as *kereis* also use it as string to tie beads on. When we get sick, we use the young stem in our healing work. We find these plants on the banks of small rivers. If they cut down the trees, these plants will be crushed and we won't be able to find them any more. What will we do to protect our health and heal us from sickness?

'So the village head of Taileleu explained to the minister that I was a medicine man. He said that although I was small

Above: Journeying into the interior of Siberut, Amam Maom in his pink hat, chattering away to me in front.

Right: A *kerei* concocting a medicine from herbal ingredients.

Previous page: To me, a fascinating eco-system, but to the Mentawai the rainforest is not only a resource but also home to the ancestral and forest spirits.

Above: Amam Dirikogo's father giving me a tattoo, a lengthy and painful beautification process which the Mentawai endure to make their bodies attractive places for their souls to live in.

Left: Bojuok with Amam Maom (seated) at his field house. In the Mentawai world, even inanimate objects have souls which must be kept content, and to this end the *umas* or clan buildings are decorated with palm flags and toy birds.

Above: Amam Gresi (left) and Amam Dirikogo, trying to explain to me how they go about the process of divining, by means of a pig's innards.

Right: Amam Maom, Amam Gresi, Amam Dirikogo and a fourth *kerei*, Sakigege, calling the souls of the ancestors to join the feast.

Below right: The skulls of hunted monkeys are hung in the *uma* rafters to ensure their souls still have a home, and are content.

Opposite: Amam Dirikogo leaving for the forest equipped for a downpour.

Opposite above: Although during ritual dances the *kereis* are in a semi-trance state, guided by ancestral spirits, this is also a performance – done for the pleasure of the community and for the ancestors.

Opposite below: If overcome by a spirit, a *kerei* may need to be reassured and spiritually strengthened by the others.

Above: *Kereis* are invariably male, but their wives play an important back-up role, and are heavily adorned at rituals to further attract the ancestral spirits to feasts.

Right: Sakigege ridding the *uma* of bad spirits with the help of cleansing herbs.

Overleaf: Amam Maom – although his long, *kerei* hair has been removed to comply with the authorities, he is still respected.

and young, I had the experience of an old man. Regarding the new settlements they wanted us to live in, he told him that we didn't need them when we got sick because out there in the forest, beside the small streams, *there* were the medicines. We said we also had all our food out there... we had vegetables like the young leaves of the *aren* palm which we could find in the forest. We could walk in the streams and rivers and find shrimps, eels, *teppe* fish, *lolot* fish, crabs... everything.'

No doubt the last thing that the minister wanted to hear was that the primeval forest was a better home than the nice modern villages. He wanted the Mentawai to end their self-sufficient lifestyle, and adopt one in which they were dependent on the government, which could control them. Amam Maom's attempt to dissuade the minister from his intention to log the forest was about as successful as you can imagine.

Later, we saw Amam Maom put his knowledge into practice, when we went to visit his neighbour Teutakpuiba. Amam Maom nodded with approval when he saw the household's large pigs, and then settled down to the business in hand, which was offering advice about a sick baby girl. She lay silently in a rattan basket hung from the ceiling, and wore a blue bead collar that was adorned with numerous bells. More bead necklaces and herbs too lay around her, like the bedding of a nest.

But the bead charms and herbs were not the cure, they were normal procedure: such was the fear – and likelihood – of losing children, who were said to have souls that are less developed, and therefore more liable to stray. There was also a danger that a malevolent spirit might be attacking a child, and a *kerei* might suggest its name should be changed, to confuse the spirit.

We learnt, however, that in this case an even more radical measure had been recommended: the mother should give up her baby to her younger sister. And, after listening to various members of the family, Amam Maom confirmed that this was also his opinion. 'Her soul feels it needs to live in another *uma*.'

This was the reality of living in the forest – death and uncertainty. Amam Maom's first wife had died, and Sarti herself was an adopted orphan. As for the hunchback, his whole life seemed to have been a tragedy. First all his children died, then the child of his wife (by another man) died, and then his wife left him. Now he couldn't be called Amam, 'Father of...', because he was no longer a father. 'Bojuok' was a name denoting someone who had no one.

Death was all around you here; your house walls were often painted with *takep*, representations of the hands and feet of the dead. Here, you soon learnt an acceptance of what came your way. As and when your loved ones died, you remarried or changed households. In this respect, Mentawai women were disadvantaged – if their husband died, they went almost empty-handed back to the family *uma* which they left on their marriage. 'You mean taking only a pig, or something?' I asked Yan.

'A pig is actually a bit big,' Yan said. Normally, she might get a chicken or two, and her clothes.

On one of our walks, Amam Maom went off to gather a little heap of leaves and bark scrapings, and then sat on the forest floor to talk about how, with the help of the herbs, he made the necessary preparations prior to going hunting. It was a privileged moment – in all my travels, rarely had anyone charged with handling the spirits, these powerful forces, been so open with me.

Amam Maom now talked about how he went hunting the forest animals – creatures that belonged to the spirits. But the picture he went on to paint, as we sat flicking away ants and slapping the occasional determined mosquito, was one of his total involvement in the ecology around us – a family of animals, plants, ancestors, wood spirits, earth spirits, wind spirits and more, all of which you had to get along with, or else die.

Again, I have laid out his words, his forest:

'When we prepare to hunt monkeys it is so early that the monkeys are still asleep in the tops of the trees... We walk a little way, and then we put some earth and a mixture of herbs on a wooden plate as an offering to let us catch monkeys. First we ask the Earth Spirit for permission to hunt the monkeys: "We are here, we are here, calling to you... help us to be light and quick so that we can catch the animal that screams, that makes the *aggak* and *bago* sounds.

'Then we say, this is an offering especially for you, Wood Spirit, so that you will allow the monkeys to fall easily through your branches. This is the offering from my clan, from my family who is with you, who is the same as you.

'And you, our ancestors who settled here in Masiasiat, we have for you a beautiful offering. Accept our offering on your fallen leaves…

'Then we take the herbs we have gathered, and we take them in turn, and call them one at a time by their special names. We address this, the *panopsop* plant, as "*sakalat papaiak*", "light", so we too can be light and can catch the monkeys easily. And this plant we call "*sugguru-sugguru*", "together", so that we can be sure that we will be brought together and have meat in our house. This one we call "twisted" so that it will make the stomach of the monkeys twisted so they cannot sit still and hide from us.

'Then we call to the monkeys, "We are the clan who has a field house here and we look after this land… come, please, soul of the monkeys… Here is your offering…"

'After we have given the offering, the best hunter says, "Friend, we have offered herbs to you, the Wood Spirit, and we will now start to hunt the monkeys… help us, help us… And, bowstring, please help us… we touch you and caress you… be the eyes of our path… lead us."

'After we have done this, we open a bamboo tube and split the sago inside into three parts. One bit here, one bit here and one bit here for the different spirits we have called. We say, "Watch which way I am shooting and help me, please, touch me." We open another bamboo tube. "Bow and arrow, these offerings are for you. Shoot and hit the monkeys who make the *mago* sound. Here is my offering for you and for the monkeys. Make my eyes clear. Come, souls of the monkeys, come and join us… Your stomach is not straight any more and you are cold out there. I can see you coming closer, climb towards us and prepare yourself to meet us who call for you."

'After we have given the offering, even if we make a lot of noise when we walk beneath the trees it doesn't matter because the offerings have been accepted. Our friends come to us having accepted our gifts and we kill them as they come towards us.

'If we get a monkey, we cut a little piece of its left ear off as a gift for the ancestors... We say, "We are the only ones honouring you and giving you this present, please take it and let us get more of your monkeys in the future. This is our offering, we will take our share."

'We do not know where they actually live, but they are everywhere and in every hill.'

Sometimes during our stay with him, Amam Maom would cook a chicken or small pig for us – a procedure that started with him first gently passing the animal over the heads of each of us in turn. He would brush us with the feathers, saying, '*Areuake besi oringen kasatakogaku*,' that is, 'Go far away, sickness, from my "children".' It was a blessing on us, but also an explanation to the soul that it was valued, and therefore shouldn't be angry. That said, whenever we heard Amam Maom talking kindly to one of the animals, effectively they were receiving their death sentence.

And this is the central dilemma of *kereis* but also every type of medicine man around the world – that we must maintain harmony with the spiritual dimension, not disturbing the souls of the plants and animals around us, yet we must kill in order to eat and build our shelters.

In the Mentawai islands there is an extra problem: wild animals are the domestic herds of the ancestor spirits. You could perhaps legitimately kill a wild boar if it 'comes your way' – as, for instance, had happened in Taileleu when the wild pig had been trying to seduce a household's sows – but otherwise it must be done carefully, often as part of a ritual. In short, the act of killing puts you yourself in danger. It is no surprise to hear that meat is not a large part of the islanders' diet.

To add to all this there is the compelling problem of the Outsiders. I asked Amam Maom to talk about his persecutors – his practices banned in 1956 and the waves of repression following more or less ever since.

'The first time the police came, they took our bells from us and broke them up. The second time they came they took more of our things and sold them. The third time they came they didn't sell or break our things but confiscated them and put them in the police office in Muara Siberut.

'At this time everyone in this area, *kereis* and laymen alike, had long hair. My hair was long, all the way down to my knees. Teteu Batja cut my hair and used it in his back bag, part of our regalia. He was my teacher, my adviser, my uncle and my father. He told me that unless I cut my hair the policemen would punish me. It was very sad. I was very proud of my hair. I used to treat it with pineapple juice, *kakainau* flowers, *totonan* fruit, coconut oil...'

In about 1970 all the *kereis* were told to give their regalia to the police – the necklaces, bells, everything. The police chief, Nikodemus, from a southern island in the Mentawai, ordered them never to practise as *kereis* ever again, on pain of punishment.

'Even though he is from the Mentawai, Niko didn't understand what he was doing. It is the same for everyone – for those who eat sago, those who hunt monkeys, for everyone. The moment someone breaks the bell, the *kerei* vanishes in fire. The ancestors choose who becomes a *kerei* and allowing your regalia to be destroyed is disrespectful. You will die.

'We had to leave all of our *kerei* regalia with Niko when we returned to Taileleu – sixteen *kereis*, all without regalia... Then a man called Rikdik came to us and said that he had heard our bells in our houses and around the village as if we have been walking along wearing them. We asked him when he heard them, and he told us that it was last night. We couldn't understand it because none of us now had any bells as they had all been confiscated. They heard my bell in my own house when I wasn't there.'

Eventually the *kereis* were given back some of their things, but even then they were forbidden to do their healing rituals and people died. So to heal people they had to break the law. There was a change when they healed a policeman's wife who had been bitten by a dog spirit and was dying.

'We said to the village head, "If you don't let us heal her she will die." What else could we do? We could hear her sickness in the plants we gathered. We could see the feet, teeth, hair and ears of a dog. We could hear it. So we made an offering. We rang the bell to call the spirits. We could hear the bells in the river and we started to see a dog's bone, dog's teeth, his fur, his feet, his intestines and his heart...'

The *kereis* performed their ritual for the woman, discovering that the dog spirit was angry because her husband had eaten a dog – a Batak tradition but taboo for the Mentawai.

'When his wife got better, the policeman wrote a report about it. He said in his report that we were like doctors in the western sense. "They help sick people. They are not political agitators. They give medicines. Look at my wife, she is better again and her sickness is gone. They gave her a ritual bath in the river Kurei and her sickness has been driven away." The policeman told us then that we could continue being *kereis*.'

Sometimes, after hearing Amam Maom talk, I would walk down to the river, and look around at the butterflies dancing through the air stirred and cooled by the passage of water. They each have a soul and Amam Maom also speaks of their *bajou*, their life force. The tree ferns, flying squirrels, even the stones of the river, slimy with algae, have a *bajou*. It is as if they are emitting radiation – and if this is disturbed, harm must inevitably follow. It shouldn't be so hard for westerners to believe in this invisible force, dismiss it as a belief in 'magic' – we accept it when our scientists claim that every object exerts a gravitational pull.

In Siberut, everything turns out to be surprisingly logical. Here there are no Heathens, cowering in the darkness of their ignorance. To the *kereis*, like medicine men everywhere, the universe is governed not by strange happenings, but by clear and indisputable physical laws. And, if someone is ill – that is, his soul has drifted away to the other, spiritual dimension of our world –

an animal offering is made to bring it back. This isn't a 'backward' notion; it is an act in compliance with a law that every school-child learns – that energy cannot be created, only transferred. Thus, to receive a life force, you have to give one back.

The Mentawai do accept that there are some illnesses that can be cured only with western medicine, but still the root cause of a malady will be explainable in spirit terms – it's just a question of finding that explanation. So, if you consistently fail to shoot anything with your bow and arrow, it may be that you haven't respected the *bajou* of the bow when cutting it from the palmwood. Likewise, *kereis* have to have a strong *bajou* in order to deal safely with powerful forces – and this means that when *kereis* meet they must sit together, performing a ceremony to harmonize these energies and avoid the risk of causing danger to each other.

Another indication of the perils awaiting the unwary in the forest was given by Anjel, Yan's quiet brother. His first-hand account had all the more potency coming from such a reticent person. But Yan coaxed him to tell us his story – about the time he was attacked by a malevolent spirit, while on a journey in the centre of the island.

'I was on a trip with my uncle Laiming, to buy a chicken,' said Anjel. 'We walked and walked, and then for a while travelled by canoe. And my uncle said to me, "When we get to the hill called Leleu Baja don't say anything about it or you will be bewitched. Leleu Baja doesn't like to be noticed and if you do, Kelak Kulit, who lives there, will be angry." Well, I was very young and I didn't listen to what he had said. When we passed the hill, I said "*maeru*", beautiful, and looked for a while in amazement.

'After we had stayed two days in Lita village I started to get hot. I got a headache, I started throwing up. My uncle Laiming was very worried about my sickness as it was getting worse. He asked some people to take me to Simabuggei where I could be healed. It took seven people to carry me there.

'A *kerei* called Tupilaggai did a long ceremony for me and on a small stream off the main Saibi river, our uncle Juda completed the healing with a week-long ritual. I started to feel light on my feet again and was no longer bewitched.'

Amam Maom announced one morning that he had slept badly. He said he felt that someone had died at Taileleu and he wanted to go back. Soon we, too, were packing, knowing that we had to leave for Taileleu with him, but wondering where then? In the back of my mind was Anjel's story. If Anjel was affected by looking up at the hilltop, then what about me? What if I climbed to the top – maybe even I would feel this force, one of the spirits the Mentawais believe in.

Amam Maom, whose first wife was killed by sorcery, he said, wasn't enthused by the idea. In fact he wasn't keen on going anywhere far with me at all. He said that such sorcery is often used on a visiting *kerei* by *kereis* fearful of the visitor's power and intent. So *kereis* tend not to travel – and it turned out that, although Amam Maom nodded learnedly while Anjel was describing the whereabouts of the hill, he'd never even been to the centre of the island. It's not just him – no one travels very much, and as a result customs vary radically from place to place. In some places you roll your cigarette in nipa palm, in other places banana leaf. In Taileleu you don't say *oinan*, that's river valley dialect for water, because there it means 'urine'.

We agreed in the end that Amam Maom would come with me at least some of the way, to meet another *kerei* Yan knew, called Amam Dirikogo. John would take him back and I'd continue with just Yan and Anjel towards the Malevolent Spirit.

We trekked back through the mud and leeches, having waved goodbye to Sarti. After a talk with Amam Maom's son, absolving him of blame if anything terrible happened to his father, we were back in our canoe, speeding north up the coast to Muara Siberut. A school of porpoises came towards us, very slow in their rising and dipping. Towering cumulus clouds, lit from below in neon yellow, flared and then disappeared into the night.

The next day we turned inland up the Batreiket River, where Amam Dirikogo lived, and found ourselves passing a line of three new, rather suburban, settlements. Puro 1, Puro 2 and Puro 3 were much like Taileleu, official villages that were to replace the forest *umas*. They were extremely *maju* – 'developed' – tin-roofed and small. We wouldn't have stopped except that, as we passed, we heard the drumming and singing of a *kerei* ritual. We slowed and saw, beyond the riverside palms, a T-shirted throng enjoying what might have been – but for the thumping drums and the chorus of men singing – a wedding celebration. Then we spotted two men wearing what seemed at first to be only flowers and leaves. Nearer, we saw they were wearing red bark loincloths, their skin was dyed yellow with turmeric, and the feathers and flowers were tucked into bead crowns and arm bands. This might be a government-approved village, but these men looked as traditional as the two *kereis* I remembered from my first trip. Furthermore, one of them Yan recognized as Amam Dirikogo, the man from further upriver whom we'd come to see. It seemed that he'd come to help out the inhabitants of Puro 3, who didn't have their own *kerei*. They'd called him out from the forest, calling him as if from the past.

We tied the canoe to some exposed roots and came ashore, standing a little way off – we had turned up with our own *kerei*, whose powerful *bajou* might upset the balance of forces here. For a while Amam Maom wouldn't even leave the canoe – he just sat firmly there, patiently looking about at what was going on.

Soon, Amam Dirikogo caught sight of us and came striding up. He was about thirty-five, totally at ease, and what impressed me as he came nearer was not the unashamed floral display that sprouted from him, nor the ceremonial splodge on his cheeks – apparently applied with lipstick – nor the realization that the best hibiscus blossoms, neatly tucked behind his ears, were actually plastic ones, but that he still had his full *kerei* hair. There was a mass of it, bound with red ribbon and extending down his back.

He grabbed any hand that was in reach to shake. He smiled and smiled, a home-made cigarette sticking out through his teeth, which were stained as brown as an old teapot. Not speaking much Indonesian, he was unable to engage anyone other than Yan in conversation, but somehow he was still the centre of things. Amam Maom now came ashore, but still stood rather apart. It was strange seeing him not in the centre of a circle but fiddling with his fingers in the background, like a small boy who'd been left out.

The next day we came back and picked up Amam Dirikogo, heading on up the Batreiket to his home. Now that the ritual was over, Amam Maom behaved more normally with this other *kerei* – soon they'd have a ritual to harmonize their *bajou*, but for the moment they were happy to talk. Or at least Amam Maom was, and he talked on and on, sitting at the front of the canoe, giving this young *kerei* the benefit of his years of wisdom.

Hours later, we moored the canoe and, picking up another young *kerei*, Amam Dirikogo's brother Amam Gresi, we walked along winding forest mud tracks to Amam Dirikogo's *uma*. It was small, positioned in the curve of a stream, forest pressing in around it and the pigs scouting beneath. Yellow flags of young *poula* palm had recently been placed in the ceiling. Known as *katsaila*, they were adornment for the pleasure of the *uma*'s soul but also protection for it, because the *katsaila* deflected bad forces – *saila*, I now knew, meant 'other direction'.

Soon the three *kereis* were quietly sitting down together to perform the *paruwak* harmonization ritual for *kereis*, in the midst of them a platter bearing the cooling *ailéléppet* leaves, and *malatchat*, the 'clear' fish. Together they sang a gentle chant, soothing each other's souls, and introducing them to each other by touching each other's necklaces.

Afterwards we shared our tinned fish, diluting them with fresh *laipat* ferns, and Amam Gresi and Amam Dirikogo discussed that strangest of all modern phenomena, the *orakturi*. This word proved to be a distortion of the Indonesian *orang torist*, that is, 'tourist'.

'When the *orakturi* come,' Amam Gresi said, 'we hide our wristwatches in the kitchen. They prefer it that way. It's very funny. The watches are given by previous tourists, but they don't want to see us wearing them. They all like to imagine that they are the first to visit our houses and our forests!'

'And if we leave them on,' Amam Dirikogo added, 'the guides say that they won't bring them again!'

'We don't use our real names,' said Amam Gresi, whose *uma* was festooned with photos sent by grateful tourists, rows of portly Germans in bulging loincloths. 'Do you?'

Amam Maom nodded silently, as he did on occasions when he didn't have a clue what was being talked about. The truth was, he had hardly seen a tourist in Taileleu. Only Australian surfers came to his bit of the island, and they were more interested in the offshore rollers. However, elsewhere he had seen a bikini, and he hadn't liked it. 'They should bathe in secret, these women.' It wasn't the breasts, which traditionally in Siberut were uncovered, but the sight of thighs.

'When we are with the *orakturi*,' Amam Dirikogo continued, 'we give ourselves funny names.'

'I'm called "Sprite",' Amam Gresi said. 'It's the name of a drink which bubbles in a bottle!'

'And if my wife wants sugar,' Amam Dirikogo said, 'she takes it from them without asking – and we all secretly have a good laugh at the poor *orakturi*! But I like them. It's the guides who are bad – they come from Bukit Tinggi, where they gather *orakturi* as we gather herbs from the forest. And then they pay us and we have to perform a Dance For No Reason.'

'But I enjoy that,' Amam Gresi interjected. 'I love doing a Dance For No Reason.'

'The best things are the Polaroid photos!' Amam Dirikogo suddenly exclaimed. 'Have you seen them? It is like a penis coming out!'

Over the next day or two, I began to get to know Amam Dirikogo, a man who was fascinated by everything new – and that included us. He examined our soft feet, our pockets, our cameras, and each time give a tut, smiling at our uselessness in his world.

I began to piece his life together from the evidence around me: there were his tattoos, the first of which had been those on his arms, next legs, then chest – his ankles would follow one day.

And there was the ceiling of his house – a broody hen sitting quietly in its basket, and around it the spare arrows, spears, drums, and a line of monkey and pig skulls adorning the rafters; also up there, a wooden model of a bird which was a toy for the spirits; and a lock of hair which hung with the cobwebs, and once hung from the head of his first wife, who was now dead.

Death had touched Amam Dirikogo, as everyone else. His first wife had died about four years ago, and her daughter, newly born, was handed over to a woman who could breastfeed her. Likewise, Dirikogo, Amam Dirikogo's daughter from many years before, looked after Sola, a boy born from her husband's first wife, also dead. It struck me anew that the forest sometimes seemed not an ally to these people but an enemy, uniting everyone in the common struggle. Amam Dirikogo also mentioned that a sister of his had died – and he was proud, because he still had seven siblings in all. In Siberut, it was a sign of a healthy family that only one in eight had died.

During our stay, Amam Maom would occasionally give us further insights into the spirit realm, and at these times Amam Dirikogo would sit with us, listening to the older *kerei*, who through his greater experience would have a greater spiritual power and *bajou*.

'What do the spirits look like? They look much like us. For example, the ancestors also have tattoos. When I die, I will still have my tattoos even though I am dead and lie under ground. So the spirits have tattoos, too. They also wear a small belt around their waist. We put several on a *kerei* when he dies, but despite this when we see him as an ancestor, he wears only one belt. Of course, they also wear beads and bells and they have the *leilei* bag of hair, the *kerei* necklace and crown.

'Most of the time ordinary people cannot see them, but the *kereis* can see them because they have been given the eyes to see. It is like looking into a mirror. If I stand in front of a mirror, I can see myself. If I give the mirror to someone else they too can see their body. It is like this when you see the ancestors. For the layman, if he manages to see the ancestors it won't be clear. For the *kerei* it is as clear as watching television.'

Perhaps encouraged by hearing Amam Maom talk openly like this with us, Amam Dirikogo began to add from his own experience.

As was the usual case, he had become a *kerei* following illness. The medical condition, one known as *pangoringen kerei*, wasn't recognized at first. 'It's like children crying,' he said. 'You as a parent don't know why: to find out you try different things. In the end, there was only one possible explanation: my soul's desire for my body to become a *kerei*.'

He talked about what it was like to see the ancestors, these awesome, supernatural beings. For the novice *kerei*, it seemed, contact with such power was traumatic, akin to a shockwave. 'We feel it all over our body. It starts in the feet and they begin to feel cold. We start to shiver and cannot stand. When this happens other *kereis* come to us and sing, "My child, I have come here to help you and to protect you from the ancestors."'

Amam Dirikogo soon seemed happy to share these things, just as Amam Maom had been – though his discourse was likely to be interrupted if he heard an ill-omen, such as the call from the forest of the otherwise unremarkable *kuilak*, or ashy tailor bird. Bit by bit, we heard more and more.

'There are ancestor spirits of other clans who are not close to us and who keep their distance. They are shy and can become malevolent spirits, like the sky spirit, the earth spirit, the spirit of the wind. They are not the same as us. They speak a different language and when we speak to them they do not understand us. It is impossible to call to these as they are nervous near us *kereis*.

'But our own ancestors are different and they are close to us, very close and we give them gifts. They are always close and come when we call. Our dear ancestors have mercy on us and when we ask them, they help us, when we give an offering to them, they accept it.

'Before they arrive we always first see a special sign. When there is sickness and many people have died in a village, we see them wandering about. For example, when someone died over at Rokdok I saw his spirit on the path.

'Their form is like live people, though not so clear. But to see them is amazing. Our eyes are astonished. We are in awe. Their bodies are covered in hair. Their hair hangs long and wild. Their eyes are like a gibbon's. He who sees them for the first time will be terrified.'

On about the third day we decided Amam Maom should go back to Taileleu. He had been very polite about it, but was listless away from home. And anyway I wanted to see the haunted hill. So we packed to go our separate ways, and then Amam Maom took me aside and performed a *ne-ne-nei*, a 'cooling off' procedure to strengthen my soul. This was a disappointingly simple process – he undid three little plastic bottles from a bundle that I now realized must have been around his waist throughout this trip. One bottle contained an orange liquid rather like 3-in-1 oil; the second was like green toothpaste; the last was a transparent liquid suspiciously like baby lotion. He bathed *ailéléppet* leaves in the oils and then smeared them over me. With that I should be protected against all spiritual dangers. Unfortunately in Siberut not all dangers are spiritual and, just as with medicines, illnesses can have a strong physical component, too. However, I could rest assured that my soul at least was now safe.

CHAPTER THREE

'Everything I do and everything I have learnt is to care for the soul.
If I hadn't become a *kerei* I think that my body would have died.
My soul wanted my body to become a *kerei*, so my body felt in pain
and was sickly. All because it wanted to be a *kerei*.'
Amam Dirikogo, kerei

Promising both Amam Maom and Amam Dirikogo that we would visit them later, we went our separate ways, John and Anjel taking Amam Maom back home, then Anjel leaving John (who would fetch the film crew) and returning to ferry Yan and me still further north along the coast. We turned inland at Muara Saibi, then began a three-day walk to Leleu Baja. And it was while walking along through the forest that we came across something quite remarkable. It was a small group of *kereis*, standing in a huddle, and decorated for a ritual, heaped with bells and beads and crowns of fresh *dubbak* leaves. One man, perhaps the most senior, also wore across his shoulders the *leilei* bag containing a *kerei* talisman and hair, sprouting from it a thick bunch of feathers. He was applying turmeric to the other men, yellowing them up and down.

Yan asked if we could approach, and they beckoned us over. We learnt that the man being given most of the attention, and most of the turmeric, was the owner of the *uma* up ahead. And I suddenly realized I had stumbled, by an extraordinary piece of luck, on the opening stages of an initiation. Furthermore the senior *kerei* now invited us to see what would happen next. The initiate, who was a skinny, tired-looking middle-aged man, didn't seem to get a choice in the matter, but looked up and smiled weakly, like a world-weary tortoise. He was ill, and no doubt it was his illness that was prompting him to go through this ceremony to become a *kerei*. Probably it was a last resort, western medicines – or those available to him – having failed.

We walked together back to the *uma*, and found a crowd of relatives and neighbours sitting around on the veranda. In front, three pigs were bound up and waiting – the future didn't look promising for them. To the side, boys were tuning drumskins, and at the back was the initiate's wife, who was also being prepared – in her case for her new role as assistant to the *kerei*. She already had her own crown of *dubbak*, and was sitting between the wives of the *kerei* initiators, who were trying out different blue necklaces on her.

What we were about to witness was the start of the ceremony, to enable this man to see what only a *kerei* can see. 'However long it takes,' I remembered Amam Maom saying, 'the *kereis* won't stop dancing around and around in the ritual until the initiate has been given the power to see spirits.'

Done in public this way, the initiate's progress would be witnessed and shared by the whole *uma*, whose souls he would one day have the responsibility of looking after. However, after this first stage, lasting about a week if done according to tradition, he would then spend many months privately in the forest learning herbs, songs and the exact regalia to be worn so that the spirits and souls could recognize him as a *kerei*. He would also be raising his own pigs and chickens, building them up for the final feast

We shook hands with the people gathered there – members of the *uma*, but also friends who had come to lend a hand killing the pigs, and also drumming and preparing the feast. The lavish food, together with the singing and dancing, would provide an irresistible attraction to the souls of those in the *uma*, whether the living or the ancestors. I dug into my luggage for some of the archaic little beads, handbells and necklace bells that we carried as emergency gifts, and as usual proffered them nervously, thinking they were not what the modern, almost twenty-first-century, *kereis* wanted. Sure enough, the senior *kerei* nodded unenthusiastically on seeing them. It was only when he saw one of the handbells that his expression changed. He gave a broad grin, and started chattering excitedly. Persecuted the *kereis* may be, but that didn't stop the spirits wanting people to be *kereis*, and there was a shortage of the obligatory regalia.

However, when the *kerei* rang the bell he couldn't help releasing a slight, but plainly audible, sigh of disappointment. The bell had the wrong tone. I wasn't surprised – it looked to me suspiciously like part of a kitsch door chime marketed to the new middle classes of Java. Whatever it was, it apparently didn't produce a sound that the spirits would recognize – or, I suspected, one that any spirit with taste would like.

All was not lost. A young man was set to work hammering a nail into the form of a tongue for the bell, and then it was tested alongside those of the *kerei* to make sure that the tone was just right. Then – I couldn't help feeling a little proud – our bell was presented to the *kerei* initiate.

Soon he was being settled down to work. Though it already looked like he could do with a rest, he now had to learn the first of many of the extraordinarily long and complex *kerei* songs, ringing the bell in one hand and learning each line, mimicking the *kerei* who sang at him. The songs had to be word perfect, and all in the special *kerei* language, or else the souls wouldn't come when he called them.

The ceremony proper began towards dusk, the initiate and his tutors going outside to call the ancestral spirits to attend. By now the drums were being tuned over the fire, the *kereis* wearing crowns of beads and feathers, and their wives wearing feathers that projected from their hair like a turkey's tail fan.

We had already seen the initiate watching the lips of the *kereis* as they taught him songs, now he had to watch their feet as they led him in a dance. The wives joined the group and the drums were suddenly thumping, the *kereis*' arms delicately poised as they shuffled in a tight circle, gyrating slowly among us. Slowly, he was learning to dance well and so entertain the souls.

The key task, though, was to get the initiate to see the spirits. The drummers pounded the snake skins, vibrating the air around our ears, and the loose planks of the veranda became an instrument in themselves, clacking as the dancers worked their feet harder, explosively stamping while their arms remained like outstretched wings. With the drummers still pulsing away, the dancers would pause, waiting, their extended arms still, then stamp, stamp, stamp – they would again stomp around the dance circle.

The air seemed to become denser – as if the spirits were thick among us. And we could see that the initiate was already unsteady on his feet, as he was being whirled into a state of disorientation, an unstable ecstasy. I remembered Amam Dirikogo's words: 'We start to shiver and cannot stand.' And I noticed that the *kereis* wore mirrors – devices to deflect the power of the spirits. The initiate, however, had no mirrors. He was here for the spirits to reach him – and of course he had no experience of how to handle them.

The dance continued, the *kereis* circling round and round. The crowd was enthralled, the children mesmerized, gazing at the dancers as they padded around, their arms out, hands smoothing the air, the wings of an eagle rising in a thermal; then, with the drums continuing relentlessly, the *kereis* would stop still, hovering for a moment, before again juddering on the planks.

There was only one group here who were not caught up in these events. They had placed themselves rather in the middle of the *uma* and were engaged in a card game. A bunch of clean-cut Protestants, they were making a point of slapping down their cards hard. Above and around them, the initiation continued – the *kereis* danced and their protégé followed, getting dizzier and dizzier. Now young men from the audience were gathering around the dance circle to be ready to catch him.

Soon he was swaying backwards, eyes half shut. Then, finally, he dropped to the floor – at first I thought because he was weak from his illness. But as he was carried past me, I could see he looked more dazzled than tired. It really did seem as if the moment had come – that he had seen the ancestors.

The men propped him up against a post and waved a leaf fan in his face. He sat recovering, staring ahead, oblivious to me as I filmed, and his body in utter shock, trembling. He looked like a biblical character who had encountered the Angel Gabriel and was 'sore afraid'. Here in Siberut, even a fully fledged *kerei* didn't actually deliberately visit the spirits, journeying in a trance state to their spiritual dimension like the classic shaman. On the contrary, a trance state was to be avoided – it came about if any of us mortals merely brushed with the supernatural, and was a moment of danger, when your soul was threatened. It was these weakening encounters that the initiate was learning to manage.

So the initiate sat there looking like he'd seen a Heavenly Ghost – which was more or less what he had seen. And, leaning against the very same post, the Protestant youths played on, slapping their cards down.

It was time for the initiate to begin again. He rose to his feet, still disorientated from the last dance. The drumbeat quickened, exciting the spirits, and again the initiate weakened in the mere presence of the ancestors. He was now being supported by his wrists, sustained by the *kereis* as they and the spirits swirled around.

Eventually, the initiate was slumped on his side, unable to comprehend anything. He was carried back to the post, and the senior *kerei* sat down next to him and sang a gentle song, a cooling melody to comfort his soul.

Though the initiate was no longer capable of dancing – or anything much – the *kereis* continued regardless, now involving the audience. Putting aside the business of training the initiate, they instead entertained the ancestors they had drawn here. In their dances they flew about as birds, and then scurried about as crocodiles, causing hilarity among the spectators by lying in ambush behind the posts and pouncing on toddlers and other unsuspecting members of the audience – like me, who they pretended was a giant tree.

The *kereis* were fulfilling another typical role of the medicine man, that is, the entertainer or storyteller. But this performance was not just for the sake of the living members of the *uma*, it was for those of the clan who had died – and the greatest task of the medicine man, the uniting of the living and dead, was done.

How much the initiate was taking in of this I couldn't judge. However, tonight, the *kereis* had reminded us all of the importance of their devotion to the needs of the souls of the 'departed' and those yet with us.

After three days, Yan, Anjel and I walked on, hiring a couple of young men to help carry our gear. Soon we came to a government nature reserve. It had been established without the locals' consent – and in some cases without even their knowledge. The sign at the boundary read 'Simabugai', a nonsense word that should have been 'Simabuggei', meaning 'a place of much sand'. Held in swinging cages on the warden's veranda were two officially protected birds he'd caught for his entertainment.

We had a further day's walk, through thick, untrampled forest, up hills and down. This was the rough country that Anjel had been carried through by seven people, the time he got the condition known as *kisei*, when you have disturbed the *bajou*, the life force of something – in his case, that of the hill Leleu Baja.

By mid-afternoon we were nearing the very place. We dropped into a steep-sided valley and waded along a river, scrambling up banks when the water was too deep or the algae too slippery. Somewhere along the ridge ahead and to our left was the hill, and I was wondering whether or not I could risk a little look myself. Obviously I had come here to do just that – indeed even visit the hill – and, as someone who had spent weeks in several rainforests alone I hadn't for a moment thought I would actually myself suffer ill effects. However, now that the time had come, I felt slightly less easy. Up there in the trees somewhere was a bad spirit or *sanitu sikatai* called Kelak Kulit, in whom everyone with me believed.

However, Anjel and Yan had raced ahead of me, and not only did I have no one to help me pinpoint the hill, but I could not see the effect of the haunted place on them as we approached. The two baggage carriers with me seemed unperturbed – but later I realized it was perhaps because they knew the route we were taking didn't anyway give us a clear view through the trees. You'd need a chainsaw and/or loudhailer if you were going to risk offending Kelak Kulit.

We stayed the night in an *uma* perched above the riverbank. This was actually at the very foot of Leleu Baja – and even here, we were cheated of a clear view of the dangerous place. The owner of the house was a *kerei* called Teujajak. After we'd eaten our tinned fish, he had this to say about the hill:

'If we ever get sick or bewitched here, it is because of Father Kelak Kulit. He causes it. He got the name Kelak Kulit because when he lived in our village he was struck by lightning. The lightning made his skin hard (and *kulit* means hard). When he was alive, Kelak Kulit was our uncle, our mother's brother. Once upon a time, his nephews killed a deer and beat their *duddukat* to tell everyone. When their uncle arrived he had a thorn in his foot; he said, "Please help take the thorn out for me." The nephews said, "How did you get a thorn in your foot when your skin is so hard? Is your foot soft?" He answered that it was.

'One of his nephews took the thorn out and noticed the soft skin underneath his foot. Later, when Kulit had gone, they beat their *duddukat* again [to signal a feast], even though they had not killed any animal, and put a snake tooth on the ladder into the house.

'The nephews were making arrows when Kelak Kulit arrived for the feast. He stood on the tooth and said, "Ah! There is a thorn under my foot." His brother-in-law said, "Your nephews were busy making arrows, maybe it's wood from the arrows." But Kelak Kulit saw he had a snake tooth stuck in his foot.

'Kelak Kulit said, "My nephews, I am going to die, I am going to die. When I die remember this: my home will be Leleu Baja. That is where I will always be. Remember also that when people get sick it will be because of what you did."

'He went to the top of the hill and died there. His soul went into the hill and the hill became his place. And so that we know he is still there, he sends special signs. If Kelak Kulit is angry he kicks out and there is a landslide on the other side of the hill – that is a bad omen for the people who live in the vale of Rereiket. If there is a landslide on this side, it is a bad omen for us and many people will die.'

I decided that I should, as planned, spend time alone on the hill. I wouldn't feel anything – let alone see anything – from down here. So I loaded up my pack with food for three days, a stove, mosquito net and a tent flysheet, and walked with Anjel, the *kerei* called Teujajak and the two young men up the hill. It was a beautiful day, and crossing the river at the hill's foot there seemed to me to be little chance that anything or anyone could haunt me. Men were punting by in their canoes, transporting branches of bananas and thatching material. All was calm.

I paused to fill a two-metre bamboo tube that would be my water supply, and we worked our way into the forest, rising higher and higher, stopping sometimes to catch our breath, or for Anjel, up ahead, to cut through fallen branches. What he was feeling, nearing the home of Kelak Kulit, I couldn't tell, but knowing that I was soon to be alone here I had an increasing sense of trepidation. This intensified as, nearer the summit, Teujajak waved for us to stop and called out ahead, as if some-one was there – which there was, in a sense, because this was the House of Kelak Kulit.

There was no reply – and I found myself relieved. Relieved about what? Was I already beginning to 'believe'? Was I already swallowing the story? I walked on with the others, wonder-ing if, once alone out here, I would crack up. What would it be like, when darkness fell, and the branches creaked and the bats circled? How would I feel then? I noticed we were now walking in silence: one way or another, this hill was exerting its influence on us.

To my right now, glimpses of the land below: hills undulat-ing, a carpet of forest rolling into the haze. We ducked and wove through the trees; the air cooled; and then the slope was level-ling out, and I could now see a view out through the forest on both my right and left. We were up on the ridge.

'This is the place,' said Anjel. He wasn't speaking in a whisper, but his voice was slow and considered, as if he was being careful. 'You are sleeping here? Alone? That is correct?' He was giving me a last chance.

I said I'd be fine, and carefully wedged the bamboo tube, my entire water supply, up against a tree. Anjel and the others put my things down.

Teujajak now picked some broad leaves, and laid some cigarettes out on them. The others each now got out theirs. And I realized I was the only person here with no offering. I sheepishly asked Anjel for a cigarette, and laid it gently on the leaf.

The *kerei* began talking out loud to Kelak Kulit, breaking up the cigarettes as he did so. He was speaking Mentawai, words to the effect 'Please, you who live here, we have come here peacefully to your house and we give you this offering. Please let the foreigner stay here a while. He means no harm, so please look after him.'

Teujajak sang a pleasing melody to Kelak Kulit and then suddenly all was silent except for the forest humming around us. Anjel looked to me. 'We are off then. You must stay exactly here. These slopes are steep. You must not wander, or you will get lost.'

I agreed to stay there, and the next moment they were gone, their voices lost to the leaves in the breeze, the insects and birds...

And now, here I am on the top of the hill, alone. Far down below, rising up from the valley, I can hear chickens. From further still, lifting out of the forest, comes a 'tock-tock, tock-tock' drumming sound. Someone down there has brought back a pig or deer, and his family are about to feast.

In a minute I will gather wood for a fire, and then I'll walk around, find out what other species I'm sharing this hilltop with.

Already I feel more loosely attached to the reassuring world that I came from – the clocks, my busy diary, the medicine – all the features of our cushioned existence, the life that we lead in all forgetfulness of our connection with 'nature'. I can see the importance, for a *kerei* who is being initiated, of getting away into the forest. You need to be able to understand the interconnectedness of everything. I have just killed a leech – and no sooner has it dropped to the ground than ants are carrying it away. Life and death, the eternal circle. Our Great Religions have distanced us from our origins – Christianity in the West, Islam and Judaism further East. They remind us of our specialness in the scheme of things. But, during their time in the forest, *kerei* initiates see the web of interwoven life; then they go back home, and every ritual they perform acts like a reminder to their people: the *kereis* help the Mentawai understand what we in the West have forgotten: that we are part of the system, not above it.

Now I've turned on my little dictaphone, playing the sound of Amam Maom singing a *kerei* melody. It's a quiet tune, and out here it seems lonely.

It's about to get dark. I've made my camp, and am all set for what may be a sleepless night. Just now, as the light was fading, I was looking for firewood when *something* crashed down not far away. I was startled, and grabbed my bush knife. Of course, it was probably a branch falling from the canopy. But how easily I have been absorbed by my own fears. When you are in a place loaded with fear it doesn't take very much to shear off the complacent veneer of urban civilization.

Now I look about me, trying to memorize the shape of tree trunks and thick branches, as if to make new friends. Soon they will all fade into darkness, and I'll have only the voice of Amam Maom.

The middle of the night, and a strong moon is up. A passing troop of heavy monkeys woke me. They were joja, I think, and they crashed through the leaves above my head. I found them comforting. The silver light plays on the shadows, stretching gnarled branches into the shape of hands. Fruit bats flick across the open sky.

Generally, I feel at ease. Of course, any encounter with Kelak Kulit will change this. And I lie here, and I drink from my flask of coffee, and I look around me, wondering: half wanting to see Him, half definitely not wanting to.

Even though I'm not feeling scared, I've found that I cannot bring myself to say the name of Kelak Kulit out loud. I tell myself it's not because I might conjure him up but because I want to respect the local people. I haven't come from Europe just to play a game with beliefs they hold sacred. Or am I fooling myself? Maybe the spirit of Kelak Kulit, after all, can reach even me.

And now it's over – towards five in the morning and the chickens are starting to call out from the *uma* down below, the dawn a magenta glow in the mists. Soon I'll hear Anjel zigzagging his way up the slope towards me, and then he'll be peering into my camp, wondering perhaps if an ashened face will meet his.

A few days later, I was back with Amam Dirikogo.

'It's impossible,' he said when I told him I hadn't seen anything much up on Leleu Baja. 'Impossible for you to see.'

'I know, but I was hoping something might happen.' I didn't dare reveal that I'd had the cheek to spend a night alone there to provoke Kelak Kulit into action.

'You want to see the spirits but you are a layman. If you try to see the ancestors without preparation, without being chosen by them to become a *kerei*, they will be angry with you and bring sickness to you... And you don't know how to sing to them, how to call them properly with kind words or how to behave in front of them...'

I was reminded of a phrase that I'd heard around the world so many times from healers. 'No one can choose to become a medicine man – you are chosen.' And, it seemed, I hadn't been chosen. The consolation was, my position was no different from that of any ordinary Mentawai. They weren't chosen, they couldn't see the spirits.

But we did now seem to have the friendship of Amam Dirikogo, and maybe something would rub off. So I sat with him as he mixed up his arrow poisons, watching him bathe the arrow tips until they'd soaked up the stagnant-pond black liquid. And each evening he patiently tried to teach me a song about a bird wagging its tail up in a durian tree.

Here, there was a palpable sense of Amam Dirikogo belonging to a tight family. Brothers, sisters and cousins were always
dropping in. Even the pigs seemed to have a sense of belonging
to the *uma*. They got over-excited if a dog stole food from
a plate, knowing the miscreant was about to be kicked off
the veranda and down to them, and they could do some dog-
bashing. They would begin skitting about, grunting. And hearing
them below, the dog would begin to fear the worst, and struggle
desperately to hide. But the pigs would be waiting, and he'd
eventually have to fling himself into the forest to avoid them,
spending a lonely night somewhere out there in the bushes –
and all because he hadn't been loyal to the *uma*.

One day, something arose that took Amam Dirikogo off to
his neighbour: the man had been attacked by a crocodile spirit
while fishing. I had already learnt that *kereis* could never refuse
to help, and Amam Dirikogo was soon on his way.

We trudged through deeper and deeper mud, along the way
Amam Dirikogo mimicking my phrase, 'Oh mai gourd!'

We came to the *uma* – the usual milling pigs, chickens and
lethargic dogs – and Amam Dirikogo sat down with the patient,
a youngish man, who was yellow-eyed and cramped with pain.
It wasn't the crocodile spirit, Amam Dirikogo said; the man had
been gathering building materials, and this was probably a hill
spirit, like Kelak Kulit.

I followed Amam Dirikogo as he went gathering herbs. Rain
sprinkled down on us as we wandered in and out of the dripping
leaves, cutting a sprig here, snapping off a leaf there. It felt exhil-
arating to be extracting elements of good from the forest and
bringing them together to create a recipe to heal souls. And all
the more so because many of the species that Amam Dirikogo
was seeking out were said to signpost their potential as medicines – the so-called Doctrine of Signatures seen in other animistic societies. There was a twiggy fern called *osap*, whose
fronds spread like gnarled fingers and so would be waved over
the sick man, its leaf fingers scratching away at the malevolent
hill spirit. Other herbs, used in massage, were of spiral shape,
and had the power to 'deflect' badness.

When he had all he needed, Amam Dirikogo knelt at a brook and washed and mashed the herbs as Amam Maom had done. A crab reared from the pebbles, lifting its white clippers. 'Many ow-ow!' said Amam Dirikogo, piecing together two more English words he'd gleaned.

The ritual was a modified version of the one I'd seen performed for Amam Maom's grandchildren. The hill spirit was driven out of the patient with, among other things, the *osap*, the twiggy hand-like fern, and a special meal of eggs and sago laid out with cooling leaves on a dish for the missing soul. The soul was further enticed into the meal with the help of Amam Dirikogo's songs and bells, and the patient swallowed his herb medicine and some of the now soul-enriched food; he was massaged with spiritually 'cooling' herbs to further welcome the soul home.

How did the jaundiced, shivering patient know the sickness was gone? With a flourish, Amam Dirikogo split open a bamboo, and showed its remarkable contents – not a hollow tube, but one spilling a red, blood-like liquid. The implication was that he had extracted this gore, this badness, from his patient. 'As you see, you should now be safely on the road to recovery,' you might imagine his doctor equivalent in the West saying, bolstering his patient by enthusiastically proffering the X-ray photos before gathering up the case notes to leave.

Or was it just cheap trickery? Medicine men have sometimes admitted their use of illusion – a healer for example dramatically produces a stone which he has 'sucked' from a sick girl's stomach, saying a sorcerer placed it there. But such tricks are also a way of convincing patients – who, unlike them, haven't the benefit of being able to see the spirits – that a change really has taken place. The stone is merely a physical representation of what, he genuinely believes, has really happened.

All in all, how helpful to this patient was the ceremony? The physiological benefit of the massage – at least in circulating the blood and alleviating discomfort – was obvious. And in the West we now begrudgingly accept the very real medical value of theatre: improvements, even cures, can in many cases be effected through 'the power of the mind'. As for the actual efficacy of the medicine he'd swallowed, I could imagine a team of pharmacologists being kept busy running their five-year trials on each herb – and researcher Wanda Avé has noted that some medicines contain forty herbal components. A full examination of only one 'curative' might take many lifetimes.

As we left, Amam Dirikogo's patient was looking better for the treatment. I couldn't say whether it was the medicine kicking in, but his morale, his 'spirit', at least had been raised – so maybe you could say his soul was, indeed, back. Sadly, however, when we called round the next day he was again yellow, again looking terrible. The ritual was repeated with a different collection of herbs. Perhaps it was malaria, or perhaps it was the crocodile spirit after all.

John, the BBC producer, arrived at Amam Dirikogo's *uma*, bringing with him our small film crew – here to pick up specialist shots – and, to our glee, they had lost the Government Minder, who was supposed to be assisting us in not filming any illegal activities, like tattooing or the wearing of loincloths. He was last seen at Jakarta airport, in bell-bottom trousers and Cuban heels, unable to get on the full plane, waving his documents forlornly the other side of the ticket barrier.

The crew settled in over the next few days, and Amam Dirikogo gamely extended the porch to accommodate their gear and repair the slats that had been smashed by their boots. And, having done the house alterations, he now began preparing a house rejuvenation ritual, a *liat sapou*, for the spirit of the *uma*, which might have been disturbed.

Before this got under way, a thin, middle-aged man with large Javanese teeth came gingerly along the path. It was the Government Minder, and he had staggered here alone, rather admirably, against all odds through the mud. He was now in jeans and T-shirt, and was leaning heavily on a staff. 'At last I've arrived at the chicken house,' he said, mistaking the *uma* for a shed. The women ran to cover themselves in sarongs, but Amam Dirikogo stayed exactly where he was in his loincloth, drawing on one of his home-made cigarettes and regarding the man and his mud with amusement.

Despite our fears, over the next few days we found ourselves warming to the Minder. He was nearing retirement and had lost interest in curbing foreign films. One of our biggest concerns had been that he would try to stop the ritual, but, as the members of the *uma* gathered, drifting in like leaves from the forest – Amam Dirikogo's daughter and her husband, and Amam Gresi – he showed no sign of wanting to interfere. Though a Muslim, he was even spotted secretly nibbling pork.

The ritual proceeded along familiar lines, starting at the *bakkat katsaila*, the shrine near the kitchen hearth. Spirits were called, enticed with trays of coconut and flowers, and the Minder scuttled back and forth, trying to avoid the moment when the pig was sacrificed.

Finally, Amam Dirikogo was doing the divination with the pig entrails.

'Are they looking all right?' I asked, sitting with him.

'I am happy the way the future looks,' he said, looking over at our sack of presents. 'It looks like a gong is coming my way!'

The ritual wouldn't be over until Amam Dirikogo brought food from the forest – the Mentawai speak of needing to 'go to the hill', as if their invitation to the spirits was now to be reciprocated. Amam Dirikogo said I could come along – a big chance for me because I would at last be alone in the home of the spirits with a *kerei*.

We both gathered together some food and sleeping gear and left in the mid-afternoon, walking swiftly along the track. We hadn't gone far when Amam Dirikogo stopped me, put down his quiver and bow, and squatted right in the path. He gestured that I should do the same. I sat down beside him, waiting. It was as if he'd brought me out here only to tell me a secret. Then he got up again, and took two palm leaves, and he laid these before me across the mud.

I realized then that he was performing a *panake*, a 'permission' ritual – like the one done for me on Leleu Baja – to make sure we could stay in the forest unharmed. On the leaves Amam

Dirikogo placed different herbs – I found myself marvelling once again at the ease with which these *kereis* reached out for the species they needed – then a strip of cotton and a stick of baked sago, and once these gifts had been assembled he gently called to the monkey souls – '*kourna, kourna…*' – to be here.

We hadn't gone much further when rain came down in torrents. Amam Dirikogo swiftly built up a palm-frond shelter, patching the gaps with banana leaves. As the rain dripped down around us I got a fire going to make some tea. Amam Dirikogo and I sat drying off on our floor of sodden palm leaves. The light began to dim as we drank tea and munched my choco-ring biscuits.

After dark, while we were sitting there, Amam Dirikogo began issuing strange mumblings and mutterings. Was he talking to himself? Or to some spirit? Next, he moved me aside – as if allowing space for someone. He chattered on, and I clearly discerned my name. I was being talked about.

I stepped outside as Amam Dirikogo rigged up his mosquito net. Moisture was coming down through the darkness, drifting through the palms, trees and ferns like the breath of the forest. There were fireflies and there was blackness. There were screechings, and there were the itchings and scratchings of a hundred thousand species. 'How much more can I ever experience here?' I wondered. 'I haven't seen a spirit, and I can't see a spirit.' In the end I could only guess.

Back in our shelter, Amam Dirikogo was already snugly in his mosquito net. I put up mine, and blew out the candle.

I woke sharply some time later. It was not yet light. There was a slight drizzle but the air was still. Amam Dirikogo, somewhere very near, was singing. I looked, and the candle was flickering a silver glow on his face, and he seemed to be half-way into the spirit world. I turned on my torch and immediately felt very separate from him – belonging elsewhere, to a life shaped by concrete and electrics. I turned the torch off.

Amam Dirikogo walked off into the blackness. I heard water being disturbed in the nearby brook. He came back a minute or two later with a large prawn and a frog. These he put into a leaf package and stuck in the roof. They would be taken back to the *uma* and given to the children, signalling the end of the trip to the forest, and the beginning of life back to normal.

Then we heard a faraway monkey – short, deep calls. 'A joja,' Amam Dirikogo whispered. 'He's sad because of rain.' I'd got so used to him talking to the ancestors it took me a moment to realize he was speaking Indonesian. He was talking to me. And I realized then that we had hardly exchanged a word since we'd entered the forest the day before.

And then, nearer at hand, the whooping calls of the *bilou*, Kloss's gibbon. The sound was light, soft, heart-rending. It soared around the tree canopy, calls first from one gibbon, then another. It was a moving cry of what seemed to be both loneliness and exquisite beauty. Without even needing to talk, we headed off in the direction of the sound.

We stepped through the dawn light, Amam Dirikogo first, his bow and arrow quiver to hand. Without breaking stride, he picked up a tortoise from a stream and placed it upside down on its back for collection later. The long, slow whooping of the *bilou* was nearer now. Nearer and nearer. Finally, way, way up in the canopy, there they were: a troop of small, gangly black figures against the dawn sky. They had already seen us, and were gazing down – they were not alarmed, but intrigued. They were spread around a vine-draped tree, most dangling from one arm, casually hanging from the creepers; some were fidgeting with leaves, others cautiously clambering through branches to catch up with the others. In the midst of them was what must have been a wayward youngster, tumbling through foliage and oblivious to us and everything but his game.

But we both knew that Amam Dirikogo would not be getting his poisoned arrows out. There was a taboo against *kereis* hunting them and, listening to their calls – that cry from a broken, desperate heart – it wasn't hard to see why.

That doesn't stop ordinary Mentawai killing them; the *bilou* are classed as animals that are *matai ketgat*, literally 'spirit of ones who have to die' – that is, the edible. Shotguns are banned by government, so the old Mentawai use their bows and arrows and the young use air rifles, with traditional poison on the pellets. But they eat *bilou* meat in the forest, not at home, and they do not hang the skulls in their houses. And listening at dawn to the beauty of its voice, the sound of a lost human soul, many huntsmen must have lowered their bows.

Amam Dirikogo gazed in silence for perhaps half an hour, watching the gibbons as they watched us. And perhaps one sign that I did, after all, feel something of the ancestors and forest spirits was that I came away instinctively talking, just like Amam Dirikogo, in a whisper. The trip had done its purpose – whether you bring home meat or not, the act of hunting forces that respect on you.

We stopped at the camp, folded our mosquito nets and sat for a moment to share my tin of pineapple chunks. '*Mananan!*' Amam Dirikogo said, gulping his down – 'Delicious!'

I'd been on Siberut for six weeks, feeling increasingly absorbed by life here, and one day found myself being absorbed further, as Amam Dirikogo's father set about tattooing my leg. It was something that seemed strangely appropriate, perhaps because I'd found something here that I'd been dwelling on in my thirteen-year absence. Or perhaps because I was endorsing something of their way of life. I knew I could never belong, but this was a sign of further commitment to something I'd spent most of my adult life investigating, a mark saying that I'd somehow progressed a little way. *Matéu* is the word used to express the reason for tattooing. It means 'fitting, something to make the body finished', Amam Dirikogo said. 'As a plant needs a flower.' And it did feel '*matéu*'.

His father, a rather humourless, lean old man, made the ink by chewing sugarcane and spitting it into a wooden bowl blackened by paraffin soot. Next, he began the business of driving a blunt safety pin, attached to a stick which he tapped with his other hand, into me for three and a half hours. It felt the same as running a slow sewing machine up and down your thigh, and afterwards, still raw, it had to be rubbed with the *laipat* fern to prevent infection.

Now I was indelibly stamped by the island. And, oddly, it seemed right – even though I couldn't yet even sing the song I was meant to be learning. So far I'd only managed the song's name – *urai ngorud*, a dove-like bird.

Soon after this, it was time to leave Siberut. I saw Amam Maom again – we brought him up to join another big ritual at Amam Gresi's house. There, for the first time, I saw Amam Dirikogo dancing, reinvigorating the soul of Amam Gresi's *uma* with the help of another *kerei*, Sakigege, a dancer lighter on his feet than a bird. Together, they drew the *uma's* souls into a bamboo tube that would form a new *bakat katsaila* at the very heart of the *uma*.

During this ritual, Amam Dirikogo was flung aside by the power of the souls that they'd gathered. And another *kerei* collapsed, suddenly overcome by an encounter with a wood spirit. The other *kereis* dragged him to the side, protecting him from the spirit with their own souls. He was weak, he was dazed. But he had seen what you and I can never see.

'To see them is amazing. Our eyes are astonished. We are in awe.'

SIBERIA
SHAMANS IN THE STEPPE

Arctic Ocean

RUSSIAN FEDERATION

SIBERIA

Tuva

Lake
Baikal

MONGOLIA

JAPAN

CHINA

CHAPTER FOUR

'I find it hard work, healing, but the trials I face from dangerous spirits make me more powerful. The more I heal, the stronger I am. And these hardships are necessary – they help you understand patients in their suffering.'
Ai-chourek, 'urban' kham

L eaving Siberut, I found myself thinking back to the men and women I'd seen with similar duties in Borneo, the Australian bush, the Amazon Basin, the African desert and savannah – in fact, I'd seen them operating almost everywhere outside the reach of the main religious empires. I remembered a woman called Tsend in northernmost Mongolia, and even she, living in the cold and arid mountains of inner Asia, would have recognized the spiritual dimension that Amam Dirikogo described; she'd have understood his talk of the need for harmony with the living forces around us, his commitment to the souls not only of the living and dead, but of everything around.

However, the techniques of the *kereis* differed in one important respect from those employed by Tsend. She was a shaman in the classic sense – indeed, like the very word 'shaman', her family emerged from Siberia, though fled with their reindeer herds into Mongolia to escape Stalin. To communicate with the spirits she went into a trance, 'riding' her reindeer-skin drum into their spirit realm, which was composed of upper, middle and lower worlds. She talked about it as a place that was the mirror image of ours, and for that reason wore a crow feather headdress that seemed reversed, ribbons like tresses of hair hanging right over her face. She wore a *khalat* or long coat – spiritual armour to protect her against dangerous spirits she might encounter – and was guided through the perils of the cosmos by the crow spirit, her personal ally whom she had learnt to trust during her initiation. The exact nature of her experience I could only try to imagine, but I had watched while she underwent these trance-journeys – seen her laughing and crying, reacting to the spirits she was consulting or with whom she was battling. It was all with one aim in mind: to bring back sacred, healing information that could improve the life of her people in the physical realm. The *kereis*, on the other hand, did not journey to this spirit place. They called the spirits to come to them; then they interpreted their needs or the needs of the patients 'given the eyes to see'.

After Siberut, the obvious next step was to get to know one of these more orthodox shaman figures, who healed the world through their cosmic journeys. I travelled north to Siberia and the land that the shaman Tsend had fled, the republic of Tuva. The previous winter our Siberian fixer, Misha Maltsev, from Yakutin, had identified some promising areas of investigation.

Siberia may have given the world the word 'shaman' (from the Tungus *samán*, the term used by Evenk herders in the north to describe their medicine man) but now it was rapidly adapting to more 'modern' needs. Following decades of communist perse-cution, some sort of spiritual rebirth had taken place in Tuva.

After the Soviet Union's collapse in August 1991, the shamans had found acceptance in the eyes of the Tuvan govern-ment as a symbol of the newly independent country. The unthinkable had happened: these strange, chosen people – who around the world were maverick by the very nature of their calling, outsiders by the very exclusivity of their profession – had somehow been organized into clinics. Nowadays, the shamans diagnosed their patients from behind desks. It sounded like a new use had been found for Tuva's communist legacy of centralized bureaucracy.

A hand-woven carpet had been rolled down the aisle of the plane, and on our plastic trays we were served horsemeat. The flight attendant slammed on some cassette music, a quixotic ballad from somewhere in Russia. With me was Ruhi Hamid, the BBC producer on this leg of the journey, and Misha. We landed at Abakan, then began a long car journey to Tuva over the Sayan mountains, down a road built by prisoners in Tsarist times.

Though it was mid-May, spring was just arriving. There were two-metre drifts of snow and, as we dropped down into the arid steppe, following rivers churning with melt-water, the banks thickened with burgeoning plant growth. Everywhere sap was on the move again, pumping through hitherto frozen soil. The trees seemed to vibrate with newfound life, thrusting out pine needles that were pale and tender, delicate in what was still a biting wind. I remembered Tsend decorating certain sacred trees in Mongolia; looking around me now at them, leading the return of life, I could see why any tree might be venerated.

And I was thinking, as we drove, that whatever shamans there were here, most must have learnt their knowledge after Tuva was incorporated into the Soviet Union – it had been part of Mongolia until 1921 and lost its independence when swallowed by its even larger neighbour in 1944. So how, under the communist regime, did they learn? Despite the repression, the traditions had somehow been transferred down. Or had they been made up? Endorsing the shamans – in Tuva they are called *khams* if male and *udagans* if female, but to avoid confusion I have referred to all Tuvan shamans as *khams* throughout – had been the government's way of encouraging the country's grass roots. Except that the communists had scorched those grass roots, and who knows what really had been left over?

However, I would be able to tell more once I'd got to know Ai-chourek, a female *kham* we'd arranged to meet. Brought up in the countryside, she now worked with one of the officially recognized clinics, and had even been abroad to demonstrate 'Tuvan shamanism' for New Age workshops. The government had given her money for a flat: 'She is classed as a spiritual resource of Tuva,' Misha had learned on his reconnoitre trip, 'a piece of heritage.'

Eventually I also wanted to meet Mokur-Ool Sevenovich, a *kham* living well away from the goings-on of townsfolk. He was living the traditional life of a nomadic herder, moving his yurt from pasture to pasture. If all else failed, he might reasonably be expected to be the 'real thing' – or closer to it. One of our contacts, a Tuvan craftsman and musician called Gendos, was making a drum for him. Later we would join Gendos when he went to hand it over.

We arrived in Kyzyl, the capital, which seemed to be composed almost entirely of communist housing blocks, each substandard brick placed with half-hearted applications of cement. We were installed in a rented apartment – graffiti'd dark corridors, their light bulbs stolen. And we looked out at our view: playgrounds made of dust, balconies of scrap iron, decked with clothes that were clean but still grey. Everything here looked second-hand. If shamanism of any kind exists in this place, I thought, it'll be a miracle – a triumph of faith. Or a last resort.

We'd been told that, before we did anything else, we ought to pay our respects to Mongush Kenin-Lopsan, who was said to somehow 'oversee' the official *khams*. An old man now, he had done an enormous amount to document Tuvan shamanism, and was a key element in the founding of the original clinic, the Düngür ('Drum') Centre, in 1992. Here in Kyzyl, he was highly respected for having preserved the spiritual tradition of Tuva – and, it seemed, rather feared. However, by the time we'd rested and phoned his office, we'd missed him. It didn't seem too important at the time.

We focused instead on Ai-chourek, the female *kham*. I had already seen footage of her from the recce trip, drumming away, cleansing a pregnant woman. She'd worn an overly lavish feather headdress that would, I was rather afraid, have bewildered Tsend. Human figures decorated the back of her cloak – they were rather like a child's simple cut-outs. All in all, she'd so far failed to inspire.

Our Tuvan translator, a young woman called Aldynai, came to the flat and, soon after, Ai-chourek herself. She seemed a little shy standing in the doorway, placing her palms together in greeting. She was also quite small, and looked younger than she had in the recce video tapes. She had two plaits – her left one hung with a clutch of *kabarga* deer teeth, earrings and bead jewellery that seemed fresh from the more ethnic stalls of a western street market. However, I recognized one item as local: around her neck was a *küzüngü-eeren*, the protective device I'd seen Tsend wear, a metal disc containing a helper spirit that reflected evil and focused power. And after Ai-chourek had taken a seat and talked a while I was very pleasantly surprised. Underneath, there was something very genuine about this person.

Ai-chourek took a seat and gradually composed herself, telling us of her plans, talking glowingly of her forthcoming trip to address a conference of New Age Italians. Mainly, though, she was a countryside woman, she said, and she hoped we would join her on her trip in a few days to her home village, Bei-Dag. But later today she wanted to take us to one of the clinics, to see how the *khams* operated in Kyzyl. The Düngür Centre, the original clinic founded largely by Kenin-Lopsan, was now being refurbished, so we would visit a new clinic, the Tos Deer ('Nine Skies') Centre. Its name was drawn from an ancient concept of nine divisions in the Upper World – the nine planets but also nine energy-charged realms that oversee us. We arranged to rendezvous after lunch, at the Centre of Asia Monument.

With a couple of hours to spare, Ruhi, Misha and I had a chance to see the sights of Kyzyl. I couldn't help noticing odd splashes of blood on the pavement from the drunks stumbling home last night, and there were men still stumbling – even now, at midday. Some of the women, however, were in the tight, impractical, showy clothes I'd only seen on cable channels, and looked as if they were still out clubbing. I was getting the impression that Kyzyl was not a content place: as if people were trying to lose themselves – in drink, in the fantasy land they'd seen on MTV. And I was beginning to understand why they might want to: with the collapse of the Soviet empire, there'd also been a collapse in infrastructure. We passed through the open market – and learnt that many of the women behind the stalls used to be teachers, who'd had to give up because they were never paid.

The Centre of Asia Monument turned out to have been made – like the *khams* of Tuva – a national symbol, part of the effort to rejuvenate the nation. I doubted if it lived up to its name (somewhere in Mongolia's Gobi Desert would be a better guess) but here anyway was the monument with its plaque, a giant globe and obelisk reaching to the sky. It was as if being at the centre of Asia was an achievement of their nation.

The translator Aldynai turned up but Ai-chourek was rather late, and while we stood there I began wondering if 'Tuva' actually existed at all. What did they have of their own, apart from their language and an interesting set of triangular stamps? There was a fine tradition of *khöömei* throat singing – which wasn't unique to them. They also had nomadic horsemen, they had the steppe, they had shamans – but so did Mongolia, next door, and Mongolia had for centuries, undeniably, been a nation, a very considerable one in fact. This wasn't so much the Centre of Asia so much as a bit of outermost Outer Mongolia. Tuva was a sponge loosely attached to the fringe reef of the great Mongol nation, and furthermore thumped by waves of Russian culture, squeezed by Soviet philosophy, and now, released, sucking in whatever lay in the turbid sea around it.

Oh well, I thought. It's probably just my jet-lag.

Then I saw Ai-chourek. This time she had dressed up in her finery. From her ears hung silver feathers, from her plaits real feathers and threads. Through my bleary eyes she looked as if out of *The Sacred Drum*, a New Age magazine I had read – not so much Tuvan as an interesting blend of Sioux, Hopi and other American Indians.

Misha went off to find Gendos, the musician making a drum for the nomadic *kham* Mokur-Ool, and the rest of us walked along to the Tos Deer Centre, a low wood building above the Yenisey River, where the birches were bright with their unfolding greenery. In we walked. I was already bracing myself for the worst: shamans tend to work alone, and medicine men around the world tend to go into action only when the place and time are right for the spirits. Not here. Not any more. Now the official talk in the Republic of Tuva was of unity, being together, working together – and shamanism was no exception.

Ai-chourek led us into a corridor and told us to stay behind her. On the wall there were photos of each *kham* and lists in Cyrillic of their specialities. 'Kidneys, backbones, pregnancies,' Aldynai translated. 'Hearts, bowels, flatulence … ' We passed one door that was ajar. Beyond, a woman in a white coat was manhandling a little old lady.

'Just a masseur,' Aldynai said, as we quickly moved on. 'Bio-energy,' a voice corrected her. It came from a girl sitting at the cash desk at the end of the corridor. She said we could go back to have a look. So we darted back while Ai-chourek wasn't watching, and the woman in the white coat invited us in, packed off the old lady, and told us she couldn't cure bad spirits but had the power to rid people of negative energy. She demonstrated her work, flicking the negative energy out of an imaginary patient and into the wastepaper basket.

Ai-chourek then found us and we were hoiked out and led into a room where a man wearing a trilby hat was sitting behind a desk. Around him on the wall were an assortment of garish headdresses and tambourine-like hand-drums. There was also a fish head and a bunch of bird feathers and a little rag doll with ribbons hanging from it – these I recognized from Mongolia as *eeren*, amulets or spirit helpers, like Tsend's crow. We didn't know what we had come to see the *kham* for, but we smiled at him and he smiled ingratiatingly back. And, before I could ask his name and role here, he began what I can only describe as 'dressing up'. From a cloak peg behind him he began putting on clothes which might be a child's idea of a Red Indian costume. His trilby hat was now replaced by a Hiawatha headdress. It really did look like make-believe, a re-creation of Never Never Land, as if Tuva was a nation of Lost Boys seek-ing hope in Redskins, not even sure what a *kham* was any more. In some ways, that was all right: who could deny that the West hadn't also lost its way? My worry was that this clinic might be preying on the Tuvan people's desperation; and if such criticism could be levelled at all religion, at least the major faiths didn't normally change the rules quite so obviously as they went along. Let's face it, were these *khams* likely to be in trance through the night as the spirits sometimes called Tsend to be? Or would the clinic doors close as advertised at 5 p.m., to suit the convenience of the *khams* (who like all shamans, in theory, are the spirits' appointed messengers) instead?

'What now?' said the translator, Aldynai, turning to me. A very good point. The *kham* had been joined by two ladies who I'd thought were secretaries but who now were also dressed up. They stood beside the Red Indian, waiting for us just like extras on a film set. But we hadn't come to film an act.

I asked them to introduce themselves. We started with the Red Indian. He produced his shamanic ID – a bit of typed paper with a stamp – just as, a few years ago, he might have offered his Party card. Did his credibility rest on this? He seemed proud of the card and no doubt it was given only after some sort of selection process: but it brought us back to the central problem. The medicine man is invariably someone a little different from normal – often even an eccentric, an oddity – an outsider because, as Jesus found, a prophet is not welcome in his own home. The spirits had singled them out, if not through their personality then by an affliction or illness or brush with death. Often they were physically disabled – they were subject to epileptic fits, or blind, like Tsend. In this respect, the *kereis* had been unusually 'normal' – but even they, with their long hair and flowers, stood out from the crowd. Not in modern-day Tuva. Here the medicine men were not the shamans of old – the epitome of freedom, warriors guiding their community by means of their lone, cosmic revelations – but instead children of new-found capitalism.

However, I was again judging too harshly. Some traditional shamans would have been feared for the use to which they put their power, and here they were not. And besides, the shaman's role is, after all, to serve the needs of his society. Perhaps, I thought, this society needs a Red Indian.

Through Aldynai I explained that I'd lived in Mongolia a while, and met a powerful shaman there, a woman called Tsend.

'She'll be less powerful than any of us here in the Tos Deer Centre,' the Red Indian said.

Hmmm … It was hard to believe anyone here would ever fly far off into the spiritual realm – or anywhere too far from their cash desk. We were just beginning to look for excuses to get out of here, when a young lad was brought in. He had a soiled shirt, worn shoes and a face that was burnished by the wind – a country boy, and possibly a bit of a wide-boy as well. He smirked as he sat down in front of us. 'Looks like he's been brought in as a fake patient,' I murmured to Ruhi. But I was being unkind again. The boy had been produced only to give us the general gist of what went on here.

Ai-chourek put on her garb, the coat with the cut-out figures across the back, and now the little demonstration got under way. The four *khams* slowly began to drum. The boy, whose name was, I think, Mingi, sat with that faint smirk, eyes closed. He wasn't taking this very seriously. And, I was tempted to think, who could blame him?

Tsend, the shaman I'd met in Mongolia, had worn a *khalat*, the coat that was her protection on her divine journey into the spirit world. These *khams* were wearing what looked like embroidered dressing gowns. And where were the ribbons and mirrors tied to them – the pendants representing spirit helpers that helped fend off the arrows and other weapons sent by demons? Where were the pendants that transformed the *kham* into an animal – an eagle, a bear – to better negotiate the wilds of the spirit world? Where were the pendants to communicate with the souls of the dead and the living? And where were the rattles and bells to signal spirit helpers and warn away demons? If you needed to confront Erlik, the great lord of the underworld, you might need two sets of ritual vestments for your spiritual journey.

But not here, not in the Tos Deer Clinic. You weren't going anywhere.

I almost didn't bother filming. But as they began to drum, closing in on the boy, he swayed just a little. The Red Indian began throat singing, *khöömei*, an otherworldly, peculiar sound composed of two varying tones and which, like the sound of the drumming, is said to reach out to the spirits. Then the boy's eyelids started quivering – a surprisingly good act, I thought. However, it would have been better if we'd left earlier, giving the Red Indian the benefit of the doubt. Now these people had ruined any chance I had of believing in their institutionalized shamanism.

But the next thing, Mingi's eyes were dramatically rolling back – I could see only the whites. I was suddenly alert, aware that I was seeing something that wasn't an act at all. The boy without any warning keeled over backwards, on to his head. I could hear a sickening thud as it hit the floor. No actor would have risked that. 'Oh my God!' Aldynai whispered to herself. 'He *isn't* a charlatan!'

The *khams* moved in closer still, drumming by his head, and the two 'secretaries' stopped to lift the boy on to a bed at the side. Ai-chourek massaged Mingi's chest while the Red Indian burned some *artysh*, a sprig of juniper that is said to release a purifying smoke. The boy sat up and began crying. He was confused, scared. The Red Indian took off Mingi's shoes and socks and poured water over one of his feet. 'I saw an old lady!' Mingi wailed. 'She beat me with a rod and it hurt so much.'

Ai-chourek opened her mouth for the first time. 'She was a spirit.'

'He'll be all right,' the Red Indian said. Everyone kept on repeating it, as if to convince themselves. 'He'll be all right.'

'Maybe the lady was telling him to become a *kham*,' Ai-chourek said. 'If she comes again, maybe she'll beat harder – then he'll have to start listening.' It was an interesting thought. I'd witnessed an extraordinary thing, something that reminded me of the illness or crises that Amam Maom had talked about when the spirits chose you to be their messenger.

Mingi was helped outside, and Aldynai and I stayed to poke about the clinic for a while, talking with the girl at the cash desk, who was the daughter of the clinic's founder. She said patients were often sent here from the hospital, which was in a sorry state now that the Russian support had gone. Then the

Red Indian came up, placing his hands together and bowing to me as a thank you. 'Any gesture would be welcome,' he said, his head bobbing up and down. He began a long address in Tuvan, bowing all the while. 'He wants payment,' Aldynai said, translating with admirable succinctness.

As we paid our fee, the other *khams* came one by one to cash-in chits from their own patients. It was the close of another day's satisfactory business. The last patient, a pregnant girl in a minuscule mini-skirt, scuttled away past us, excited at the portents that had been revealed to her.

Outside, we caught a word with Mingi, who was now very much back on his feet. He explained that he hadn't wanted to be part of the demonstration, but his mum was the masseur – he meant the woman who rid people of 'negative energy' – and she'd dragged him in. 'And then, it all happened like a dream,' he said, looking at his feet.

'Did you know that the others said you'd make a good *kham*?'

Mingi was incredulous. He said he was someone who just enjoyed singing *khöömei*. It made him feel better if he was ill or depressed. He'd never thought of being a *kham*. 'What if you are chosen to be one?' I said. He shook his head. 'Then I'd have to accept it. But I have no plans in that direction – and really,' he added with emphasis, 'I'd *rather not be*, thank you.'

I walked away from the clinic feeling healed somehow by it, just like a normal fee-paying patient. I'd come to Siberia as a non-believer in 'Tuva', in paying for Magic by the Minute, but I had now seen a lot more happen than just fakery – though I still suspected there was some of that here as well. But the ancient system of healing, shamanism, had been crushed and yet was surviving, even outliving, the communist system. Despite the extraordinary rise in health care and literacy during fifty years of Soviet control, it still hadn't profoundly dented people's belief in the *khams*. For the average person there was still something beyond the rational.

Outside the clinic, and leaning his massive frame against the balustrade, was Gendos, the musician–craftsman who was making the drum for Mokur-Ool. I'd been expecting an introverted craftsman from the backwoods, but, standing with his hair in a long neat plait and wearing sunglasses, home-made cowboy boots and a black leather jacket, Gendos looked like a rock star – or perhaps a Hell's Angel, a biker without a bike.

Gendos, Ai-chourek and the rest of us went on a long walk together, down by the river. The soft new leaves were quivering in the afternoon wind, men were fishing with rods, boys were sitting in a row whacking sticks at the boulders. As we strolled, Ai-chourek told us that when she was a little girl, she felt like an old woman. 'I was a child of nature,' she said, plucking birch leaf buds as she went by. 'I would leave the house at sunrise and come back at sunset. My parents thought I was odd, even mad.'

We walked along, Gendos saying little, his small hands together behind his huge, bear's back. He seemed in awe of this *kham*, and listened like a child to her story of how it all began for her. I felt he wanted to be like her somehow.

'The feelings got stronger,' Ai-chourek continued. 'At the age of five, I could predict certain things. And I used to worry myself that I was mad. It was only later that I could make sense of it all by becoming a shaman.'

Shamanism, then, seemed to give a structure to all these odd feelings. And as long as she stayed with nature, she felt strong. 'Nature recharges me,' she said. 'Nature cannot be deceived. It is a way to truth.' *Pravda*, she kept repeating, truth. We drifted on back to town and went our own ways, agreeing to meet in the morning to see two sites that meant a lot to her.

I still had lingering doubts about Ai-chourek's outfit – the one that belonged to an Indian squaw. And she called herself a child of nature, surely a phrase she'd picked up from a New Age workshop. No medicine man that I'd met would ever see nature as we do, that is as something 'out there', separate from us; for them we, the land, even our towns and cars are natural, and have souls and spirits. But I also felt that she believed in whatever it was that she did do. 'I have my own shaman mystery,' she said. 'I work on my own, in nature.' And there was something to be said for someone whose inspiration was the land, not symbols plucked from nature and hung on the sterile walls of a clinic. And another thing: I could also sympathize with why, in this disturbed, confused country, she felt the need to keep going on about truth.

The next morning, we were up early, Gendos arriving with two decrepit cars for us supplied by his musician associates. The drivers looked green-faced and hungover. Perhaps last night's jamming session had only just ended.

We picked up Ai-chourek and drove together to her first site, which was on the other side of the river, in a birch grove below a sheer rock outcrop. We followed her from the cars, lugging a picnic we had assembled at the market. Gendos was ahead, walking in Ai-chourek's footsteps and bearing firewood like a pageboy. Ai-chourek seemed to enjoy the attention he gave her. He was a follower in need of a teacher, and she was a teacher in need of followers.

'During Stalin's regime everything was destroyed, shut and wild,' Ai-chourek said. 'But even before the communists left I learned that this place was blessed with a living spirit. I came here in 1993, and performed a ritual to open this place to people again. Now the spirit is alive and people come all the time to pray.'

Approaching down the cliff path, I could see several trees had been adorned with cotton ribbons – prayer offerings, just like in Mongolia. And for the first time in Tuva I was excited. Here at last, people were doing just as Tsend would have done.

Below an older birch, growing from the outcrop and possessed of more ribbons than leaves, was a spring, or *arzhan*. This was, I saw, the focus of this holy site.

We edged down the slope, to find the area around and about decked in plastic wrappers and beer bottles. 'It makes me sad, how people misuse this place,' Ai-chourek said, placing her drum and bag of regalia on a smooth rock. 'People come for picnics and leave litter here – they even shoot the beautiful birds that come. I went to the police and complained but they said, "What can we do? There is no shamanic law!"'

Not yet, I thought.

Gendos began to clear the bottles away – though, as we drove here, he'd been chucking all last night's bottles along the road. Meanwhile, Ai-chourek was taking her drum from its white canvas cloth. But it wasn't at all like Tsend's drum – nor, for that matter, like any drum I'd seen in any book on Siberia. It was a lovely drum, better perhaps than any shaman might have hoped for, but it wasn't Tuvan. I made a mental note to get a closer glimpse of it. It wasn't large and plain, a great round shield, it was smaller and pretty, decorated with images inspired by – well, by whom? Perhaps Sitting Bull. Or did J. R. R. Tolkien have a hand in it? It was a drum a Hobbit would have used.

Now Ai-chourek was setting to work. She made a fire and laid a silk cloth out on a rock that Gendos had heaved into place and as she scattered tobacco around the fire and burned incense sticks, he looked on reverently.

Needing an offering for the ritual, Ai-chourek walked over to our picnic supplies. She took an extremely generous chunk of our precious cheese, half of our sausage and chicken, and plundered all the best biscuits, the ones with thick chocolate. 'These are for the master spirits,' Ai-chourek explained. 'And the Old Lady.' None of us knew quite who the Old Lady was – the spirit of this sacred place, perhaps – but she had an impressive appetite.

We were here to witness what Ai-chourek did from time to time at sacred places right across Tuva: keeping them 'open' as she called it, by calling the spirits, making them welcome. She began by blessing the site with a wooden spoon called a *tos karak*, 'nine eyes', one with nine notches carved into the bowl, so that once you had dipped it in the purifying milk and flicked the spoon in the air, nine lots of milk blessed the nine skies.

Putting her spoon down among her collection of tools, Ai-chourek pointed to one that I'd hitherto thought rather pretty. 'It's made out of a human skull,' she said. She winced a little at the thought, then laughed at herself. 'It frightens me! And soon you will hear me sing, and I can never tell how my voice will sound, and sometimes that scares me as well. My power rests in these places – every tree has a soul, but this is a sacred healing place. And the voice coming out of me is the voice of the Old Lady here.'

She lit the fire – using our entire supply of picnic margarine – then asked to be left alone. We went a little way off, and I watched Ai-chourek go to the tree and hang up offerings that she'd brought – a sheep's shoulder blade, ribbons, and feathers from her necklace. She began conversing with the tree, first talking, then listening. This was not for us, but for herself and the spirit she believed in. I could be sceptical about her regalia, perhaps, but not her sincerity. She was exactly as she presented, a child of nature.

Gendos produced a *doshpuluur*, a Tuvan guitar-like instrument, and sat himself down beside the river. He began lightly plucking the strings and to this pleasing, easy mandolin tone added the strange vibrating sound of *khöömei* from his throat. It was pleasant being here, imbibing the peaceful atmosphere, and good to have along someone like Gendos, who was so visibly altered by this place.

'You know,' he said, putting down the *doshpuluur* after a while, 'towards the end of my time at school I performed on stage in front of various dignitaries – that is, for the Party. I played the part of a *kham*, and up there on the stage I had to hide behind a drum, then jump out, dance a bit as if around a fire, and then chuck my drum to one side and the drumstick to the other – as if I was throwing it all away. Then I had to wrench off my shamanic cloak, revealing Party Youth clothes underneath. The final part of my act was to jump up and down on the *kham* garments, dirtying them on the stage. "The Last Shaman", my performance was called. I was part of the propaganda machine.'

'And now?'

'And now I am making a drum for a *kham*,' he said, his huge chest and stomach swelling. Gendos told us that in a week or two we would see him hand it over; Mokur-Ool would perform a ritual to empower it to carry him to the spirits.

We went over to Ai-chourek, who was putting on a small headdress. Affixed across the front were the spread wings of a bird; bright blue and red strings of beads hung as a fringe from it. She raised a conch shell to her face and blew, slowly, three times. Next she rang a small handbell, just as Amam Maom and Amam Dirikogo had done to call the ancestors. 'Look!' whispered Gendos. He pointed up at the leaves of the birch tree, now quivering – disturbed, it seemed, by the coming spirit.

Ai-chourek next took her drum and began pounding it slowly, and sang *khöömei* to that heavy, resolute beat. The sound from her was low – disturbingly so. I could see why Ai-chourek said it sometimes frightened her. As a foreigner newly arrived, I had no belief in the Old Lady she had mentioned, but could almost believe that this deep, vibrating rumble was from some-one other than this young woman Ai-chourek.

We watched her, time disappearing as we were embraced by these sounds, and finally the drumming came to a halt, and the ritual was all done – the sacred site refreshed and sanctified. Ai-chourek marked our foreheads with ash and we drank some purifying milk. Then she bent to look into the fire ashes, divin-ing the state of things as, in Siberut, a *kerei* might have read the intestines of an unfortunate pig.

We waited for the diagnosis. 'The small bits are fine,' said Ai-chourek, 'but there's a long piece.'

'And what does that mean?'

'You will be fine,' she said, and we nodded with satisfaction. She frowned. 'I, on the other hand, will be in conflict with those who are jealous of my work.'

'Jealous of her work?' I said to myself. 'Is Ai-chourek talking about Kenin-Lopsan?' I wondered. From all we'd gathered, he had absolute say over what he called his '100 shamans'. Before leaving for her trip to address the New Age Italians, Ai-chourek would have to seek authorization not just from Italian Immigration, but this man who now guarded the name of Tuva's shamans.

We walked up reverentially to the birch tree – it was time to leave a *tchalamlar* or prayer ribbon. Ruhi, Misha and I didn't have one, so Aldynai helped us out from the supply in her handbag.

I tied my ribbon, and realized as I stepped back that I had enacted a ritual that was common to people across the globe. In front of me was the Sacred Tree, a living thing connecting our world to the upper and lower ones – but it was also the pole carried through the Australian bush by the Arunta Aborigines because their creator god Numbakula had used it to climb to the sky, after his work forming the earth. It was the post at the centre of the sun dance of North American Plains Indians – the Sioux – who renewed their contract with the sacred by gyrating around this symbol of the cosmic axis, the creation and perpetuation of life. Participants acknowledged that life was composed of suffering as well as joy by suspending themselves with cords tied through their flesh, and dedicating their agony and prayers to the great spirit Wakan-Tanka. In England, on the other hand, dancers celebrated the renewal of life in spring by weaving bands around the maypole, as if participating in the stitching together of the fabric of the cosmos. And so it went on – the tree as the Axis Mundi, the centre of the world. It was a Tree of Life on which the Nordic god Odin hung suffering for nine days and nights, and in the Middle East on which Jesus died for man's sins. It was the Tree of Knowledge from which Adam was forbidden to eat because, as God warned, 'then your eyes shall be opened, and ye shall be as gods, knowing good and evil'.

The tree was resonant with many such themes, and specifically in Siberia was the home of the souls of shamans who had died, and others who were yet to live. The tree connected the different cosmic planes – the roots were embedded in the earth, the underworld, the branches embedded in the heavens. The tree trunk was a conduit, a passage through which the shaman ascends or descends. And in this task, he or she is helped by the drum, which is itself cut from a sacred tree – usually birch and preferably one singled out through being struck by lightning. The drum was the tree, and so gave access to the other worlds. And as for the tree in front of us, bedecked with the prayers of a thousand Tuvans, I could see why anyone would want to reach out to it – especially after the communists collectivized their herds and put these nomads into housing blocks.

And it's no use westerners saying that tree-worshipping is far removed from life back home on the cutting edge of the twenty-first century. It seems that we all partake of this ritual, once a year. It's probably the very same tradition that came to us from the nomads of northern Europe, and evolved into the decorating of the Christmas tree.

We walked up the cliff and back to the car. 'We are now going to a second sacred site, this one out in the steppe,' Ai-chourek said, and she had a smile on her face just picturing it. I had visions of the horsemen I had seen in Mongolia, cantering through the arid expanse. But this was a very different place. The road that took us there sliced straight through the plain, scarring the land as it went. There was a roadside café, and a huge, light-blocking sign to tell you about The Sacred Site. And where you might once have found a natural salt spring, and quietly breathed your prayers to the spirits of the steppe, there was a cemented wishing well.

However, on closer inspection, I again had to acknowledge I was being unreasonable. Shamanism was once banned, but now soldiers weren't shooting shamans, they were joining in with others busily collecting sacred water in plastic bottles to take home. And their presence here was a tribute not to the site but to the people. Despite all these years of suppression, still they wouldn't be put off. The Tuvans, just like we in the West, wanted to be connected back to 'nature'.

Behind the wishing well, just where the cars drew up, there was a heap of stones and pitched on this were three interlocking poles. Numerous people had been before us, hanging up their prayers on the structure. They flapped in the wind: myriad ribbons, small-denomination banknotes, tobacco, necklaces and horsehair.

'This is the spirit's home,' Ai-chourek said, and indeed, it was clear that these were the larch support poles of the tepee-like homes in which reindeer herders like Tsend still lived.

Ai-chourek lit a fire, blessed the wishing well with milk, beat the drum and sang *algysh*, the ancient songs and prayers. She was happy to see the cars trundle up, the kids and grown-ups tip out to fill up their bottles. Nowadays, instead of the traditional stones, they flicked coins into the water, and that didn't matter. As we crammed into the cars again, Ai-chourek said that the master spirit was a bull, and that she had managed to get the place renamed 'Nine Bulls' – Tos Buga. It was previously 'Nine Kilometres'. In that way, the place had been reclaimed for Tuvans and the spirits, incorporated back into society.

Later that day, back at our flat in Kyzyl, I thought about this – Ai-chourek doing her repairing of the landscape. She was giving colour to the greyness of the centralized, housing-block era, and though I hadn't at first liked the gentrification of the sacred spring, I was beginning to have a profound respect for her. I'd found out about the 'jealousy' that she mentioned, and it seemed that the Düngür Centre had told her that it was not correct to do her rituals at springs and other sites where there were water spirits. She was meant to work mainly with *tchalamlar*, the prayer ribbons – this was more correct according to their classification of shaman types. But Ai-chourek ignored the instruction, saying that she couldn't resist the spirits' call to her. She would carry on doing what she felt she had to do. And this she did, a lonely, isolated figure working out there for the water spirits whatever the official *khams* said.

The next day Ai-chourek specially asked us to join her on a trip to two other favoured water sites, this time to bless a group of four women. Another invitation so soon was too good an opportunity to miss – so unfortunately we again neglected to see Kenin-Lopsan.

Her chief client was a medical doctor who wore an elegant Mongol silk robe – she would have called it 'Tuvan'; being up for an important job at the university, she wanted to better her chances. The others were her friends – an amenable lady with more Russian features, and a third lady with a dicky leg and an adolescent daughter who had the cream-faced look of a vegetable-lacking Soviet. They went ahead in one car, we followed in two others, meandering along while the musician drivers puffed away on their cannabis.

A couple of hours from Kyzyl, the steppe grass thickening, the hills rising, we turned off the main road and bumped through open birch forest to a pine-covered hill. There were greens, mauves, purples – the colours of spring in Siberia. We drew our cars up well within the woodland, beside the tree at the end of the track with strips of cloth flapping from it. Over the years, people like us had got out of their cars and adorned the first thing within reach.

We tiptoed along the marshy path towards a glade, beyond which was a birch tree wound with more cotton blessings, most quite old – the effect was of a tree covered with frayed bandages. Behind was a second tree that was lower and more convenient for putting your blessings on, and as a result this was so laden that it looked in need of healing itself.

The ladies told us enthusiastically that we must each wash three times in the water nearby to purify ourselves, and this water turned out to emerge, still almost frozen, from a pipe in an incongruous wooden hut, which sat like a garden shed slightly to the side. After we had recovered from that, Ai-chourek laid out her special objects on a tree stump in front of the main birch.

She began, as usual, by burning a juniper sprig. With this sweet smell in the air, she then blew on her conch shell to the master spirit, and started her drumming. The ladies knelt, hands to the sky, absorbing it. And after the drumming Ai-chourek again performed a purification – not making the women drink milk as we had done but, rather more dramatically, cracking a short leather whip across their backs as they knelt. Though they winced as they were struck, they didn't complain but acknowledged this need to be rid of bad spirits by whispering admonishments to themselves, shaking their heads with sorry frowns and even taking the whip to thrash themselves.

Afterwards, we sat and ate our picnic lunches together – or would have, if the musician drivers hadn't taken our share already – then left, walking out of the glade with that fulfilled feeling of coming out of church. The women had received a blessing, and it was easy to understand that such an act of worship was also a blessing of the site. And this was something Ai-chourek was doing right across Tuva, revitalizing sacred places, just as in Siberut the *kereis* periodically revitalized their *umas*.

We returned through the steppe, leaving the road to cut through the grasses and anemones to an impressive outcrop of large bare boulders. 'The master spirits have marked it out for man as special,' Ai-chourek said, as we got out of the cars to climb the final stretch. This was a strange place, where caterpillars hung by the million on silk threads from the birches, and spiders wove webs across the rock slopes in sheets broader than any I'd seen in the Amazon.

Of particular importance was a boulder set right on the top of the hill. From what Ai-chourek had said as we arrived, this had a bath-sized hole scooped out of it, sculpted away somehow by the wind or rain. The hill itself was named after this bowl – Suluk Dash, literally 'water stone' – because always, always, it had water sitting in this natural basin.

But not today. Nothing but dust.

I simply put it down to a dry spell. As for Ai-chourek, I missed her reaction because she had trotted ahead, leaving us unpacking ourselves from the cars while she sped excitedly up the hill to see the sacred water. She must have been profoundly shocked – at least, judging by what was to happen before long.

Ai-chourek got on with her next ritual for the ladies, taking them off to where the outcrop overlooked the valley. The ritual followed along the usual lines – the juniper incense, the conch shell, then drumming. The ladies placed their hands at the sky, soaking up whatever goodness was there. The lady doctor was also trying to gain a blessing from a tree spirit here, and one hand was clasped around a thin, poorly looking branch. Then the beat slowed, calming, and the ladies gradually lowered their heads and went limp. They looked utterly relaxed, almost satiated. But Ai-chourek was not relaxed. Normally at this stage we would get out our notebooks and she would give an explanation of all she'd done, but now she began a fast, rather impersonal speech first about her role in Tuva, and then Tuva's role in the world, then its role in the universe – her speech became a hectic stream of consciousness that rose into anger. We hadn't had the translation from Aldynai yet – she hadn't been able to get a word in – but now she was like a screaming wind, shrieking and with tears streaming down her face.

'Maybe she's possessed,' I whispered.

'Maybe she's drunk,' said a driver, coming up to watch. Out it all came, anger sparked by the natural water bowl being empty. 'You Europeans didn't bring enough food to share, and you, Aldynai, do not translate properly and you are all earning money out of *my* gift from the spirits. Even the drivers are earning money from me. I am not asking for money, I do not want money – but it is corrupting everything and Tuva needs truth, and what does it have but lies, and...'

We stood there, listening to all this, and the ladies still sat there, still busy absorbing the sky, and I remembered what someone had said about Ai-chourek. 'Once, she lost her power to heal. It was gone from her, and she got depressed. She began drinking – and that for a shaman is dangerous. Bad spirits can at last have power over you. She's damaged.' Maybe it was true, she was damaged. It was also true that Ai-chourek herself had said her mother had thought she might be mad, as a child – and among the world's medicine men it had to be said that there did seem to be a tendancy towards being highly emotional; scientists have even speculated that a tendency to schizophrenia is a prerequisite for being able at will to go into trance. It's surely no ordinary person who can easily detach from our world, our reality, and enter another one.

She was still ranting and raving, having already brought Aldynai to tears. Ruhi and I looked on glumly, and Gendos sat stoically at her feet, nodding understandingly.

And I couldn't help think that Ai-chourek was right about the money. The *kereis* of Siberut had worked almost entirely out of duty. And just supposing for a minute that I myself was Ai-chourek, perhaps a genuine child of nature, a little bit lost in my regalia, but genuinely called by the spirits – and just supposing that the Official Shamanism of Tuva was at times governed not by the spirits, but by, say, the chance of earning some cash – then I would also occasionally blow a fuse exactly like this.

Ruhi and I sloped off to the car, wondering what we ought to do to make amends. We also needed to bolster the translator, Aldynai. 'I'm not worried about the insults,' she said, a tear dribbling down her cheek as we drove home. 'I'm worried about my little daughter. She might send some black spirits or something.' We stopped for a bite to eat and I said we could go to another *kham* to get spiritual protection for her, and by the time we were back in Kyzyl, and Aldynai had smoked a whole packet of cigarettes, she felt better. Which was just as well because in our flat we found an angry message from Kenin-Lopsan himself, demanding to see us in his office first thing the next morning.

CHAPTER FIVE

'I repair our world. This is my job. People, animals, plants and also the spirits form this world, but there are Other Worlds too. You cannot see these, you cannot feel them, that is why it is important that I exist, to do these things for you: to take my drum and heal our world when it is broken.'
Ai-chourek, 'urban' kham

The next day was stormy, turbulent – not the weather, but again the people around us. Maybe Ai-chourek was a mad shaman, a John the Baptist raging in the wilderness, but we were also beginning to see how deep run the scars here – maybe scars from Stalin, or even scars from the Mongol armies that overran Tuva centuries before, or scars from despots unnamed even before that.

Still wondering how we'd mend bridges with Ai-chourek, we traipsed to the rear of Kyzyl's museum, through the gate and into the back yard, where Kenin-Lopsan had his office. Gendos had come along, but said he'd prefer to stay outside. He said that our meeting would be fine. I remember saying to myself, why wouldn't it be? We were under no obligation to see him – we'd just thought it a courtesy.

We turned to go into the office, and saw to our surprise that coming out was our landlady, a granite-faced woman called Zoya. She had just been to see the man herself, and we were immediately suspicious. We'd already had dealings with her and had had cause to regret it – she was an unfortunate by-product of the Soviet system, and had learnt that to survive you must manipulate. She eyed us impassively as she passed, then she was gone. But we knew already that she had left damage behind.

Before we had set a foot further, Ai-chourek turned up, here to get her permission from Kenin-Lopsan to go to Italy, and we spent the next ten minutes apologizing and trying to restore relations – all through a translator who wasn't on speaking terms with her.

'He will see Ai-chourek alone first,' said a brutish lady, coming out of Kenin-Lopsan's office, while we were still in a huddle, trying to get Ai-chourek to talk to us and Aldynai to talk to her.

We waited our turn to be ushered in. Tuvans began to queue outside his door, some sitting, some standing, but all of them waiting as if for an audience with the pope. Or, in fact, a Living Treasure of Shamanism. That was what the sign at the museum said, noting the visiting fee to see him was ten roubles. 'Must be a title given by the government in recognition of his important work,' I wrote in my notebook. But I was wrong. The title was bequeathed by Michael Harner, who had set up a Foundation for Shamanic Studies in the States, and ran work-shops attended by New Age Americans who, I rather feared, felt could become shamans themselves.

Kenin-Lopsan didn't need long with Ai-chourek. She emerged pale-faced and looking a little dazed. She spluttered that he had told her she wouldn't be going to Italy on her special trip, because she had showed her skills to us without permission. 'Everything I have worked for is destroyed!'

'I'm sure it isn't … '

'*It is!* And you must film all this with your cameras,' she gulped. 'Everything!' She wiped tears away with her wrist. This was a woman who had been raging at us yesterday; now we were at her side, comforting her.

'Kenin-Lopsan is waiting,' the brutish assistant said.

'Keep your heads bowed,' Aldynai instructed as we went in and, feeling like serfs, we lowered our heads in the prescribed manner. Ai-chourek followed on behind.

At last, our first view of the man himself. His hair was shocking white – straight and yet unruly, sitting like storm-damaged thatch on his head. He was a bulky figure, and his face was severe – maybe it was just his mood. He said, 'Sit, sit.' It wasn't exactly a greeting. Our presents, a bottle of decent wine and my favourite fountain pen, stayed exactly where they were, inside the duty free plastic bag.

'You have done great wrong. You have come here and talked to *khams* and filmed without my authority. Now Ai-chourek will not be allowed to go to Italy.' Ai-chourek had seated herself behind us, and she now began to whisper a pleading kind of protest. 'Shut up,' Kenin-Lopsan muttered. He turned back to us. 'And your project will be stopped.' By now the voice of Aldynai was trembling as she translated. 'Here we have a hierarchy,' Kenin-Lopsan continued, 'and we are very strict. I rule like Genghis Khan.'

Ruhi and I exchanged raised eyebrows. He was comparing himself to a medieval warlord, and, though he in fact had no legal power at all over us, judging by Ai-chourek's sorry state he did indeed even in 1999 have total power over her.

'Shamanism is more precious than gold in Tuva – and is not to be abused.' Kenin-Lopsan's anger was making his face ugly – his jaw was tight, his lower teeth projecting sourly. 'I won't speak further on the matter. I am too old to bother with this any more.'

Then we found ourselves dismissed. Out we went, bowing, our hands together as a sign of respect. In the yard, Ruhi and I recovered ourselves. 'Phew!' Ruhi said, 'I haven't had a roasting like that since I was a schoolgirl in front of the headmaster.'

Poor Ai-chourek. We felt so sad for her – this woman who had yesterday been spitting tears at us. 'We'll talk to him,' we told her. 'We'll sort it out.' It didn't look very promising.

Ai-chourek sat down in front of a regiment of monumental deerstones that had been gathered by the museum from the countryside. The oldest were etched with leaping reindeers, creatures from Scythian creation myths; others were bulky figures with long noses, and with funerary beakers in their hands – they were from the gravesites of heroes, the product of an ancestor cult. However, just as interesting, here among us we had a living cult – and it was centred on Kenin-Lopsan. He was a new Joseph Stalin, a new Vladimir Lenin. The ladies were queuing as if just to be in his presence, though actually he gave them divinations; he would scatter forty-one pebbles across his desk and use his power to tell the future. The citizens of Tuva had lost faith in politicians, and were turning to new figureheads, these neo-shamans instead.

Kenin-Lopsan was having a busy day. Fortunately for us, among his stream of visitors was a kindly museum employee called Ludmila Salchak, a friend of Aldynai. Luda listened patiently while the story was unravelled to her, and said she'd try herself to talk to Kenin-Lopsan. 'I know his mind,' she said.

She disappeared, deftly side-stepping the brutish secretary, and we waited. Among the deerstones, Ai-chourek was still weeping, only occasionally managing to splutter, 'Keep filming, keep filming!'

Next thing, Kenin-Lopsan himself appeared, storming past us and out the gate. 'His lunch break,' Ludmila said, apologetically. 'Nothing interrupts that.' She'd try later.

We took Ai-chourek for something to eat. In the restaurant, she sat stunned beside us, not the slightest interested in the special roast chicken that we'd ordered to cheer her up.

We waited for the chicken, Aldynai still unable to forgive Ai-chourek for yesterday's outburst, and Ai-chourek now raging about Kenin-Lopsan. By the time the chicken arrived, an uncomfortable hour later, we had to get back to see how Ludmila had progressed with Kenin-Lopsan. We told the waitress to keep the chicken for us, and raced back to the museum. At last the great man strode in from his lunch, and Luda shot off in hot pursuit.

A while later, she beckoned us in and we took our seats beside Luda. Ai-chourek sat at the back, sobbing.

Luda addressed Kenin-Lopsan as she must have been doing for the last ten minutes, her hands together like a child in prayer. She begged and grovelled, her hands shaking with her pleas. Slowly he got out his typewriter and began typing a letter – a deliberate, heavy thumping of two fingers. We guessed that the letter was *the* letter of authority, granting Ai-chourek freedom to go to Italy. Kenin-Lopsan still hadn't spoken to us – no comment, nothing. So only when it was stamped, and then signed, were we sure it was going to be all right for her. Taking the letter, Ai-chourek ducked reverently, placing her hands together in gratitude. Tears of relief were slipping slowly down her face.

Kenin-Lopsan now spoke. If we agreed to work in co-operation with the Düngür Centre, he said, we would be allowed total freedom to talk to the *khams* of Tuva.

'At a price, no doubt,' I said to myself.

'There will be a payment of $500,' he went on. 'We have to work in conditions far worse than the Christians and Buddhists.'

'$500!' exclaimed Aldynai, involuntarily. 'That's big money here.'

'Our first substantial payment,' said Kenin-Lopsan, nodding with satisfaction.

As he was speaking, a secretary produced a blue silk cap and gown and placed them to the side, ready for use. For what? It looked like Kenin-Lopsan was rather expecting to give us a filmed interview. Duly, we requested one and he said, of course, it would be a pleasure. In a moment he was in his silk robe, and a long but actually first-rate dissertation on the shamans of Tuva followed. I began to admire the man for the first time. We learnt about the different *kham* types – 'Each has his own mystery, his own attributes,' he explained, and talked about the category called *tudurzhu khamnar*, who helped those with broken bones, others with herbal knowledge, and others who worked with particular spirits. 'For example, there are shamans like esteemed Ai-chourek, who work according to the classification of the Düngür Centre, with the sky.' He turned meaningfully to her. 'Others with water, or forest nymphs.'

He talked of his grandmother, who had been a shaman – only released after fifteen years in prison because Stalin died – and of more recent politics, how with the coming of democratic Russia the parliament had recognized for a while only the other religions, 'as if they were the only great ones', he said. Of course, there had been Buddhism here for a long time – for centuries, most Tuvans had been both Lamaist and shamanist – but for Tuvans it wasn't the 'root religion'. After a year, though, the government accepted his shaman movement. 'Now, we are the only lawful shamans – and we each have documents proving that we are really a shaman and a member of our organization. There are also some fraudulent shamans and we don't accept them. They are subject to prosecution by law. And they are in hiding…'

'And who says they are fraudulent?' I asked myself as we listened on. 'Not the spirits, but the shamans of the Düngür Centre. Who sometimes don't seem very much like shamans at all.' If I had brought Tsend from Mongolia to sit in on one of their rituals, she would have been fascinated, excited – many things, but most of all bemused. 'Wonderful,' she might have said. 'But I am a tired old lady and when are they going to begin?' Because one of the key features of a shaman, according to Mircea Eliade's classic book on the subject, was that they went into an ecstatic, trance state. So far, I hadn't seen that – not even in Ai-chourek. But at least her heart was in the right place. And she had been chosen to become a shaman in the classic way – her disorientation as a child had come to a head in a bout of severe sickness. For her colleagues in the Düngür Centre, though, there was no crisis, no life change. It seemed to be a commercial decision, pure and simple. They simply chose to become *khams* because it was convenient – profitable. Not a way of life but a living. In angst-ridden, modern-day Tuva, people were looking for answers – and these neo-shamans were able to provide them, given the right fee.

We thanked Kenin-Lopsan, and got up stiffly to leave. Aldynai stopped us. 'He'll be expecting something for himself,' she whispered. 'Some money.' We struggled awkwardly with our money belts and the smallest we could find was a $50 note – almost a month's wage for ordinary Tuvans. We handed it over.

We were now taken to the Düngür Centre to make a contract with the head man, Sailyk-Ool. The place was still under repair and with the banging of bits of wood going on in the background we wrote out an agreement. The tools of his trade, all his shamanic kit, were laid out on his desk: a bear's skull, claws, bells, an incense burner from which issued a long thin line of blue smoke. It was like a market stall, and on sale was hope.

Sailyk-Ool told us he was about to found a school for *khams*, and that was where our $500 was going. I tried to picture them all sitting in a row like schoolboys at desks. How could it be done? How could shamans be grown like seeds in the town, cultivated en masse according to traditions developed for nomadic existence in the steppe?

Ruhi said that Ai-chourek must get part of this payment, say $100. Ai-chourek sat beside us, not saying anything. A school for *khams*? She seemed to have given up being surprised long ago.

'So, you give $500 for Ai-chourek and the Centre – and how much to me?'

'For you?' Misha, Ruhi and I said together. And together we all gave a despairing sigh.

It was only by mentioning Kenin-Lopsan's name that Sailyk-Ool relented, angrily slamming down his file as if we had mentioned a contact in the politburo. 'OK,' he said. He had somehow been thwarted by the old system, though it was now meant to be working for him, one of the good guys. He took the $500 and waved it over the incense burner – though you'd need a far more substantial ritual to purify this particular payment, I felt.

'This is the first time I have ever accepted proper money for my work,' Ai-chourek said, taking her share. She walked away sadly.

She seemed such a pure person, just then. And was this the beginning of the end of that purity in her? She had been alert to, but apart from, the day-to-day political machinations of society – as shamans have generally been. Now she was joining this new system, the new Tuva. The interests invested here were too big for a country girl to fight. She was a Joan of Arc, but succumbing to save herself. If she protested about the money, this new hierarchy, she'd be a real spanner in the works, undermining what the new system stood for – which sometimes seemed oddly similar to what the old system stood for.

We followed her out. It's so ironic, I thought. The *khams* who were once so repressed are now repressing each other. Each spiritual movement starts out with a visionary, a medicine man

Above: The taiga land-
scape of northern Tuva,
Siberia.

Left: Mokor-Ool's yurt.
The nomadic lifestyle
has declined, and with
it shamanism, a spiritual
practice suited to living
intimately with the
elements. By the yurt,
Gendos is crafting
the sheepskin of his
drumstick.

Above: Ai-chourek drumming at Suluk Dash, just prior to her dramatic outburst.

Right: Gendos, urban musician and would-be shaman, playing his *doshpuluur*.

Opposite: Ai-chourek and New Age drum. Traditionally, the drum is a vehicle to the spirit world. It is a symbolic piece of tree and, like the adorned birch behind her, a conduit to the upper and lower worlds.

Above: Children of Teeli.

Right: Mokur-Ool, shaman, shepherd and someone I began to deeply respect.

Opposite above: Villagers of Bei-Dag placing ribbon prayers on a newly erected shrine in response to Ai-chourek's call to them to re-invigorate the spirits of Tuva, following years of repression of shamans by communists.

Opposite below: Kenin-Lopsan, revered leader of the movement to restore shamanism, even in modern-day, urban Tuva, beside an earlier cult hero – an ancestral gravesite figure from Tuva's nomadic past.

Right: Mokur-Ool, sharing a moment with apprentice Gendos, resplendent in his stage costume.

Below: Ai-chourek giving me a blessing of milk, by means of a human-skull ladle.

Above: The Little Stars, dancers at Kyzyl's school for the deaf, an impromptu performance for us at a roadside *ovaa* or shrine.

Left: A quick purification ritual for me in a water tank – a modern adaptation of a holy spring.

Overleaf: Shaman with a drum adorned with prayer ribbons and *eeren*, spirit guides which should ensure her protection from mal-evolent forces in the spirit world.

or quasi shaman. A Jesus, a Mohammed. Then they are engulfed by others – society clambers on board and takes over. It takes possession of that spiritual impulse, uses it for its own, various ends. That day in Tuva we seemed to be witnessing the birth of a Higher Religion. No longer a spiritual revelation but formalized into something convenient for the state.

We went back to the restaurant to rescue Ai-chourek's special roast chicken.

Ai-chourek wasn't leaving for Italy until the following week, so the next day we set out together to Bei-Dag, her home village. It would be a relief to get away from here, for us and no doubt for her. We were looking forward to the trip into the countryside – going closer to the source of Ai-chourek's inspiration – and we would tread more carefully with her, knowing her volcanic nature.

Ai-chourek's plan was to perform a ceremony to reinvigorate a sacred tree monument, something that should be done every nine years. It would be an important moment for her – she had left the village aged five, when her mother died, and this was a rare visit to the community she still thought of as home.

Steppe gave way to thin taiga forest as we drove, stopping at sacred sites for Ai-chourek to continue her mission to re-enliven the spirits, waking them from their dormancy now the communist winter was past. She was doing what women have always done: safeguarding the hearth, tending to their culture, acting as its guardian in times of change. Around the world – Arabia, New Guinea and India spring to mind – it is women who have been slower to leave behind traditional garments and adopt T-shirts and jeans. In the same way, the last vestiges of the traditional religious culture of Europe were the old ladies who still knew the ancient 'spells' and herbs. They became known as witches, characters we think of as ugly, spooky hags, not least because they were demonized by the new, rival, religion, Christianity.

At one site there was a collection of three tepee-like spirit homes. The communists had deftly driven a road right through the original site, but in 1995 Ai-chourek had erected these fresh tepees, and, for good measure, a circle of nine stones, placing on each a pebble she'd collected while on trips to New Age workshops in Italy, America and Canada.

Now wind had blown down one of the tepees and, as soon as she was out of the car, she was propping it up. 'The local *khams* don't like me, a woman, restoring this place,' she muttered. 'But what do they ever do?'

As before, she laid out one piece of everything that we'd brought for our picnic – a banana, a tomato, a Pringle … She lit the incense, blew her conch, drummed and chanted, circling around the stones. After, she sat for a moment in contemplation. The sweet pine fragrance floated to us from the forest behind. We quietly ate our lunch.

A crow flew over and let out a raucous noise. 'A good sign,' Ai-chourek said. 'The crow says the villagers know we are coming.'

Whatever the crow said, it went against all available evidence. At this moment Gendos was down by the road, trying to wave down a car to hand over a note for the villagers, telling them to expect us. This vehicle, like all the others, speeded up seeing this great lumbering man coming out of the forest like a bear.

Ai-chourek was calm, and happy just to be here. The weather was fine, the air fresh and rich, the auguries good. The rest of us could also breathe easily – Ai-chourek wouldn't have a tantrum for hours. I seized the chance of a close-up look at her drum, her vehicle into the spirit world. In particular I wanted to see these drawings – not traditional Siberian cartoon-like depictions of animals, gods and shamans, but careful artistic expressions in glorious technicolour.

On the outer side, there were three motifs. Uppermost was a blue wave and a serpent riding it. This represented the sky, the upper level or what westerners equate to heaven. Below was a green dot, which represented where we were now. And spiralling out and around it were the wiggly branches of a tree, the tree of life. Underneath was a reddish-brown figure, part human form. He belonged to the lower level, the underworld.

I asked Ai-chourek about how she used the drum and she answered awkwardly, as if we were discussing her body. 'As I beat the drumskin, these three different sections resonate differently. That is, I can tell if the master spirit is responding well to my ritual. You could say that my drum speaks to me, it is my companion.'

Reluctantly, she turned over the drum to reveal the inner side. Various ribbons and bells, attached to the crossbars, rattled and flapped. On this side was a motif centring on a plan view of a fortress – a box with turrets bulging out at the four corners. I could see, without Ai-chourek having to explain, that these turrets were part of a defence around her. She was within this fort, represented by the dot in the centre, and safeguarded by other, inner, defence lines. Beneath the fortress, at the bottom of the drum, was a brown monster, a creepy character with outreaching twiggy fingers and a haunted, thin face. He must represent the ever vigilant, ever threatening malevolent spirits.

Ai-chourek turned over the drum, to stop me examining the image further. I could quite see why. This was like a glimpse into her soul. We had seen a depiction of the turmoil in her, the neurosis that her calling kept at bay.

'Can you explain a little?' I asked, softly.

'I said that my drum is my companion, but it is more than that. The drum is my guardian. It protects me. I am always vulnerable when I am quiet. That is why I must use my drum as much as possible. I have to drum.'

As we got up to go, a bus choked its way up the slope, crunching its gears until it cranked to a halt. A bevy of young teenage girls gushed out. It was only as they spilled towards us, each with a ribbon to tie on the tepees as an offering, that we realized they were oddly quiet, flapping their hands frenetically and looking to each other, cross-checking each other's intentions. These were the urgent, frustrated gesturings of the deaf and the dumb.

As the girls tied their ribbons and bowed with their hands together in prayer, we learned from their teacher that they were a dance troupe, the Little Stars, who were travelling about the countryside raising money for their school. She asked if the girls could perform a dance for us. Dressed in shiny yellow finery adorned with ribbons, they performed a balletic piece called Ornamentations of Nature, creating waves with their swirling limbs, arching their necks, inclining their heads – all totally quiet, except for the rustle of their garments. They were a flock of birds, the gold of sunset on their wings. We watched, entranced.

Afterwards, they knelt around Ai-chourek's stone circle to receive a blessing. Ai-chourek circled, drumming for them. They must have been able to feel the vibrations of the drum as she passed by, a tingling of the air and ground. Even their silent world could be reached, united to ours by this, the shaman's sacred tool. The girls seemed at greater and greater ease, and Ai-chourek finished the ritual with a cleansing splash of milk over the Little Stars' hands and faces.

Then it was time for them to tumble back into the bus; they blew kisses and waved as it faded into the dusk.

'It is a special blessing on this place,' Ai-chourek said, tears trickling from her eyes. 'They are so pure.'

Pure, I thought. That was a word I used yesterday to describe you.

Our journey continued, and I was still thinking of those dancing children. Ertine, the teacher, had said she felt so guilty: some of the Little Stars were leaving school soon, and then they'd have to fend for themselves. 'They face total isolation,' she said. 'Even their families can't communicate with them, and some are embarrassed and just chuck them their food, as if they are animals. These children are going to be just thrown away ... '

Hearing this, I felt sick. We had been forced to give $500 to the Düngür Centre. The *khams* did need money to live in towns, of course, but their people would support them if they valued them, just as they did in Siberut. And if they had no need for them, they would not, and that was forever the way.

The road wound up to a plateau backed by conifers and laid open to the sky. The night was coming on, the moon beside a dazzling Venus. We dropped down to Bei-Dag, located one of Ai-chourek's friends, and arranged ourselves on her floor.

The next day was the day set for the re-sanctifying of the village's sacred tree monument. I was worried the event would be a disappointment to Ai-chourek. Perhaps no one would turn up. Already it wasn't looking good: just as I'd feared, the village wasn't, after all, expecting us. Perhaps we should brace ourselves for a tantrum.

Ai-chourek, Aldynai and I walked up through the wide, pale, dusty street, towards the hill where the ritual would take place. There were low houses of wood, many fenced in, and a school with girls skipping over a rope and boys kicking about, their satchels on their backs. Opposite the school, a sorry heap of old boulders – once an *ovaa*, or sacred cairn, but long since lost to the Party. Ai-chourek scattered rice from her cloth shoulder bag as she passed, feeding this near-dead site, bringing it back.

Still with absolutely no sign of interest from the good citizens of Bei-Dag, we made our way up the bare hill. Towards the top there was a small tree banked around with stones. It had been placed here, not planted, and was merely a representation – the tree of life. There were many cotton strips on it, but they were old and hanging like dead leaves. The tree looked like it was in dire need of Ai-chourek's attention.

Ai-chourek was visibly angry, seeing that the place hadn't been cared for. She stomped around, inspecting the hilltop, which was said to be the grave site of nine shamans, each marked with bedded-in boulder circles. The hill also featured a lone, disused telegraph pole, shoved there ineptly in the Soviet era as if a symbol of material progress, an alternative to the sacred tree.

I waited, bracing myself for an explosion from Ai-chourek. However, within minutes of our arrival, a few aged ladies could be seen wending their way uphill to join in whatever was going to happen. The rumour must already have gone around that Ai-chourek, the little girl who'd gone to the capital and who was now an international shaman, was back.

Once they'd arrived at the summit, the ladies bent to move stones here and there, tidying them into something a little bit more symbolic than nature itself provided. Schoolboys walked up the hill, each with a stone. They tidied the heap around the tree, while others took stones and put them in another spot, to await the arrival of the poles, presently being cut from the taiga forest for a new spirit tepee.

More and more villagers were turning up, as word spread. Ai-chourek sat down to address a few, and found herself speaking non-stop as more and more came to listen about the spirits. Soon there was what the Bible would have called a 'multitude'. And all were silent, looking on steadily – one man at the back rocking a baby's pram back and forwards, lost in a trance-like state. It was by now very much a sermon on the mount.

Already, it looked good from the point of view of crowd attendance. The fresh poles were erected and were soon flapping with fresh cotton prayer offerings. Women arranged themselves around the spirit tepee, and the men tacked on to their circle. The most senior village elder, an eighty-three-year-old man with a russet, wind-battered face, was delivered up the hill in a decrepit Russian car, to be given the honour of lighting the fire. He staggered over to it, beaming to his villagers, who bowed their heads in respect.

'I remember the time of Stalin,' the old man told me, after Ai-chourek settled him by the fire tinder, stuck a stick of incense into his hand and told him to keep holding it. 'The ceremonies done in secret, at night. And today is a very fine day for the village, as the ritual will be done openly, which is exactly as it should be.'

The village elder's wife was also here, and I asked her for her memories. 'I can't remember any rituals ever being performed.'

'Even in secret?'

'Even in secret.'

It was not the correct answer – or at least not what everyone wanted to hear – and her husband jabbed her with his elbow. 'She is a fool,' he said.

After more sermonizing, Ai-chourek blessed the assembly by flicking milk over them, then began her drumming, until, after a long, long time, and cries of '*kurai*', 'Amen', and the final three slow drumbeats, there was only one sound to be heard, the squeaking of the baby's pram as it was rocked forward and back.

A few seconds' pause and then the villagers stood up, some going over to the fire to do a spot of divining. Some older men, who'd apparently been at the vodka, wanted to make a speech, but the elder had had enough and slapped his great leather hands together to end their blathering. 'Take me home!' he said.

We were invited to the village hall, where we were given a feast of boiled sheep and blood sausage, washed down by salted tea. Ai-chourek was presented with the best of the sheep, its fatty tail, and after various speeches asking us for 'humanitarian aid' – this to go to their various family business enterprises – we loaded the sheep tail into the car and were on our way.

Dusk fell and then night, as we stopped briefly at each shrine, placing a little bit of the sheep as a present for the spirits. These were our last moments with Ai-chourek, and it was poignant listening to her in the dark singing her prayers, this lone voice. But she was invigorated, just like the land and people she had blessed, and was leaving for Italy freshened by the rising sap of the land, and cleansed from what, at times, must have seemed the rotting log that was the town.

CHAPTER SIX

'My drum is a sounding bowl. As I beat it, it talks to me,
informing me if there is something wrong in the Other Worlds.
I drum clockwise, sensing the drum, feeling if all is well out
there, and then the drum carries me.'
Mokur-Ool, nomadic kham

I was still on my quest to discover something akin to a shaman
of the original tradition. We would now go on with Gendos
in search of Mokur-Ool, the old nomad living out near Kyzyl-
Dag, in Gendos's own home region of Bai-Taiga far to the west.

First we watched Gendos construct his drum at the riverside. To my surprise, its frame would not be the traditional wide
band of birch, but a lattice-work of young willow. He bowed as
he cut the saplings, showing respect to each, and then produced
a sheepskin, wet from curing, and carefully stretched it over the
frame. He neatened the skin with his knife, scraping off the last
of the fleece, and then stood up, announcing that the drum was
finished. 'It can dry on our journey,' he said, a tad optimistically
I thought.

Gendos had taken to the idea of his journey being a highlight of the film, and was impatient to get on with it. But the
film crew had arrived only the previous day and needed a rest,
so we had to wait till the following morning.

Equipped with two vans, we headed to Kyzyl-Dag along
straight, state-manufactured roads. We passed through steppe
hemmed by craggy hills, and occasional yurts sprinkled across
the unfenced land. Gendos played on his *doshpuluur* as we
passed mountains both bare and capped by dark taiga forest.
Occasionally we stopped to leave offerings at shrines; Gendos
would tut, wagging his head at the majesty of places. At

Khayirakan, a severe and stark but very sacred hill, he placed his *doshpuluur* under the poles of a spirit tepee for a blessing. 'Energy!' he said, backing out after depositing a cigarette for the spirits. And as we went along, Gendos seemed to be partaking of more and more elaborate rituals, bowing more, waving more and more incense. It was as if he was trying to get into a role.

That night we reached Kyzyl-Dag, not far from where we thought Mokur-Ool might be living, and stayed with some distant relatives of Gendos. The lady of the house, Ana, brewed up some tea as we got out our sleeping bags. She lived in a typical wooden bungalow, the yard of which accommodated her livestock at night and was shared by a neighbour whose prize possession was a vicious dog. This wasted no time in planting its teeth in the leg of Nick, the soundman.

It was no minor bite, despite his thick trousers, and a doctor was called. In due course, a kind lady turned up and opened her bag with much aplomb – it proved to be empty apart from some iodine and a stethoscope. She cleaned the wound and said he'd best go to hospital in the morning.

This Nick did, and got a first-hand insight into Tuva's non-traditional healing practices. 'They didn't even have spare bandages to go round,' he reported after. 'The scissors had blood on, the autoclave didn't have a plug, and the hospital staff pounced on me before we could get my BBC medical kit out.' We could see now why the Tos Deer clinic was a popular place. The Tuvans really were up against it.

While Nick recovered from his hospital visit, we strolled about the dry, empty town of Kyzyl-Dag. As elsewhere in the former Soviet Union, there were fences everywhere, even around the yurts – as if, like the herds, they had been rounded up by the communists and collectivized. It was a graphic illustration of the end of shamanism – perhaps in every corner of Tuva. Shamanism is a belief system associated with those having a nomadic lifestyle. The practitioners here, as anywhere else, were intimately connected with the land, on which they entirely depended. Once people began settling, they lost this relationship with the elements; they were no longer tied to rhythms of the world around them. Being stationary, they could afford to keep possessions and then they began fencing these things in – and fencing out 'nature'. Man began to require gods that were more human, and to abandon the spirits of the animals and plants that had served his needs until now. And so the major religions moved in, along with their hierarchy of priests, and the shamans were lost.

We came across a new Buddhist temple – like the Tos Deer Centre, built since the collapse of the Soviet Union – and found that it housed the local museum. We persuaded the director, Saaya Kögel, to show us around. The prize exhibit was a shaman's coat, the *khalat*, and drum.

Discovered in a cave in the 1970s, this dark relic was laden with mystique. The discoverers were cursed, just like Egyptologists who had unearthed pharaohs' tombs. Before they died, it's said that the *kham's* drum had rolled around the cave. Saaya Kögel, an unshaven, stern-faced man with a jutting, almost aggressive jaw, wasn't going to be put off by anything. He removed the dusty glass of the display cabinet, and we were face to face with something unquestionably of the original Siberian tradition. At last, I thought, feeling the thirst of an explorer who'd wandered a vast desert.

The costume was stiff and blackened, perhaps a hundred years old. On it hung thin tongues of metal containing spirits; their noise would help in the journey by driving away unwanted demons and calling others. There were also tassels of leather hanging all over the costume, each one representing an auxiliary spirit the shaman had made his partner. They signified snakes, which had protective and surveillance roles: gathered during the shaman's life, they created a patina of souvenirs from the different cosmic journeys, like the scars of a well-worn traveller.

Beside the coat was a headdress with tattered feathers, perhaps, like Tsend's, from a crow. There was a *moos*, a fat creature resembling a bulbous toy dragon that was like a companion adviser to the shaman, and there was a drumstick and the drum itself – ripped, as drums always were at a shaman's death. It was made the traditional way, from a solid band of birch, the skin, according to Saaya Kögel, from reindeer. A drum more different to Gendos's huge willow-lattice creation would have been difficult to conceive – though Ai-chourek had done quite well with her own version.

Noticing my interest in the drum, this rather imposing man, Saaya Kögel, surprised me by suddenly launching into a humorous anecdote.

'I know a *kham* who had a drum made for him,' he said, between his teeth, his jaw still tight, but his eyes now alight. 'And the craftsman chose to make it from sheepskin!'

'Oh really?' I said. Did he know about Gendos's drum? Was this a joke on us, who were meant to be here documenting shamanism, but focusing on a man conveying a drum made of sheepskin and willow-lattice?

As Saaya Kögel continued inexorably to his punchline, I became convinced he did know. He was extracting the most out of his story, delaying the denouement by going off on a tangent. 'In prehistoric times, when man had no shelter and used to be very frightened by thunder, he used to beat a drum to frighten away the roaring sound from the heavens. So the drum was in use before man could really communicate, talk or sing. It was an early way for people to communicate not just with the gods, but each other.'

We all agreed that this was an interesting thought, though we'd already heard it from Ai-chourek.

'And now back to my story,' Saaya Kögel continued. 'You know what he said – the *kham* – when he received this funny drum? The one not made out of reindeer skin?'

'Tell me,' I said, not wanting to hear it.

'The *kham* said, "If I drum that too much, I'll be turned into a sheep!"'

What Saaya Kögel didn't know was that our drum was getting worse by the minute. Stretched over the lattice frame while it was still wet, it was now warping the whole structure – and it still hadn't finished drying out.

Before we left the museum, I learnt that many Buddhist texts were hidden in caves round and about, just like the *kham's* costume. Remote places had been a sanctuary, as churches were in medieval Europe. They were a resource – a fountainhead, a place where shamanism and Buddhism could later re-emerge. It reinforced my feeling that the place to discover any relics of the original shamanistic techniques was out in the countryside – the place of the caves, the place where shamans had always operated.

So, on to Mokur-Ool. He wasn't going to be easy to find, being a nomad, but we travelled on to Teeli, near Gendos's home village of Shui, and based ourselves with some of his relatives while we asked around.

The family there did us the honour of killing a goat, and while it was boiling away in the yard for our feast, Gendos began work on Mokur-Ool's drumstick – not like the spoon-shaped one in the museum, but rounded, like a cosh. I sat with him as he worked on it, the goat bubbling away nearby. The drumstick now needing only last-minute touches, Gendos moved on to another job. He picked up a garish thing from his feet; an object I slowly realized must be a sort of headdress.

'You are making this for Mokur-Ool as well?' I asked. With his round fleshy fingers, he was positioning a little snake of green beads to run across the front headband.

'Oh no,' Gendos said, suddenly portentous. 'No, it's not for Mokur-Ool ... '

I had a terrible sinking feeling. It looked like – I didn't dare ask – Gendos had decided he would become a *kham* himself.

Next, he sewed on a fringe of beads. 'Like Ai-chourek,' Gendos said, with an enthusiasm I hated to dampen. I left him as he got to work with the feathers, which he'd gathered from an unlucky crow, run over by both our vehicles yesterday. Putting aside the fact that you couldn't just 'become' a shaman, and that this headdress was modelled on a female's, and Gendos was a male, the idea behind it was actually fair enough. Gendos was a Renaissance Man, wanting to play his part in the renaissance of his culture.

Still with no news about Mokur-Ool's whereabouts, and time ticking by, we decided we must go and find out for ourselves.

We squeezed into one van – there was a petrol shortage, and we needed all we could save – and were off then to the *kham* I'd been waiting to see for so long. Mokur-Ool wouldn't have a drum covered in New Age doodles. He wouldn't compare himself to a medieval Mongol warlord. He wouldn't run a school for shamans, telling them what they should be, in order to serve their people. Or would he? I had low hopes, nowadays. I wouldn't mind if he was too old, or unused to articulating his knowledge. I would accept almost anything if it had that seemingly rare quality in Tuva: deep, undamaged spiritual roots.

We left the road, jarring our way along a track into the hills. We stopped at yurts to ask Mokur-Ool's whereabouts, and occasionally I got glimpses inside the yurts, and saw that none of these families had the customary altar. In Mongolia, even a dyed-in-the-wool communist would reserve the altar space for something special – say, a beloved granny's photo of her visiting the capital. Again, I had that feeling – these people were like Mongols, but Mongols who had lost almost everything.

Slowly we made our way, the shepherds we came across pointing further and further up the valley. Eventually, Gendos and I left the van behind, and continued on foot to a clutch of yurts that lay beyond a patch of snow and bedded in a tight valley bowl rimmed by pine forest. We crunched through the deep snow scraps, striding excitedly towards the first of three yurts. A flock of sheep passed by; horses turned their heads to view the valley's unexpected visitors. 'Mokur-Ool!' Gendos panted, waving me onward with his large hands.

As we came nearer, a little man appeared from a brook below the yurt. He wore a flat cap, and even from here I could see that his eyes were bright, impish, and that he had precious few teeth. He greeted us each with a bow, hands together, and like a city gent raised his hat – this act revealing a bald pate and grey hair fluffed out around his ears. Gendos gave him a cigarette – Prima Nostalgia, the packet with a picture of Lenin across it. He beckoned us into his yurt. The interior was much the same as the others – a stove in the middle, a bed to the left and right –

though this time, beside the cupboards at the altar place, there was a picture of the Buddha and also of an astrological wheel.

We were sat down on the left side, the half of the yurt reserved for visitors, and, when Ruhi, Misha, Aldynai and the crew had arrived, his daughter served us tea and deep-fried dough biscuits. He was a little overwhelmed by us flooding his home from nowhere– there were eight of us, and the five bulky foreigners alone almost filled the yurt – so we just chatted on about his herds, the state of his family and so on, until he was a little more relaxed. We learned that he was only in this valley each spring. His favourite place in all the world was down by the forested banks of the Khemchik.

After some time, we felt we could broach the subject of his role as a *kham*. Though still not entirely at ease, he was a civil man, and I could tell he was trying his best for us. He told us how it all began. 'When I was about five,' he said, 'I was out on the hills, alone with the sheep on the hill, not far from here. A whole cloud of butterflies came down and settled on me. It was very strange. And then I suddenly fell into a dream. My father woke me up, much later. And not long after, I began hearing voices – and I knew I was different. But it was years before I became a proper *kham*.'

'How did you know when you were a "proper" *kham*?'

'Oh, I mean I had *eeren*, I had spirits to help me. For example, the crow and wolf, and other animals like the eagle.'

I was already warming to this man. He wasn't relaxed, but everything he said was straightforward, clear and articulate. He spoke not to the translator, Aldynai, but directly to me, as I sat cross-legged near the altar not understanding a word of his Tuvan.

He got up and rummaged in a plastic bag of clothes, and produced a tassel of ribbons tied to a few talisman-like objects. There was a little bell and a crystal and a bear's claw, all in a rather untidy bundle. It was an *eeren*, but not one guaranteed to make an impression.

'This one helps my family not to get sick,' he said, proudly jabbing his finger somewhere into the bundle, 'and this one is for my patients.'

'Can you explain how it works?'

He took the *eeren* in his left hand – I noticed that the hand didn't have a thumb – and knocked my chest with it. He did this with rather unnecessary force, and it made me realize that he was no longer overwhelmed by us. Answering all these questions, he was in a role that he was comfortable with. He had been given centre-stage, and like any shaman seemed to feed off the energy we focused on him.

Mokur-Ool continued his little demonstration, first knocking me on the forehead, and, when his sharp rap produced a satisfyingly startled response from me – 'Ow!' – he finished off by whacking me even more sharply on my skull. As I rubbed my head, he buckled up with laughter.

He was in his stride, and it wasn't long before he spotted Nick's bandaged leg and was taking it on himself to do a cure. For a while, Nick just sat trying to finish off his tea while Mokur-Ool waved the *eeren* about, trying to get the right bit of crystal and claw in position.

'He wants you to roll up your trouser leg,' Aldynai said.

Nick put down his teacup, and did as instructed. 'As long as he doesn't do anything too radical.'

'And now he wants you to undo the bandages.'

There was some tutting from Nick, but he said, 'Well, it can't be worse than the hospital,' and unfurled them. Mokur-Ool hung over him, expectantly.

Now there was just a dressing left, sealed tight to the wound by dried blood. 'He wants you to remove that as well,' Aldynai said.

'I hope this is a good idea,' I said. Nick, who'd been with us in Siberut, and worked in Namibia and Morocco and seemed to be a stranger to nothing much, obediently teased the dressing off. It wasn't a pretty sight. Aldynai saw the bed of pus between the stitches, and closed her eyes.

With Nick's leg exposed to the world, Mokur-Ool turned to the stove. He began fishing out burning red coals.

Wayne, the American cameraman, who'd also in his time filmed the world – even the dark internal workings of the Ku Klux Klan – said, 'Hang on, I think we ought to clarify what exactly is going to happen next ... ' No doubt he'd noticed that I was still suffering from Mokur-Ool's previous activity, thwacking me on my head with a crystal. And there'd been nothing wrong with me – up till then. So would Mokur-Ool hold back, now he had a real patient?

We sat gawping, horrified at what we might be about to witness. Michael, the director, himself a veteran of many a grisly ritual – notably Asian ones – exclaimed, 'He's going to cauterize it! He's going to cauterize it!' As for Nick, he was rather quiet, sitting on the floor with one leg out, holding it at the knee and just staring at those coals.

But the panic was soon over. Mokur-Ool applied the coals to light some juniper. Soon the sweet, calming smell of the *artysh* was wafting over us. We laughed at each other for having been so stupid. Of course Mokur-Ool wouldn't do anything so rash. What were we all fussing about?

But Mokur-Ool hadn't begun his treatment yet. Soon, he was again waving the *eeren* about, once more taking a very long time to sort it out in his fingers. Next, very gently, he pressed the *eeren* up and down the leg. Nick – large and strong, not the sort to be trifled with – looked on suspiciously.

Mokur-Ool was moving in, now pressing the wound without gentleness. Nick released his first protest. 'Aargh ... ' After letting out his involuntary sigh, the first of many, he clutched his knee harder, trying to maintain a grip on himself.

The rest of us were silent, no longer wondering what was going to happen but dreading it. Ruhi was filming Mokur-Ool, his gleaming, excited eyes; I was filming Nick's pale and taut face. Aldynai was just staring into space, translating only occasional words. Michael, the director, was now holding the reflector shield. Wayne didn't have his camera even to hand; his head was down, baseball cap blocking the view, just one hand up to hold the microphone. Every one of us was doing the wrong job – the cameraman doing the sound, the soundman doing the presenting. Our world had been transformed, stirred and shifted. Such was the effect of the shaman, whose job was exactly this, to stir energies, transform worlds.

Mokur-Ool now took out his bear claw. Was he deliberately brandishing it to scare us? If so, it worked. Our thoughts were now racing. Mokur-Ool was a man who, typically for a shaman, showed none of the normal social restraints – in this lay much of his power. By seeming to be a man whose actions knew no bounds, he had an edge. He was no longer old and little, a nomad living in the sticks, but like a king over us. We were voluntarily letting him do this. 'No!' Ruhi said. 'That's enough!' Michael said. Yet we let it go on.

And Mokur-Ool, what was he feeling? I think he was in a kind of ecstatic state. Five foreigners were in his thrall and, holding this power over us, I suspected he was fulfilled in some way. He was satisfying this peculiar need of the shaman to be the outsider, be the centre of attention. We were giving all of ourselves, letting him rule us. And he was thriving, squeezing the drama for all it was worth.

We watched, frozen, as what we feared all along happened. The claw was dragged down the wound, across the two hospital stitches, and out again. Mokur-Ool didn't do it hard, but quite hard enough. He opened the yurt door, saying, 'Buh!' and sweeping away the sickness with his hands, as the *kereis* of Siberut had done, clearing their *umas* of badness.

'That's right!' said Nick, trying to hurry the healing ritual to a close. 'Get rid of all the bad stuff.'

The healing was nearly finished, all except Mokur-Ool's finale, which was to spit thoroughly into the wound.

'That's really hygienic,' Nick said. 'An old man's fingers and now his spit. Go on, do some more, why don't you?'

But Mokur-Ool was finished. It only remained now to search for some fresh bandages. I asked Nick why he'd let himself undergo this. 'I'd thought it was going to be fairly harmless – I mean, I didn't know he'd spit. And because I didn't know what was coming next, there was nothing concrete to fear. The hospital was worse because I understood the principles of western medicine and they were breaking the hygiene laws – walking in and out of surgery still wearing their face masks and coats.'

Strangely, the wound didn't seem to be hurting Nick as much as it did when he arrived. 'It must be the shock, I suppose,' he said.

Before we left for the night, Mokur-Ool applied a poultice to the leg, a noxious-looking herb he called wolf's tongue, and then got out his drum – which looked like a brand-new version of the museum one – and toyed with it for the camera crew. He kept doing little dances for us, repeating them until he judged we'd got the right shot. He was revelling in this attention – doing little bows to us, each time he finished. There was self-evidently the performer in him, but we all agreed that Mokur-Ool also deserved to feel pleased with himself. He'd greatly impressed a load of seasoned foreigners who, between us, had seen some of the most extraordinary things on the planet.

With the bump on my head still growing, and Nick's leg now throbbing, we clambered into the car, and went back to the village of Teeli to sleep.

The next day, Nick's leg apparently on the road to recovery, we got up to find Gendos inspecting his creation, the sheepskin drum, swinging its warped form about in the morning breeze. He had now also finished the drumstick. He was ready for this evening, when he would formally hand over the drum and stick, to be given the power that would enable them to carry Mokur-Ool into the Other Worlds.

All that remained, it seemed, was for Gendos to stitch red bead eyes onto the green snake that straddled the front of the headdress. 'It is a powerful shamanic symbol,' he said. But how true an *eeren* could that snake ever be to any of us whose life is not of animals and plants but of cars and solid houses? And even if he was tonight made into a *kham*, there still remained the problem of the drum. It was not made from the skin of a reindeer, the animal that you rode to the spirit world, but of a sheep. How far could a sheep carry anyone?

That said, Gendos was, in the end, doing an honest thing – stitching together scraps of a broken culture. The green snake served a purpose – in the same way that mistletoe, though no longer regarded as having religious significance, gives those who kiss under it a blessing at Christmas, even today. These things have ceased to be associated with their spiritual origins. We include them in our rituals because we have always done so. They give us a connection to our ancestors, a security, a tie to the past. We still use the same icons – that of the snake spirit, of the sacred mistletoe or the Christmas tree that once joined northern Europeans to the Heavens and Underworld – and maybe it doesn't matter why.

Once back at Mokur-Ool's yurt, the new drum carefully out of sight, horses were gathered and Mokur-Ool, Gendos, Aldynai, Ruhi and I rode up the valley to a quiet spot at the tree line. With the sun blazing, the spring gentians and buttercups still bursting out through the grass, we sat and talked with the old herder about the business of being a *kham*.

First he spoke about his drum, talking as Ai-chourek had done about how it represented the upper, middle and lower worlds. 'I use the drum to call the spirits, and then hold them there in the drum,' he told us. 'It is the focus of all that happens in a ritual. And the drum also helps carry me to the spirit world. I keep it high, in order to be lifted to the upper world, not the dangerous underworld.'

'Ah, so you do trance-journeys … ' I said, still grateful for any sign of behaviour resembling that of the elusive, classic shaman. I asked Mokur-Ool about the cosmic journeys I'd seen, as an outsider, in Borneo, Mongolia and elsewhere, but not yet in Siberia. I told him of shamans on perilous quests, by air, foot and canoe, into the spirit realm, and of reading how they talked of passing through deadly clashing mountains, and traversing treacherous narrow bridges, the valley below littered with the bones of shamans who had failed.

Mokur-Ool's reply was typically honest but, ultimately, a disappointment. He did go on journeys, but, it seemed, remarkably short ones, and there was no indication that this other component to our existence, the spirit realm, was a world like ours but in reverse. 'I can only speak to you with authority about what I experience. And I reach into the spirit world with my drum. I see the bears. I can hear the cry of eagles. I can see the spirits of the good, and the bad, and of the dead people. These are all around me, and I can feel the danger to my soul from the malevolent ones.'

I listened to Mokur-Ool for an hour, around us the crows, and occasionally a buzzard, with its lonesome shrill cry. There were wagtails, skylarks and, passing like clouds across the slopes, sheep and goats. Ai-chourek, also from the countryside, had found a role in modern society, an arena where she could be fulfilled. Mokur-Ool carried on as he always had, answering his calling to his fellow herders, as and when they needed him. Neither reached as far into the Other Worlds as the shamans of old, but both felt and used a powerful, guiding resonance from there.

At dusk, Mokur-Ool put on a dull purple cloak and we gathered ourselves for the handover of Gendos's drum. The ceremony was to take place at a very unpromising spring further downslope, in the crease of the rolling hills. It had been fenced off – though some fence posts had now been borrowed by needy nomads. The water flow, which dribbled as if from a gently weeping hill, was conducted along guttering to a metal tank. This was festooned with cotton strips, which flapped beside the water container like the remains of a thousand abandoned bathing towels.

Closer, I saw that there was a little bush upslope where the water first emerged, and this had more cotton ribbons on it than leaves – it was another of those sacred bushes that was going to die if people carried on venerating it. At the foot of the bush was a collection of objects – the knick-knacks of herding people, each belonging to a sick or desperate person. A cuddly bear with huge ears, a cheap purse, coins, plastic hairclips, a syringe – they were each part of a prayer, and each told a story, mainly of sickness, and always simple hope. Hundreds of ordinary people were reaching out directly to the land that supported them, with no Kyzyl career shaman to get in the way.

It was time for the ritual to begin. Gendos lovingly placed his new drum, still hidden from Mokur-Ool in a cloth, to the side, and we stepped back as the two men quietly assembled a pile of wood. Mokur-Ool lit the fire and Gendos stood, head bowed, before it. He seemed bigger somehow, perhaps swollen with pride at this, what I saw was a momentous moment in his life. For years he must have been yearning to find his roots, the True Heart of Tuva. Gendos was here not just for the enlivening of the drum, but the enlivening of his culture – and he hoped to be a part of it. He quietly knelt as the flames gathered.

First to sanctify the site, the spring. Mokur-Ool threw milk to the nine planets, then gradually began tuning his drum on the fire, afterwards beating it, softly at first. And then something rather odd happened. Gendos got up from his knees, and while Mokur-Ool sounded his drum around the fire, he slipped away to the van. He came back with another, older drum, and an ominous-looking bag. 'That headdress!' I thought. Opening the bag, he drew out not just the headdress but something to go with it, a shiny, satin gown of blues, reds and pinks. As Mokur-Ool drummed away, Gendos ceremoniously started putting on the garment. Skulls adorned the lower skirts; there were silken, voluminous sleeves. The general effect was of a collection of lady's scarves, stitched together by someone who was extremely colourblind. Gendos breathed a deep sigh of satisfaction as the technicolour garment settled on him. Then he raised the lady's headdress, the one with the little green snake, and placed it on.

From somewhere among the film crew, I heard an astonished gasp.

However, Mokur-Ool was in charge here, not us, and when Gendos joined him again, kneeling by the fire as the old man drummed, he didn't seem the slightest bothered. We'd just have to see what happened next.

Mokur-Ool finished this first part of the ritual and invited Gendos to sit with him, resting a while. Gendos produced some vodka, in fact a whole bottle. That vodka they didn't perhaps need, nor a second bottle that followed the first, but indisputably there was charm in the moment: the young apprentice accepted by someone who belonged in the countryside – that hitherto ailing spiritual resource of Tuva.

Now for the next stage of the ritual. Mokur-Ool stood up and again began a slow, controlled and deliberate beat of his drum. Gendos stepped forward and joined in on his old drum. He beat louder, stronger, and he beat with an attractive rhythm – that is, as a musician, creating crafted patterns of sound, not as a shaman whose drum, with its simple, regular pulses, was a vehicle into the spirit world. Together they walked around the fire, Mokur-Ool uncomplaining as Gendos followed piously, listening, copying the guru, and adding his own improvisations, these culminating in a sympathetic rendition of *khöömei* throat-singing.

Evidently, I had underestimated Gendos's ambitions. He was here not just to find his roots, but to fulfil what he saw was his destiny. Now he would be able to go back to the town having been endorsed by the Real Tuva, the land itself. As he circled around as if on stage in Kyzyl Theatre, he thought he was a *kham*. It was a fantasy world, like the one inhabited by the girls of Kyzyl who walked the streets in lace and plastic skirts as if on MTV. Looking around, I noticed that Ruhi, Misha and everyone else were gaping. Gendos was upstaging a *kham* on the hillside, upstaging the hillside itself in his garish reds, his electric blues.

Gendos echoed and enhanced Mokur-Ool's call to the spirits for a good half-hour, but by now we had all but stopped filming. We stood around, muttering discontentedly, as dark fell about us and the moon came up. 'He's hijacked the ceremony,' I said.

'We should have known better,' someone said. 'He's a showman, an actor. We've given him a stage – he's responding to the cameras.'

Wayne, the cameraman, tried to make the most of it. 'Reminds me of filming the Ku Klux Klan. Maybe it's the fire, maybe it's just that costume.'

'For me it's the Druids,' added another voice. 'Druids with runny noses at Stonehenge. People trying to re-create what once was.'

The only enthusiast was Michael, not just the director but also an anthropologist. 'Don't you see what's happening? It's immensely exciting! He's an urban *kham*, gaining recognition from a rural one!' But there was no time to analyse the thought. The new drum was about to be handed over.

In the darkness that had now descended, Gendos lifted the new drum out of its cloth, struggling a bit to ease its warped frame free. As it was brought into the light offered by the flames, Mokur-Ool now had a chance to feast his eyes on this artistic creation.

Really, I thought he took it very well – simply smiling in silence at it, as you do an unwanted Christmas present. This must be partly because he's such a gentleman, I thought, and partly because we caught him having a secret glimpse of the drum yesterday. He was over the initial shock.

Standing by the fire embers, Gendos, now established on centre stage, took the initiative. He took up the new drum and began beating it. The sound was actually quite good – a little soggy, the skin not fully taut, but strong. The *kham* and his apprentice stood side by side by the fire, the flames lighting them from below, creating masks of their faces. Mokur-Ool beat his own drum and for a while both these instruments seemed to have a conversation with each other.

Watching this, I had to admire Gendos. After all, there did seem to be many qualities shared by him and a shaman – notably the sense of theatre – and, however easy it was to mock, he was undoubtedly equal to the occasion, and undoubtedly accepted by Mokur-Ool.

Mokur-Ool invited Gendos to throw him the new drum. Gendos threw it, and Mokur-Ool threw his back. They now had each other's drums and stood there as if equals. Mokur-Ool beat the new drum slowly, then waved it over the fire, holding it horizontally there – not to tune it but to scorch it, purifying it in the sacred flames.

After a moment, Mokur-Ool turned again to Gendos, and carefully threw him his drumstick. He waited, expecting Gendos to throw his back. This would be a symbolic exchange of their shamanic energies, and – if done without a hitch – a sign of the spirits' blessing on them both.

It should have been a straightforward transaction. Perhaps it was that vodka, or perhaps it was his silky garment that complicated every movement of his substantial torso. Or was it the will of the spirits that Gendos was not ready yet to be acclaimed a shaman? Whatever it was, Gendos was incapable of catching the thing.

He tried, and tried again. Time after time the drumstick dropped to the grass. It was picked up, tossed back. 'One, two, three,' the two men would count aloud, and each toss his drumstick to the other. And Gendos would make a mess of it, and kneel to ask forgiveness. As the evening dragged on and a full moon rose, clouds unveiling and veiling it, the fire dimmed. Now Mokur-Ool, an old man trying to see the drumstick in poor light, also couldn't catch it.

I felt sorry for Gendos, kneeling there, all of us watching. A man of great talent, and this was his big moment. It hardly seemed a ringing endorsement from the spirit worlds.

Nick's voice said, 'There's a god out there somewhere laughing.'

The firelight went completely, and all I could discern was the huge figure of Gendos stumbling about in the moonlight. Mokur-Ool was somewhere there as well, and I wondered if he was more in command of Gendos than I'd thought. Perhaps he was putting him through his paces, establishing his control just as he'd done with me that first day, cracking my head with his *eeren*.

There was a final drum salvo, and that seemed to mean it was all over. We loaded the car – Gendos to return to his urban world, Mokur-Ool to his. The last to leave was Gendos, saluting the moon with both hands outstretched. He inhaled deeply and rather loudly. I left him to it. Was he fooling himself? He seemed to have created a fantasy world, a spiritual dimension to Tuva – a land I'd always had difficulty believing in, even in our physical dimension.

My mind was full of questions as we drove home, the driver drunk with vodka that Gendos hadn't spotted. Had we, or Gendos, steam-rollered Mokur-Ool? He seemed happy to go along with everything we'd wanted – so was he, indeed, controlling events? And what did he make of Gendos – and us, who were of the same, confused urban kind?

Ruhi and I had one more opportunity to talk to him, when we went with Aldynai to say goodbye. Taking Gendos's sheepskin drum for closer inspection, we went and sat against some tree stumps, where the last patch of snow was melting into the stream. Mokur-Ool talked clearly and concisely as usual. Just sitting with him was enough to remove any doubts either Ruhi or I had about whether he'd been forced into a performance, either by Gendos or us.

I began by asking him if Gendos was really a *kham*.

'He has a lot to learn,' Mokur-Ool said, adjusting his cap. 'He has a lot of talent, and is a powerful person. He also listened to me carefully and was *ready* to learn.'

'And what about that awful – I mean awesome – costume?'

Mokur-Ool was diplomatic. 'It's true that it is not conventional. But I knew it was originally designed for his stage performances. I can accept that.'

'It was a female outfit … ' I said.

'It might seem strange, yes, but actually this was a ritual meant to be performed by males and females together, so it was entirely appropriate. It seemed very fitting and I was very pleased.'

I felt extremely guilty. How nasty I had been to Gendos. If he had been acting out a fantasy, maybe that could be said for anyone who believes in gods or God. And believers make up an extremely large portion of the world. However, there was that drum.

'It does need some improvement,' Mokur-Ool admitted. He flapped the woven willow saplings, twanging their ends. 'These need to be cut off and I need to redo some of the wood,' he said, making the best of it. 'As for the sheepskin, it needs to be dried out. But the sound is good – it is an even sound throughout and that is the most important thing.'

As for the dropping of the drumstick, I told Mokur-Ool that I'd seen a shaman called Tsend throw her drumstick to people, to test if the spirit was happy with them. She'd done it to everyone present and the ritual couldn't end until the spirit was content with all of us.

Mokur-Ool wouldn't be drawn. 'These things happen,' he said, lightly. 'I'm not here to judge Gendos. He has some things to learn, yes, but that is all right, you see.'

And I did see. I came away from this quiet, intelligent and sensitive man feeling an enormous respect for him. And when I'd had a moment to think a bit more, thumping down the road into the valley, and later flying out by helicopter to look for *khams* even further afield in Tuva, among the remaining reindeer herders of Todja, I felt better about all I'd seen here.

I'd come here wondering what, if anything, would emerge from the ashes of the communist era. And I had actually found a great deal here. Journeying on to Todja, a remote taiga habitat of the sort from where the word 'shaman' was coined by the world, I heard from the reindeer herders that the last true shamans had left them – either they had died or had left, like nearly everyone, for the towns. But all was not lost. In Tuva we had found Mokur-Ool, a herder operating in a way not very far removed from the old days; he was a relic, trying to keep his nomadic community in balance with the fragile land as *samán* had always done.

There was Ai-chourek, abused by the townworld, but genuinely 'called'. And there was Gendos. He wasn't the traditional figure, man of the taiga and steppe, nor did he know herbal medicine and the subconscious mind, or possess the full range of the shaman's impressive array of skills. He was a performer – but what is a shaman if not, in part, a showman?

As I'd learned in Siberut, medicine men survive as long as they are needed – and in Tuva we were seeing that, as people adopt a town life, they continue to have these needs, but in more specialist guises. Thus, in the West, the medicine man is still alive – he is merely split into a multitude of characters: doctor, psychotherapist, musician, historian, TV presenter and so on. We only lack him in his role as guardian of the environment – and the New Age movement is trying to put that to rights by reminding us, like the shaman-figure once did, that we are all dependent on the life and elements around us. The shaman has left behind a hunter–gatherer existence, and settled into urban life.

And what of the 'Legal Shamans' of Kenin-Lopsan? One of the medicine man's greatest roles is, of course, the priest. Once we are no longer hunter–gatherers, it seems that we humans get together to form a very fixed Church. Sooner or later, we have our first reformation, as Tuva was having now – the new pushing aside the old, the no longer relevant. The simple, spiritual inspiration of the medicine man was being sorted into an organized religion. Kenin-Lopsan was now a bishop, and soon there'd be sacred texts. One of his key *khams* – a man rumoured to have been taught his neo-shamanism by a New Age American lady – was presently proselytizing like a Christian evangelist in other parts of Tuva. Who knows, one day these medicine man missionaries might convert the young – those in leather jackets and mini-skirts who presently bow not to the tree but MTV.

But my admiration was reserved for Mokur-Ool, the closest I had come in Tuva to that original all-in-one figure who embodied all those roles. And this figure will die out. As the plane flew across Siberia, I wrote in my notebook beside his name, 'N.B. Here lies the real Living Treasure of Shamanism.'

HAITI
VODOU BEYOND THE SHANTY TOWN

CHAPTER SEVEN

'The dead are more important than the living; they look after our
future. And you have to keep feeding them – maybe a chicken,
maybe even a fat cow. This is what Vodou is all about – giving food
to the spirits who oversee us.'
Rosela Duras, Vodou devotee at Saut d'Eau

As I left Britain for my next destination, my sister Katie said,
'You will take care – I mean, you're not going to subject
yourself to any ritual, are you?' I assured her that I wasn't. Well,
probably not.

But why was she suddenly worrying? I'd lived alone with
numerous remote peoples; and in New Guinea, to understand
one culture, had even gone through a male initiation ceremony
which involved being beaten for six weeks.. The answer: because
I was now heading for Haiti, *the* place of 'witchdoctors'. In our
minds, this is *voodoo* land. The word itself is so laden with associations that it has been cleaned up. It's no longer correct to spell
it 'voodoo' – the word so beloved of those ghoulish Hollywood
B movies. The acceptable form is now 'Vodou'.

So, was it just the fault of Hollywood that the religion's
image needed a makeover? In Haiti did they or did they not
believe in zombies? By looking at the real Vodou I might be able
to tackle the doubts many of us share about the way some medicine men in general go about their work. What of the sorcerers
I'd heard of in Borneo, Sumatra and elsewhere, who projected
magical poisoned darts at their adversaries? The *kereis* of Siberut,
and Mokur-Ool, had spoken of these darker characters, and
others of the Evil Eye. Few medicine men would deny there are
downright bad individuals among their profession, sorcerers
who plant harmful objects in their victims. In Australia's Gibson

Desert I'd lived with aborigines who had had a real fear of being 'sung' to death; a fourteen-year-old, an otherwise apparently normal schoolgirl, was isolated from the rest of her community because a curse had been worked on her by a 'doctor'.

Christians talk in terms of the world being a battlefield of Good versus Evil. For medicine men, judging by all I'd learnt so far, the situation is more complex. To them the spirits have personalities like ours – indeed, many of these characters are our ancestors. They are jealous, fickle, generous – and yes, sometimes vicious. And here lies the problem: sometimes the medicine man's job is to deal with malevolent forces, and this means having to have power to battle with them – power he could, potentially, use to do harm. Or power that could overcome him if he is unwary, eating him up and turning him into a sorcerer.

So, now to scratch a bit more at this 'darker' side. Kyzyl had no shortage of manipulators, tricksters and conmen, but they were not 'traditional' practitioners. And there are no traditions more suspect, in many a westerner's imagination, than those within, or stemming from, Africa. In those traditional cultures the medicine man is seen as the very epitome of the 'witch-doctor', the scary purveyor of mumbo-jumbo.

The plane began its descent into Haiti, the western, formerly French third of the island of Hispaniola. Beside me was Chantal Regnault, a distinguished photographer who had been to Haiti countless times and would be my translator this time round. And below me were the tired hills of Haiti – forested when Columbus landed in 1492, now mostly dust. How did they come to be this way? It is a story of tragedy, the story of Haiti and the story of Vodou.

The population of Haiti is descended almost entirely from slaves brought over from West Africa, officially from 1510 onwards. The French attempted to weaken slave power and their sense of origin by outlawing their traditional religions. The Code Noir of 1685, prepared by Louis XIV, enforced conversion to Christianity. However, the African religions we clump under the title 'Vodou' continued to be practised in secret, often under cover of Catholicism. And in 1791, encouraged by the French Revolution and Declaration of the Rights of Man, and galvanized by a ceremony at Bois Caïman dedicated to the spirits, an insurrection got under way. Though Napoleon sent troops to re-establish slavery, the struggle triumphed and Haiti was proclaimed a republic in 1804.

However, 200 years of self-seeking rule followed, both in Haiti and the other Spanish portion of the island, nowadays the Dominican Republic. The mulatto (mixed race) and black heroes of the revolt, Toussaint L'Ouverture, Dessalines, Pétion and Christophe, now persecuted Vodou priests who threatened their control and the Vatican began instigating various 'anti-superstitious' campaigns. Desiring to control the 'windward passage' – the Panama Canal had recently been opened – and alarmed by increasing instability (evident in the lynching of the president), as well as German influence in the country, the Americans stepped in. Though the blacks of Haiti had, in theory at least, had freedom – and in the States there was still segregation – the Americans occupied the island. During their stay, from 1915 to 1934, they sent thousands of peasants to hard labour, and resisters to US concentration camps – one of them, at Chalbert in the north, claiming the lives of 15–20,000 people.

This particular era of unhappiness culminated in the arrival of François 'Papa Doc' Duvalier and his not-to-be-messed-with wife Simone in 1957. A qualified doctor and an authority on Vodou, he called for the rehabilitation of the religion as the soul of the nation, the African roots of the people's culture – a device that usefully challenged the powerful mulatto elite and the Catholic Church. His arm was strengthened by the recruitment of Vodou priests, *oungan*, who suppressed opponents through fear of sorcery, and his dreaded Tontons Macoutes – secret police, named after the countryside bogeyman character Uncle Straw Satchel – their habit was to place bodies strategically on street corners as a message to others.

Papa Doc's son Jean-Claude ('Baby Doc') succeeded him but proved less competent as a dictator and was ousted in 1986 after public unrest. The following year a new constitution was approved, and Vodou decriminalized despite campaigns by American Protestants to link this 'diabolical' religion in the public mind with the excesses of the Duvaliers. For the first time in Haiti's history, the people had a chance to choose a leader for themselves.

In 1990 they elected the leftist priest Jean-Bertrand Aristide, who had been rallying the poor against the Tontons Macoutes and had recognized the contribution to be made not just by Catholics and the newer Protestant churches but also vodou-ists – though to this day it's impossible to say how many Vodou devotees there are, the overlap with Catholicism at times seeming total. It marked a break in the system based on old privileges, barely changed since the days of slavery. For the first time in two centuries, on 22 August 1991, and despite more Protestant demonstrations, a celebration of that historic Vodou ceremony at Bois Caïman took place.

The following month, the army, the Church and the mulatto elite, threatened by all this democracy, staged a *coup* and forced Aristide into exile. Three years of military rule followed. Another US army force, a 'Support Group', was again brought in to keep law and order – and, back home, to win Black American votes and stem immigration. This time, the force was genuinely welcomed. Aristide was restored as president in October 1994 and invited several hundred *oungan* into his palace, an important public recognition of the people's indigenous religion.

When I came to Haiti, Aristide was again out of power – his term of office was up and, ironically, the new anti-dictator constitution now meant he couldn't return for a consecutive term. While the people waited for the return of their man, the Americans, who felt they had done their duty in restoring democracy, reduced the number of soldiers from 20,000 to a more discreet 500.

However, the future Haiti faced was, in many ways, no better than 200 years ago. At the time of Independence the slaves burnt the hated plantations to forestall the return of the slaving system, and maintained their little bit of Africa – it was what they all knew. However, in this act of destruction they had condemned themselves to crippling poverty – from having had the most productive region in the Caribbean. And, for whatever reason – ecological, political or religious – until this day Haiti has offered most of its people only an elusive freedom, and very real hardship.

In short, I was flying over the poorest country in the western hemisphere, and one of the poorest in the world.

As we came into land, passengers raised their hands in the air to thank Jesus. Some were holding Bibles. They were Protestant youth evangelists from the States, come to wage war on Vodou. 'Most Catholics gave up fighting it years ago,' Chantal murmured lightly. 'They have simply adapted.'

The plane was coming to a halt. Strong gusts of wind swirled around us as we walked down the steps, into the blinding light of midday. Out on the tarmac we passed an airport vehicle with a large badge saying that it was donated by Taiwan, a country hoping for Haiti's vote at the United Nations. There was little else that Haiti could give the world, it seemed, other than fantasy – images of walking dead and dolls prickly with pins. Or was it fantasy?

The other side of Customs, Haitian youths lunged to grab our bags. They shifted them ten paces to the left, and then demanded a dollar. Finally we were driving away past the US army barracks and heading into Port-au-Prince. The country I saw seemed as African as Africa. We wound through the dust, dodging 'tap-taps', the exuberantly hand-painted buses that you had to tap to stop, and women with bundles – or just a cucumber – balanced on their heads. I gathered from Chantal that African influence is evident too in the words of Vodou songs and rituals, though Creole, the dominant language of the island, grew out of pirate French. It is the sole language of 90 per cent of the population. The other 10 per cent, the elite, speak French.

We were passing Cité Soleil. Once called 'Cité Simone' in honour of Papa Doc's wife, it had been his pet housing project, and now seemed to be a focus of misery.

'How about education?' I asked Chantal, as we wove through a line of children in uniform. They looked smart, and one or two carried tatty books with French titles.

'The parents see the importance of going to school: the social importance of being in a uniform. But they are illiterate themselves and so cannot evaluate what they learn.'

Official figures show that between 40 and 50 per cent of adults are illiterate, but some foreign workers say it's nearer 80.

We turned into a compound, the Oloffson Hotel, one of the last remaining colonial 'gingerbread architecture' houses, on one of whose cool wood verandas Graham Green wrote *The Comedians*. 'An evil slum floating a few miles from Florida,' he called Haiti.

There were palms, and a pool. It wouldn't take very long, if you lived here, to forget about the world outside those gates. The elite had. They were the mulatto traders living in Pétionville, up the hill. 'You don't see them in the main town,' I learnt at the hotel bar, 'except as they go to the airport – shopping trips to Miami.' I imagined them on their mobile phones, the young arranging beach parties while having their pedicure.

The money was presently controlled by six families, who preferred to marry whites but, whoever they married, stuck together. They worked with Duvalier, with Aristide – as long as it didn't affect their income. 'They wouldn't want to have to start paying much tax, for example,' said one man I spoke to who had perhaps sat on too many barstools in his time.

'It's in their interests to improve the economy here, isn't it?' I asked, somewhat naively.

'Not particularly,' he answered. 'Their bank accounts are elsewhere – they are always ready to leave. They don't fix the roads, they just get bigger cars to withstand them. If Haiti erupts, it will be like 200 years ago – a total burning of everything.'

'So, hopes of the people rest with Aristide's return…'

'He's had his soul tampered with,' the barstool man said.

'You mean some kind of sorcery…?'

'Exactly. That is, he spent too long in exile in the States. He's become one of them, an American. The next president of Haiti is going to be a zombie.'

Later I retreated to my bed, wondering what else Haiti was going to come up with. Some things I'd soon no doubt get used to. I'd been talking to the hotel receptionist, Marjorie, and she casually mentioned her aunt had three beautiful wedding rings – one for her husband, plus those for the two *lwa*, or Vodou spirits, she was also married to.

In the night I couldn't sleep – not so much fear of zombies as the disturbance caused by a mad chicken in someone's yard. I thought about what I'd learnt already of Vodou from people who actually lived and breathed it.

In New York I'd met a Haitian drummer called Frisner Augustin – I was due to meet him again here on the island. He drummed for Vodou ceremonies in the basements of Brooklyn, and Chantal had taken me along to his flat in Flatbush, a Haitian quarter. Here he had an altar with pictures of Christian saints, except I learnt that to practitioners of Vodou, they were characters whose origins were essentially African. Rather than be flayed for pursuing their own religion, slaves had carried on worshipping their ancestral deities by matching a suitable Catholic saint to each one. Behind every saint, taken carefully from the iconography of the Church, a *lwa* was celebrated, bringing to them not just the life spirit of their deities but also the spirit of their ancestral traditions.

There was the figure that Catholics would have called St James the Greater, conqueror of the Moors, a valiant man always on a white horse, sword raised. 'Ogou,' Frisner said, '*lwa* of the fire and justice. He helps me when I need strength or I gotta fight over something. He likes to be offered a red cock, 'cos red is his colour. Of course, he likes a bull better, if you got one.'

Next was an image of St Patrick. He was stamping on some snakes, probably in Ireland. 'Danbala,' Frisner said. 'He gives me luck and money, when times are tough, see. He likes to be given white things – eggs and rice.' Sure enough, I noticed that below Danbala's picture was a pile of cooked rice, desiccating in New York's summer heat. Next along was St Peter by his Heavenly Gate; to Frisner the *lwa* Legba, who stands at the crossroads to the spirit world, and so at rituals must be called before any of the other spirits. Next there was the Virgin Mary, who was a promiscuous, coquettish-sounding spirit called Ezili Freda, a lover of luxury and also lover of the fiery spirit Ogou. To gain her favour, you offered perfumes and delicacies.

Frisner fetched me one of his drums, to give me a rendition. 'This is my roots,' he said. 'My heart-rhythm, the spirit in me.' He said he played the same drum at Vodou ceremonies – 'though we don't call 'em that, we just call 'em parties for the spirits'. I understood that Frisner had a vital role, because it was the drum that called out to the *lwa*, dictating which spirit would come. Furthermore, the drum controlled each one when they arrived and possessed members of the Vodou congregation. For the special power of the *lwa* was that they could displace the spirit of someone, becoming the life force that animates a person.

There were other things in the room that he explained – a rattle he called an *ason*, with which a priest himself would call the *lwa*, and other objects that, quite frankly, I felt I still needed reassurance about. Top of my list was a doll-like object in the corner which was like a sinister scarecrow but wore a top hat.

Later Frisner took me to a newly opened restaurant belonging to Edeline, a neighbour who was a *manbo*, or priestess, and thus served both earthly and spiritual needs. Edeline was a tall, mighty, sensual figure with slow-blinking eyes; a woman you would want to worship, not trifle with. As I'd found typical among the *kereis* of Siberut and *khams* of Tuva, she became aware of her calling after she became ill. 'And at that age, thirteen, I could already see into people,' she said, playing her eyes over me. I was quite prepared to believe this woman could see right into me.

She took me downstairs to see her *ounfò*, or altar. Among the stack of pictures, statues, candles and miscellaneous objects heaped in the corner, there was a picture of that sinister man again, the dark figure with the top hat. 'He is Baron Samedi,' Edeline said. 'He is head of the Gede family of spirits.'

'And what do they do?' I asked.

'They are the spirits of the dead,' Edeline said. I frowned suspiciously at the figure, realizing that I had seen him at the cinema. It was a James Bond film, and this man of death had emerged like a skeleton from behind a gravestone amid a frenzied dark ritual – writhing bodies cavorting with pythons. But turning to Edeline I saw she was smiling, thinking of him.

'He's a trickster,' she said. 'He likes a laugh, and to drink rum and say bad stories in front of the ladies.' She talked about his cavortings, how he stole money off worshippers and made them laugh with obscene antics. He was, I could see, in some way satirizing death and so helping us to come to terms with it.

Edeline also seemed to have a particular relationship with Ogou, the valiant horseman with the sword. 'He possesses you?' I asked, not sure if this was even the right word.

Edeline nodded. 'He is so strong, so tiring,' she sighed. 'It is like being ridden – this is what we say. That we are horses being ridden.'

I asked Edeline if she remembered anything while being 'ridden'. She said no. 'But I've seen myself on video – oh my God!' She gave a huge smile and covered her face with her hands.

Later that night I saw her video – not Hollywood extras this time, but real vodou-ists and in action in a real temple.

Vodou worshippers adhere to a single temple group, each one like a church parish, but autonomous, and here the congregation were, gathered around the *manbo* Edeline. She was seated shaking the *ason* rattle, and directing a flock of mostly female initiates, first in a litany of Catholic prayers and then hectically calling the different *lwa* one by one to be present. Then the drums rolled, and the temple group erupted into violent dance.

In the centre of the *peristil*, or dance floor, was a red and blue painted wood post – this, I gathered, was the *poto-mitan*, through which the spirits were said to descend into the room. Beside it I could see, between the thumping bare feet, a *vèvè*, or motif of a particular *lwa*, that had been drawn on the dirt floor in white powder to attract the spirit. And I could make out Edeline herself, now on her feet. Or was it Edeline? She seemed no longer herself – she looked physically uncomfortable, as if her body was having to adjust to the shape of something moving into her. She was being 'ridden' by one of the spirits. I watched as initiates quickly came forward and equipped her with the accoutrements of the *lwa* that was now animating her body. She was given the stick and black hat of Baron Samedi, head of the spirits of the dead.

Having his possessions seemed to reassure the *lwa*. She was now firmly Baron Samedi and got to her feet, grabbed some-one's rum, swigged it and cackled. Then her antics became wilder; her hips writhed and rolled, her legs spread and she walked like a mating insect. For, it seemed, Baron Samedi's duties were to look after not just the end, our death, but the beginning, the birth of life. He was therefore prone to sexual antics, and at present was handling his staff in a suggestive way.

Edeline later took me to her house to see her temple first hand. It was a quite ordinary, empty space: bare white walls with murals of the different *lwa* on them, and the *peristil* made of dirt 'the way the *lwa* like it'. Without people the temple meant nothing, I realized. People *were* the temple.

Edeline walked me past the post, the *poto-mitan*, introduc-ing me to some more of the *lwa*. One painting was of a pair of identical twins known as Marasa – or Sts Damian and Cosmas. These characters were immensely important, being the funda-mental powers of harmony and unity.

In the four corners of the *peristil* were chambers, called *djevo*, each with temple paraphernalia such as sets of beads for initiates and altars for *lwa* that were particularly important here. I walked around the temple, trying to get to know the assembly of spirits represented in Catholic icons. I was rapidly learning that the term 'Vodou', strictly speaking, refers to only one tradition, originating in West Africa's old Dahomey kingdom (in modern Benin), where each family's ancestral spirits were called *vodun*.

These original spirits were represented only on Edeline's left wall, and known as 'Rada' – a corruption of Arada, a city on the coast of Dahomey. The Rada category embraced traditions mainly emerging from two African peoples and their spirit families or 'nations': first there was the Nago nation of *lwa*, the powerful deities such as Ogou still recognized today by the Yoruba of Nigeria. Secondly, there was Rada itself, perceived as the *lwa* nation most faithful to the people's West African traditions. Rada was the *flé ginen*, or flower of Ginen, a place that originated as the very real land of Guinea, in West Africa, but was now only a spiritual concept, the true spirit of the ancestral home overseas. These *lwa* are seen as benevolent, and included Legba, guardian of the spiritual gates. Rooted in the profound and traditional *mistè* or mysteries of Africa, the Rada rite promotes the spiritual balance of the individual and the collective.

Edeline's other wall was devoted to the second and later branch of *lwa*, these the 'hot' and more fiery spirits often known by the general term 'Kongo'; they cover Petwo, Kongo, Gede, Ibo, Djouba and other nations. Of these, the Kongo nation were those served originally by people of the Congo Basin and Angola, and it was from this that Petwo evolved, after the slaves had been brought to Haiti. The Petwo were more concerned than Kongo with gaining material wealth, power or protection, and, emerging as they did out of the misery of the plantation system, these *lwa* were more bitter and aggressive. It was they who, in 1791, were invoked at Bois Caïman to bring about the slave uprising.

Having absorbed all this – the cool Rada *lwa*, the hot Kongo ones – I now learnt from Edeline that there isn't a rigid line between the two. Legba, keeper of the spirit gates, naturally is called first whatever nation of spirits is being celebrated; and whether a temple is dedicated to Rada or Kongo or both, Petwo *lwa* may manifest themselves violently during rituals by possessing devotees.

I was tiptoeing into the baffling pantheon of spirits, brought from different peoples spread across West Africa but in Haiti brought together and celebrated in major festivals a few kilometres apart. This was a religion without bishops, without a pope. There was no hierarchy, just priests and priestesses with their own temples and a *société* of worshippers, each of whom had personal relationships with particular *lwa*. The assembly of *lwa* you venerated were complimentary members of a family representing most aspects of your daily life. They were not so much gods as mediators – supernatural beings who organized and maintained daily existence for the Supreme Being, 'the Great Master' who exercised ultimate control over all of creation.

I now wanted to broach the other side of Vodou – at least, the side we hear about. I asked Edeline as gently as I could about Vodou's bad name.

'I'm not a bad person. People think Vodou is about putting pins in dolls. We don't do that kinda thing,' she said.

'And zombies?' I asked.

'Yeah, we believe in zombies, but if you're good that's not goin' to be something that troubles you. That's something that can happen to bad people.'

Soon after, Frisner arrived, and insisted on beating a drum as Edeline and I tried to talk. 'Some of my star peoples are whities!' he said, as I took an interest.

'And white people can be possessed by the *lwa*?'

'Sure they can!' He slowed the rhythm he was tapping with his fingertips. 'What happens if I beat the drum? Say, I beat it once, right by your face?'

'I suppose I would blink.'

'That is the first stage. You can believe in the spirits, because they affected you.'

Quite a good answer, I thought.

I met Frisner again on 13 July when he arrived in Haiti from New York a few days after me. We picked him up and headed out to Saut d'Eau, one of Haiti's major Vodou festivals. The story goes that a hundred years ago there was an apparition of Our Lady of Mount Carmel; she was perched above a palm tree by a waterfall. Haitians began making pilgrimages to the site. The father at the local Catholic church excitedly erected a statue to honour her. However, to many Haitians it didn't matter how the Church represented her; to them she must be the Vodou *lwa* Ezili. Whether she was Ezili Dantò, the black, fiercely protective Petwo *lwa* of motherhood and procreation, or Ezili Freda, promiscuous white spirit of love and sensuality, seems unclear. The devotees came, worshipping the madonna, and also Simbi, the Petwo guardian of springs and pools, and for good measure Danbala Wèdo, Rada spirit of water and rainbows – in fact whatever particular *lwa* they felt called to serve. The Vodou devotees came and came. Eventually the Catholics took the statue away, and even cut down the palm. It still didn't stop the Vodou faithful.

As elsewhere in Haiti, celebrations of the varied *lwa* – which are said to reside in trees and water – have become linked to the festivals of the country saints, in this case Our Lady of Mount Carmel. She was a White Madonna, and Ezili Dantò was black – that didn't stop the Vodou pilgrims either. They immersed themselves in the waters, hoping the luck of Freda or and fertility of Dantò – who demanded, anyway, cleanliness in her devotees – would wash off on them. Then in the church they celebrated the mass held for Our Lady of Mount Carmel, the highlight traditionally being when her statue was paraded through the streets.

Though only 100 kilometres, our journey would take a whole day, starting with an hour or two getting out of the congested, crumbling streets of Port-au-Prince. Then through the hills, spread with the maize plots of subsistence farmers or else a dry, white rocky soil that had seen lush rainforest, but now boasted vegetation ignored even by goats.

Driving on, we got a view beyond a salt lake into the comparatively wealthy and fertile Dominican Republic; the border was said to be 'porous' – Haitians of all sorts streaming that way, and, it was said, only traders and prostitutes, desired for their paler skin, trickling this way.

Up and down hills, and finally down to Ville Bonheur, a settlement on the path up to the sacred falls. There were hawkers selling beans and rice, plantains, straw hats and sunglasses. Others were proffering games of roulette – standing on the spinning wheel was a bunch of plastic figures, a mini Action Man, a gorilla, a tiger. These items, just children's playthings, seemed to serve the purpose of giving the game a supernatural aura. They were toy spirits, making luck seem more than a game of mathematical odds.

The next day Frisner, Chantal and I, tagged by the film crew, walked a few kilometres up the hill to the falls. Pilgrims progressed alongside us, most dressed in ordinary clothes but others in startling white, or the dress of the Vodou *société* to which they belonged. Up the hill they came, calabashes in their hands, shaking their rattles enthusiastically, to call their *lwa* – and encourage us to part with alms. Sometimes they sang to Ezili Dantò, sometimes to Simbi, and both women and some decorative men rejoiced in Freda; adorned in lipstick and perfume, these devotees flirted outrageously with us as they went swanning by.

The pilgrims were not just from Haiti but from the entire diaspora. We were overtaken by a flock from America, white faces among all the black ones. It is said that there are 50 million Vodou adherents world-wide – in West Africa and wherever the slave descendants ended up – while similar religions of Candomblé in Bahia, Brazil, and Santaría in Cuba evolved in other slave colonies. I was seeing the central democracy of Vodou. There was no dictating of right and wrong. It was ever evolving, just people reaching out to what they felt they knew, all based on traditions remembered from Africa.

Some pilgrims were coming back down, more of them now dressed in the clothes of the spirits that they had a special affinity with: the black and grey of Simbi; the red shoes and rose-coloured satins of Ezili Dantò; the scarlet scarves of Ogou. Others, wearing white, green and pink, carried wicker stools on their heads, as demanded by Agwé. The spirit of fishing and shipping, he was also having an affair with Freda, and demanded the chair to act as a symbolic boat that he could sit on, if he chose to possess his servant.

By a little stream, we stopped at a mapou, the silk cotton tree which is a favoured abode of *lwa*. Candles had been placed around its trunk, which had been slowly burnt away over the years through such acts of devotion. Frisner joined the cluster around the tree and, after mouthing some prayers, delivered a hefty slap to the tree trunk – as if to make a clear and unshakable bond with the *lwa*. The greetings I had received from pilgrims had been as resounding, an indisputable gesture that was a violent shake with both hands.

We came to the crest of the hill, the falls tumbling off to our left and below us a fertile plain dotted with small maize fields, palms and occasional Vodou temples topped with their red and blue flags. We dropped down towards the foot of the cascade. Ahead of us along the path were rickety stalls behind which hopeful ladies stirred their cooking pots, and others waited behind their rum and candles. There was a token attempt to extract an entrance fee by some youths, but we pushed through with everyone else, and received our first view.

It was a magnificent sight, even for me, who didn't know Ezili or Simbi. The surrounding cliffs were stacked with trees and soaked mosses in which, it was believed, the *lwa* lived. And from this natural arena came the smell of the water, the cool breeze of the updraught. Pilgrims were now running ahead, flinging their old garments into the water, calling to one *lwa* or other to bless their lives with plenty, and often, if here to venerate Dantò, specifically with a child.

I gave my valuables to Chantal and went forward on to the water-washed boulders, edging my way through the white water and bodies until I got a clear view beyond the heavy pelts of moss massed over the cliff face and feeding off the cold spray. Ahead now, the long chutes of water. Stacked up on the smooth rock steps below, men and women were singing, arms outstretched to the torrent. Some were rubbing cleansing herbs over their bodies, removing their underwear and soaping themselves in the cascade. They called to the racing current. They were talking, crying, wrapped in the furious, powerful flow of seething white water, hundreds of vodou-ists and each one of them busy – from the point of view of the World Faiths – 'nature-worshipping', confusing the Creator with the created.

I went directly under the fall itself and felt the weight and noise of the main flow. The cold itself was shocking, and the pounding – one of nature's drumbeats – might alone have been enough to induce the subconscious state that overtakes devotees when possessed by the spirit personas. Yet some pilgrims on the river bank were collapsing just on arrival at this sacred place.

As I came out of the water one woman was on the river-bank, screaming hysterically, as if unable to bear terrible news. She began to totter, her eyes rolling, and Frisner ran to hold her steady. 'That's Rosela Duras – my friend. She was meant to bring a chair with her for Agwé. That why he's angry. He says he gonna kill Rosela.' A chair was borrowed from another Agwé devotee, and Rosela was plonked on it. Calm was restored.

I walked through the possessed, watching their friends help them by providing the *lwa* with the relevant trappings – a scarf, a machete, perfume. It was mostly women who got possessed, and I wondered if it was because females are better physically, or perhaps socially, equipped to express their emotions. Anyway, what is 'possession'?

One explanation by psychotherapists is that it is a manifestation of a multiple split-personality something like schizophrenia. As children, Haitians have become conditioned to the types of personality available and, in an altered state of consciousness, these personas come forward, representing this and that aspect of life. It doesn't explain why some white people go into trance, displaying characters of spirits of which they are ignorant. And if these white people are merely susceptible individuals, open to a hypnotic state, this doesn't explain why descendants from West Africa might be somehow susceptible – they couldn't all have multiple personalities.

That night we went to see the Mapou Rasin de Azor Band – literally the Mapou Tree Roots Band of Azor. The group didn't use synthesizers, it simply played the stuff of Vodou ceremonies. There were three drummers, three men on tambourines, three female singers and the male lead singer, Azor. Through the night he sang, the ladies screeching a chorus, the drums trembling and roaring, the young men and women bouncing and swivelling on the dance floor. And as the evening wore on, more and more of the swaying crowd were gripped by this and that *lwa*, and had to be carried away by bouncers – like troublemakers in the West when out clubbing.

This was only the effect of the music, rhythms divorced from their physical context – the altar, the sacred site, the imagery. It was tapping into its origin in the soul and heartbeat. If you were part of that African tradition, it seems you didn't need the candles, the waterfall. For the first time I could see Vodou being valuable to the urban young, the future of Haiti. The Azor band gave the rhythms a modern context, made them seem hip. For the first time I could believe Vodou could carry Haiti forward.

The following day, the 16th, was the day the mass was to be celebrated for Our Lady. We chose first to walk up to 'Calvary', a hill with a crucifix at its summit. Along the path up to it were smaller crucifixes marking the stations of the cross. Around each, already blackened with the soot of a thousand prayer candles, was a fresh huddle of pilgrims. They were placing their own candles, chucking on rum, which lit up in a great whoosh. But mainly they were talking, arms out, to the crosses. 'Ezili Dantò, I have a problem at home, my husband never works...' 'Our Lady, my wife never gives birth, and really you must help...' 'Freda, remember my daughter lives in the States? We need that visa badly now...' There was a mishmash of saints from across the world, and spirits from across West Africa and Haiti.

I walked on, thinking of how, back home, I'd thought that Vodou must be an oppressive, inflexible, intolerant religion. The religion of a dark, inward-looking, trapped tribe. In fact it was the opposite. It easily accommodated the Catholic saints and anything the rest of the world insisted on, adopting other faiths' representations wherever needed. There was no written dogma, just these impulses from the heart.

I carried on up to the summit to the main crucifix, this one with Jesus upon it. It was a more formalized place of worship with benches enclosed by a metal railing. Here, rattles were banned, and a preacher directed the crowd, trying to underline the Catholic message. 'Stamp out evil!' he yelled into a microphone, and the crowds vigorously stamped. 'Long live Jesus, down with Satan!' But again the joyous vodou-ists were unperturbed. They didn't have an argument with anyone trying to stamp out the Devil. They didn't want him either. So they repeated the message wholeheartedly, ringing out the words. The Christian slant seemed to wash over them entirely.

You couldn't shake off Vodou – it simply embraced all it came across. It must have been irritating – even embarrassing – for the Church. Gripped by *lwa*, people were flopping to the ground, becoming the overly amorous Freda right at the foot of the cross. Several of these female devotees surrounded me, adoring, flirting with me, nuzzling me. The ladies themselves could not be blamed – it was a Vodou spirit, happy and alive in the middle of a Catholic ceremony.

This religion seemed unstoppable. It was constantly evolving, the spirits changing as people's priorities changed, and other qualities became relevant. Anthropologists had tried to categorize the *lwa*, but it couldn't be done. There was no Bible, no Torah, no Koran, and the people anyway were largely illiterate; Vodou couldn't be captured.

Now for the mass, the time for the statue of Our Lady of Mount Carmel to be processed through the town. Except that, for the last couple of years she hadn't, what with the mud, the crowds. And this year, the lorries and cars were more gridlocked than ever. Filling the remaining gaps were people, and mules brought down the hill with exhausted pilgrims or charcoal sacks from the last bits of forest. Then there were the beggars, hawkers, the possessed pilgrims. Our Lady wasn't going to get through that easily.

We walked to the church, through a thicket of stalls selling icons, medallions, candles. And where there was space were the beggars, sitting and standing as they proffered their bowls. It is always said to be a blessing to give to a beggar, and two rich, flashy young men were occupied tipping bags of rice into the calabashes of the needy. Children flapped their gourds aloft, trying to get them up to the level of the adults. Others were unable to get up – a gasping old mute, and a toddler with no feet. But every one of the thousands who had come to Saut d'Eau had come to ask for something. These beggars were the helpless and needy – the ordinary pilgrims were just the needy.

Adorning the huge but bland white church were pale blue and white rosettes. We entered through a line of riot police, assembled as if a guard of honour at a wedding. Inside, I couldn't help but gasp. Ahead was a heaving, swaying mob, like a rugby crowd of worshippers – humanity spread to the left and to the right, and overhead in the galleries. In fact they were everywhere. The pews were full, so were the aisles. Some people seemed to be camped here. There was one man, his mind totally elsewhere, none too discreetly rattling his *ason*, calling a *lwa* to be with him in church.

There was great applause as the priest up at the altar, a European or American wearing a white mitre, thanked a benefactor for donating the fans that now blew rather fruitlessly at the mass of perspiring devotees. Then the congregation rose, this great multitude rocking as they sung a hymn. It was a passionate outpouring of emotion that drowned whatever instrument was there to guide them. Then, rather before anyone was expecting it, the priest suddenly produced what we'd all been waiting to see. He did it with one quiet movement, as if quickly hanging a picture. It was a small statue – only about baby size – of Our Lady. He waved it a few times, then placed it down and a Haitian altar-boy whisked it away to safety.

Suddenly realizing what they had just seen, the crowd erupted. It had been only a fleeting glimpse indeed, and was only a modest statue, but it seemed enough. The people had been satisfied.

It looked like the Catholics were trying to play down the role of Our Lady in the hope of inspiring something less resonant of Vodou. However, another – permanent – statue of less modest proportions was still bearing down from an alcove above the altar. She had a pale face, brown robe and a child in her arms.

People chattered to her, they beseeched her, they thanked her. But mainly they just begged, as the children outside were begging money from us. They waved photos of loved ones to her,

IDs, passports – that great hope of Haitians, a ticket and green card to the States. Outside, the riot police filed away. There would be no procession, and therefore no security problem.

We drove back through Haiti's variously ruined landscapes – goat hills, a plain of cacti, a roadside town only populated, it seemed, by hawkers and beggars.

For the aficionados, Saut d'Eau had been quite a moment. Not the festival of Our Lady, or even the Other Ladies, Dantò and Freda, but Azor, the band. This had been what Chantal called the 'coming out' of Vodou. Its religious rhythms were being accepted into the public arena; it was going to reach the world stage.

Was this a breakthrough for Haiti as well? If Vodou was acknowledged on the world stage, it might be believed in as a force for positive change, and raise the country up. And I was beginning to think that if Vodou didn't have an answer, there was very little else here that did.

At the same time, there was still that something niggling away at the back of my mind – all those stories of 'black magic' and zombies. As we made our way home in the car, Frisner said he was offered the soul of a zombie once. 'Put it in a bottle, they did, and offered it to me to help my drumming,' he said. 'But I don't need that kinda thing. I'm a good man.'

If the beneficent and protective *lwa* of Ginen are at the core of Vodou, what of the other aspect – the darker aspect – that we all hear about?

CHAPTER EIGHT

'Vodou is like a magnum gun – not for the hands of a child.
It is strong and must be respected. Then it can be a tool
for good.'
Fabrice Charmant, Vodou devotee

In pursuit of this alleged darker side, we sought out a character called Altesse Paul, a man Chantal had known for a while, and who had a formidable, not to say frightening, reputation. At the very least he was a *bòkò*, a priest who 'worked with both hands' – that is, he worked not just with Rada *lwa* but also the 'hotter' Kongo and Petwo nations. This didn't in itself mean that Altesse was bad – it's necessary to call upon the most aggressive of these *lwa*, the Vodou rationale goes, to neutralize any sorcery being used against you. However, a *bòkò* might be more than just an *oungan* who helps you obtain justice. He might, in actual fact, be a *malfetèr*, or malefactor, someone who specializes in utilizing the most negative aspects of the Kongo and Petwo *lwa*. And this description, that of a *malfetèr*, sounded like it would fit Altesse Paul very snugly indeed.

Chantal and I left behind the film crew, to stand more of a chance of getting Altesse Paul's confidence. With our 'minder', Verdieu, in the car with us, we sped off through the countryside. On the way, I thought about the ordinary houses I'd seen so far that had a *baka*, a little glaring daemon figure, which served to protect the home. I already knew that the necklaces I'd seen in Edeline's temple were to protect initiates from evil. I asked Chantal if this was an insecurity born of being poor, a fear that the remaining peasants of Europe still have, or whether this was a character of Vodou specifically. 'And this belief in zombies.

Is it grounded in something real – I mean, *does* anyone manage somehow or other to turn the dead into his slaves?'

Chantal said that she had never known of a real, substantiated, zombie – perhaps the first tales grew out of the practice of slaves temporarily burying each other to avoid head counts. However, more recently, the toxins of the puffer fish have been demonstrated to induce a state of appropriate death-like paralysis in a victim. But whatever is behind the zombie stories, Chantal said, in Haiti some people had a genuine fear of ending up this way – a fear promoted by *malfetèrs* to increase their power over their people. Besides, she added, the *malfetèrs* are paid very well. And people want it done to enemies because it is worse than being killed – having no soul.

She had once managed to get a *malfetèr* to talk about it. 'It is very hard to do,' he had whispered to her, grimly. 'Sixty per cent of attempts fail.' It seemed that the knowledge was handed down – and the biggest problem was getting the body out of the grave quickly enough. 'It really has to be done within twelve hours. We drill holes in the coffin, if possible. And we add a certain substance to the body to make it smell as if it's putrefying. It's amazing how it hurries the burial up.'

'And what does Verdieu think?' I asked. Our 'minder', a large, ferociously loyal one-man security system, had been brought up in the countryside to the southwest. Chantal took him with her everywhere in Haiti.

He broke his usual watchful silence. 'There are zombies, of course,' he said. 'But people are not scared. At home they just cut off the legs and arms of the dead, to stop them coming back. But not always. Sometimes they poison them.'

Generally, though, Verdieu was unimpressed about the stories of zombies – as he was about anything he hadn't seen for himself, and most things he had seen. 'And if the dead do reappear,' he said simply, 'families just take them back because they are not really a son or daughter any more. Their soul has gone, so why be scared?'

I thought to myself that if my soulless child turned up on my doorstep I'd be scared. But now we were taking a left turn off the main road. To our left and right were the *lakou*, or traditional family compounds, chickens and pigs scattering ahead of us. As usual, it could have been Nigeria or any West African country. Chantal directed the driver to the end of the track. We pulled up on the edge of a paddock cropped by mules. By now I was a little apprehensive – after all, in a minute I'd be shaking hands with someone responsible, it was said, for killing. I got out, readying my camera.

It was all surprisingly pleasant – the view marred only by an altar beside a low building which must be a temple. In front of the altar, a huge black cross, emblazoned with a white skeleton. From its head, the empty eye sockets of the painted skull stared out. Behind it, an alcove with candles, incense, ropes, pictures of *lwa*.

We walked up to an old gent leaning back on his chair, under a corrugated iron lean-to. He looked a nice sort of man, about sixty, with a toothbrush moustache and a trilby perched forward on his head. Youths – who I rightly guessed were temple drummers – were playing cards around him. Seeing us, they stood up and were very friendly and welcoming, bringing forward chairs. 'Altesse Paul!' Chantal said to the old man, and, as he rose, gave him a good hug. They nattered in French for a while.

Him? I thought. Altesse Paul was a disappointment. At the very least this sorcerer was also a family man.

We sat down to have a chat to explain why we were here – difficult, because we didn't have a specific need to kill anyone, simply a need to know he could do it. Chantal introduced me, saying I was a foreigner who just wanted to see the way he worked.

Altesse told his son Jackson – quiet, lean, smooth and in jeans and sunglasses – to get some rum, Coke and ice, and we took a seat in the shade. Across the dust of the yard was the low brick building which, Chantal said, contained two separate temples, one each for the Rada and Kongo nations.

Altesse began telling us about himself. 'I was not raised into Vodou, but was born a Protestant,' he said in French, to make it easier for me. He tipped back his trilby, easing his charm and civility over us. 'I would have died if I hadn't responded to the call of the *lwa*.'

Jackson brought the rum, and Altesse opened the bottle and carefully splashed it twice on the ground. 'One drink for my Rada *lwa*, the other for the Kongo,' he explained to me, helpfully.

We talked about this and that – mostly general chat about Vodou – and once I felt that we were getting along fine, I slowly manoeuvred towards more tricky subjects.

'I noticed the cross over there…' I said, nodding in the direction of the skull glaring out at us.

'That is for Paul Kriminèl La Kwa.'

'Criminal?' I thought. This sounded more promising.

'That's a Petwo version of Baron Samedi,' Chantal explained. 'So he's "hotter".'

'He is a guard for my Kongo temple,' said Altesse, adding that only a few months ago he had been doing a big ritual at the shrine. 'I offered the *lwa* a bull, seven goats, two lambs. But, Benedict, these rituals are like contracts. I forgot to include a pig, and it was an omission from my contract. A severe mistake. The *lwa* was angry. And when I poured the rum on the cross for him, the rum exploded into flames. The flames spread, running up my leg. And they ate into my flesh.' Altesse rolled up the leg of his dusty grey suit trousers, revealing a skinny, hairless shin, which was indeed badly scarred.

'But who was angry?' I interjected in my schoolboy French. 'Which *lwa* were you offering these animals to? Paul Kriminèl?'

Altesse, now well into his rum and Coke, sloshed the clinking ice around in the cup, took a swig, and said, 'The Devil himself.'

I hadn't been expecting this unashamed revelation – not so quickly. I nodded, trying not to show surprise. I realized that, wearing his trilby, Altesse himself bore a passing resemblance to Baron Samedi, master of the graveyard. I wondered if this was a conscious attempt to engender a little respect, or even fear, as the dictator Papa Doc had done. Chantal, in the background, was laughing lightly at her old friend. 'Altesse!'

'It had been a deal with the Devil,' he said, speaking directly to me. 'The Djab.' He was staring rather, his eyes small but dark and strong – not unfriendly, though no longer twinkling as they had earlier, when he'd been chatting to Chantal. He would sometimes stop and glare, as if he had now got down to business, and was trying to show me he was a man of formidable power underneath.

'So what did you do?' I said, trying not to be put off.

'What did I do? With my leg still in pain, and at three-thirty in the morning, I went out and killed a pig for that Devil. What else was there to do? But, over the next few weeks the burn didn't get any better. So I said to the Devil, "Look, if you don't help me I'll convert back to Protestantism! I'll burn down the temple!" And that did the trick, I can tell you. The burn soon began to heal!'

Though Altesse hadn't told this as a joke, Chantal laughed again and he smiled at her, and then let himself break into laughter as well.

We went for a little walk around the two temples. The Rada temple was a simple room for worship, much as Edeline's. It might have been an empty outhouse used by teenage children for partying – the dirt floor, the murals, the *poto-mitan*. The other – Kongo – temple was rather different. A small tree, home of a spirit, no doubt, was enclosed by the four walls, and beside this was an inner room, its door firmly closed to us. On the wall were two less familiar murals: on the right side of the door was St Michael. On the left of the door was an immediately recognizable personality: he had pinched, fierce eyes, and the goat face of Satan.

'Captain Misery,' Altesse said, briskly. 'My master.' He gestured for us to follow him back out into the sun. We gathered that the tour was already over.

I lingered, trying to take in the picture of the Lucifer-like character. Was I actually looking at the Christian Devil, or was this just a Vodou *lwa* who wasn't so bad? Perhaps 'Captain Misery' wasn't so much evil as dangerous in his unhappiness.

'What's the inner room for?' I asked Altesse.

His answer offered ample clarification. 'For killing people,' he said.

Our time was up, and we left not much the wiser about Altesse Paul. He'd given us a little glimpse of something, but only that glimpse. We knew we had to go back, and so did he. 'Bring a bottle of Johnny Walker,' he called as our car moved off, 'it's my favourite.'

Whenever he returned to Haiti, Frisner was always sure not just to bring presents to all his living relatives, but also to perform a *liberà*, a salute to the all-important dead ones. It's the ancestral spirits who protect and guide us, and directly through them that the *lwa* grant favours. Furthermore, his aunt had recently died, and he must make his peace with her.

We went to where Frisner was staying – his family were all set to head off to the graveyard for the *liberà*, though all were a little quiet. The previous night there had been a wake for the aunt, and rum had taken its toll. Together, we processed casually to the cemetery. Once past the river – now laden with plastic junk but once, in Frisner's childhood, where his family used to wash their clothes – we made our way through the street children who hung around outside the cemetery, where they scratched a living from graverobbing and prostitution. Each had their plastic containers for glue-sniffing and, according to a recent survey by foreign doctors, each had their HIV. We walked through the main archway and within moments were in their homeland, a maze of graves.

They were head-high, sarcophagi of cement blocks, housing members of each family on top of each other. 'These are like houses for the livin',' Frisner said. 'Those who can't afford to pay for their space, rent it, see.' If the relatives didn't pay up, the corpses were yanked out and the graves made ready for some- one who could.

We trooped on by the unlucky dead whose loved ones hadn't paid up. The tombs were broken open, revealing their mortal remains – or those parts not stolen; there were lacy veils, femurs, ribs, all lying in dust and rubble. The skulls, prized by *bòkò* and other priests who 'dealt with two hands', had long since been stolen. Coffin handles had also been re-sold – unless they turned out to be plastic, in which case they were tossed aside or smashed.

We stopped at the family block into which Frisner's aunt had recently been slipped. Her space had been sealed with cement, her name scratched across it. Hers should be a safe haven – Frisner could pay from America. Others, less fortunate, were hostages of the living.

The cemetery's official priest, a tired, short man with an ID in plastic pinned to his breast, was running briskly through Vodou prayers; a hearty lady leaning on the sarcophagus had the job of chanting sadly in the background, and responding loudly on behalf of the bereaved. With the shoeless graverobbers loitering about us, sharp eyes on the film crew's shiny equipment, each relative said a silent or loud prayer, splashed coffee at the foot of the grave three times, then sprinkled some bread. Frisner took his turn, saying hello to his dead Haitian relatives, as he had already greeted the living on arrival in Haiti, and then I did the same. All this was beginning to seem normal to me – after all, in Haiti people were even married to spirits.

Finally, we zigzagged through the graves to the cross of Baron Samedi, chief *lwa* of the dead. Frisner slapped the chunky, candle-blackened cross, saying his prayer. Then the beggars and graverobbers began getting restless, expectant of their alms. Coffee, bread, money and more besides was given to placate the mixed rabble.

Meanwhile, a funeral cortège came by – the silent mourners all in white and black, and all spotlessly clean, the young girls like bridesmaids in their frilly dresses. And this was only a small part of the proceedings. Already a ritual would have been performed to carefully separate the deceased from any *lwa* he might have married, and from the loved ones he was leaving behind. The body is washed, dressed, and all the dead's possessions removed so that he is free to leave for the journey into the sea, where the spirits of those who have yet to live, and those who have lived, reside. With time, they might end up successfully journeying through the waters to Ginen, the spiritual homeland and Vodou paradise.

'Some families spend two thousand, three thousand dollars,' Frisner said, joining me to watch. 'How?' was all I could say. This was meant to be a destitute country, so where was the money?

The answer was, of course, there wasn't any. So relatives often sold their land, the most devoted ruining themselves if necessary to satisfy the dead. It was worth it because, if not separated off properly, the dead would drag away their surviving relatives; if not fully honoured at a funeral even your dear mother might torment you for not ensuring she would successfully manage the journey to Ginen. Nourishing her with offerings, on the other hand, could confer benefits on you, the dead having a close relationship with the *lwa*.

We watched the mourners squeeze between the crammed graves, the coffin all topsy-turvy, everyone clambering over the family blocks, and the coffin bearers adding to the confusion by pretending to lose their way, a tradition – one also practised in Siberut, I noted – to foil the dead by preventing them finding a way back. After a moment, many mourners were squeezing their way out again, lugging along a woman who had collapsed. Perhaps she had been gripped – as happens on these occasions – by the spirit of the deceased as it came away from the body.

The mourner left, screaming and writhing. Other family members followed, still shedding tears in their distress, but also so that the dead would also know he or she was honoured, and need not haunt them.

Later, I walked a little while through the streets of Port-au-Prince. After witnessing the funeral, the city seemed to me worse than ever – the poverty reached out from the ditches. Away from the city centre itself, there were still stallholders and shops but more at home seemed to be the rubble, discarded sandals, dust. And it wasn't just the capital. In country towns, there'd been children lugging other children down broken streets that were bordered by patched-together corrugated iron and sticks. From behind these stared yet more children dumbly chewing maize, and the only people who didn't seem the least downtrodden were members of a football team which came padding through. Their red shirts were clean even after their game; and on the back was a line of New Testament scripture.

Protestants such as these, triumphant in their health, discipline and vision of the future, proclaimed that Vodou was evil.

However, Vodou isn't just a religion, it's a way of ordering society. In the absence of law and order, calling on these spirits is a recourse to justice; it is a way of governing the shanty towns, the community. If someone steals a sack of charcoal, the spirits of Petwo can exact the punishment. Besides, no *lwa* can be classed as 'evil' or 'good' in the Christian manner. The *lwa* might persecute those who neglect them, but even the most dangerous can also help you. This was why it was so difficult to assess the doings of Altesse Paul. As I'd said to myself before, even an entity he called Djab, the Devil, might not be the evil figure that Christian usage of the word implies.

Besides, as I had seen at Saut d'Eau, you couldn't get rid of Vodou by getting its followers into church. Vodou already provided everything everyone needed – a complete system of understanding and dealing with the unknown in the world. Everything was explainable – life and death, good and bad fortune – through the activities of the *lwa*. So if there was a problem with your combustion engine, you turned to the *lwa* of fire, Ogou. If there was a death, you looked to the Gede family. You couldn't erase Vodou that easily.

However, there was no denying that the groomed evangelical football team was impressive. I couldn't help but think that, while Vodou is a great source of comfort to the Haitians, it might not have the same potential as Christianity as a vehicle for moving the country forward. Not that I'd go as far as the Protestant missionaries, who are fond of preaching that when the slaves gathered 200 years ago and prayed to their gods for freedom, they made a pact with the Devil. They'd get their freedom, but the Devil's price was Haiti being condemned to never-ending poverty, which is exactly what they got.

To hear the positive case for Vodou, I went to see one of its vocal advocates, Edele Joseph. An initiate of Kongo, she lived in

Port-au-Prince with her partner, Fabrice Charmant, occupying a one-room house with their little son, Sasha. Soon we were sitting in their yard and they were telling me exactly what the evangelicals wouldn't hear – that Vodou was the power that would unite and strengthen the Haitians, just as it had once before, when they rose up for their freedom.

Fabrice as a young man had known nothing of Vodou, except a distorted image provided by the Catholics. 'Everything they told me was about eating people – things like that.' Then a friend took him to a Vodou ritual. 'I felt like I was at home,' he said. Though both Edele and Fabrice wore their hair long, and seemed like perfectly matched, off-beat artists, Fabrice had come from a more wealthy background – what you might call a 'better' family. He was gentle, articulate and intelligent – and, I thought, perhaps looking for his roots through her. She was sprightly, charismatic and the servant of Ezili Freda, the Rada *lwa* who was lazy, coveted luxury and was having an affair with Ogou. Edele also served Dantò, Freda's sister, the Petwo *lwa* of fertility and motherhood.

'I am in the good side of Vodou,' Edele explained, dropping her French for a while, to hammer the point home in my own language. 'For 200 years the bad side has been strong. Now is the time for change. We have everything we need, everything, but we waste it. We don't need the West.'

'And all the foreign aid?'

She swapped back to French, to keep control of the conversation. 'This helps. But in the end, only Vodou can save Haiti. It's because the spirits haven't been respected that Haiti is undergoing hardship.'

'There is no future without Vodou,' Fabrice said softly in English. 'The cement of Haiti is made from the spirits.'

I wasn't convinced, as yet; but one thing Edele could help me understand was how vodou-ists could have such a close relationship with spirits that devotees even married them. She explained that she used to go as a pilgrim to the festivals of Souvanans and Soukri, and kept getting a condition called *sep*. She would be utterly immobilized for hours, her body gripped by a *lwa* – it was a sign. And she decided she was being told to be initiated – it is just like being baptized, she said, a further stage of commitment open to everyone. 'From then, I have never had *sep*. And I got pregnant, after twelve years.' She smiled at the happy outcome, Sasha.

Edele plucked off one of her rings. 'But you can't be married to a *lwa* without a dream,' she said. 'You are sleeping, and maybe you dream of a ring like this. And then you go to an *oungan* to find out what the dream means, and learn that you should be initiated.' This meant being secluded in a *djevo*, a temple antechamber, where you were taught the character of the *lwa* you are going to marry, and the properties of different herbs. You wore white clothes, representing death, because completing the initiation was like a rebirth.

It was much as I had heard elsewhere – in Siberut the *kereis* secluded their initiates to assist their passage into a new life, and in northern Siberia the apprentice similarly had to 'die' – be born again as a shaman with new eyes, said to be made from crystals. He often wore skeleton stripes embroidered across his costume. The difference was that here you were afterwards married to a spirit. 'You must wear a ring to show your faithfulness,' Edele said, flourishing the ruby-coloured ring she wore for her husband Ogou.

To help us understand more, Edele promised to prepare us for the next Vodou pilgrimage to Plaine-du-Nord, in a week or so. A festival honouring Ogou, it sounded most promising. It reached a climax around holy basins of mud, in which the most repentant or devoted pilgrims immersed themselves.

In the afternoon the crew and I went to a countryside school that was celebrating the completion of repairs undertaken by the US Support Group. Present in Haiti to discourage a *coup* – at least one of the wrong sort – the US army normally kept a low profile, just venturing from their barracks to undertake useful humanitarian projects such as these. The school repair was a chance to see how the Americans operated – if not within Vodou culture, then around it.

We turned up at the Ecole Nationale de Descloches, finding parking space beside an armoured personnel carrier. Marines were hanging around in their kit in the shade, guns slung from their shoulders. We were just in time for the welcoming speeches, and were ushered into a classroom where a Haitian official and some senior American officers took it in turn to address the small gathering about children being our future. Beside them stood a little squad of Haitian pupils with miniature Haitian and US flags in their hands. They smiled engagingly, and the young and over-excited Haitian press corps – heavily armed with dictaphones – captured the national anthems. Everything was going according to the schedule outlined in the press briefing notes we'd been handed. Then the commander of the US Support Group, Colonel Walton H. Walker II, made his contribution, and, in what was evidently a departure from his prepared speech, declared 'it would be amiss of me at this point not to thank our Lord, Jesus Christ...'

'A-MEN!' shouted a couple of marines, slightly startling the audience.

Outside, everyone filtering into the sunshine, I thought it would be interesting to let the good colonel expand on his religious views. They were not those of Vodou, and he was clearly having difficulty containing them.

The Embassy press attaché closed in on us, explaining how the normal procedure was to submit questions in advance to him. But next thing, he found himself engulfed by the Haitian press pack, fifteen dictaphones waving in his face, ready for a quote.

While we were standing wondering what to do now, the colonel himself came marching up to us with his own press officer. He volunteered to say a few words.

The camera started rolling and I listened, and the army press officer listened, as the head of the American armed forces told me exactly what he had to say about Vodou – the religion that had earned the Haitians freedom from slavery, had been endorsed by Aristide, the people's leader, and now cemented this fragile society together. For decades, in the absence of other means of justice for the people, it had prevented anarchy.

'I believe in a Christian course,' the colonel began. 'I think it's the light and the dark basically.'

'The dark,' I thought. 'He's calling one of the key faiths of Haiti backward – or worse.' I noticed the colour slowly but surely draining from the cheeks of the army press officer. He was standing stock still beside his senior commander – this man in charge of one of the biggest armed forces in the Caribbean, and stationed beside Cuba, in the Caribbean's most sensitive and unstable region.

I pointed out to the American commander that many Catholic priests had found a way of accommodating Vodou. 'You don't hold with that?'

'The Holy Spirit cannot compromise with Satan,' he said, swiftly.

The press officer was starting to fidget. He raised a finger to stop the colonel. But the colonel wouldn't be stopped. 'And that is essentially what you do,' the colonel went on, 'when you compromise with Vodou.'

Maybe I asked another question after this – I wasn't sure. All I could hear now were the ringing sounds of Colonel Walker, launching what in some ways was an offensive on Haiti itself.

'The people need to get past that,' he continued, 'and I think many of their leaders would agree. I believe you need a Christian consensus in the nation before you can have a democracy. Education waters that fertile ground and the seeds will grow...' ended the colonel, allowing himself a little biblical reference.

There was little more to say but thank the colonel very much for his kind contribution. We drove home debating whether or not to broadcast what the US army chief was proclaiming about the ostensibly sovereign country; the press officer must anyway have direct responsibility to the Pentagon and already be alerting them to a possible source of trouble. Whether wanting to or not, the Pentagon would surely act in some way: we had just played our part in the turbulent history of the unhappy nation of Haiti.

Some days later, with news spreading over the nation that the head of the American forces had suddenly had to leave, we geared ourselves for the festival of Plaine-du-Nord. Here, another Catholic saint was happily celebrated by the Vodou throng as someone else, an African deity.

Edele, though in the sixth month of pregnancy, was energetically buying candles, rum and perfumes in preparation, and insisted on blessing the film crew. After pouring rum three times in the driveway for Legba, master of the crossroads, guardian of the temple entrance and intermediary between people and their *lwa*, she sat on a chair and yanked me down to sit with her as the night fell. Swigging rum, she slowly became even more flamboyant and jocular than usual, while Fabrice lit candles around us. I saw that she was becoming Baron Samedi, or at least one of the spirits termed Gede, and was a bawdy man and trickster. She rocked in her chair, grabbing me boisterously, hugging me tight, and then offering advice, counsel and instructions to us in turn. There was little we could do to argue – she was Gede, not Edele. As well as a therapy service, I could see how effective Vodou was as a social mechanism to allow issues to be breathed within society.

However, we were soon interrupted by Sasha, who was turning out to be demanding even for a two-year-old. Inside the house he woke and began calling to his mother. 'Edele!' But Edele was no longer here. Gede had taken her place. '*Garçon*, Fabrice,' she muttered. 'Tell the boy to be quiet.'

Sasha came out of doors screaming for her. Gede snatched him up, and whirled him around. The Gede-possessed Edele was flinging this boy around just above the hard gravel, she had consumed a lot of rum and should be partly drunk. It was shocking, seeing what looked like a mother carelessly chuck around her child. 'Edele!' Sasha called, distressed.

After a while Gede collapsed and stumbled indoors. As we were about to leave, Edele reappeared, 'You guys! What happened?' The playful Edele was back again, and we told her about how Baron Samedi had flung Sasha around.

'Gede is an idiot,' Edele said, fondly.

I was beginning to think that to live with Edele would be difficult; to be married to her – and share her with unseen spirits – a nightmare. I asked her, as I'd asked Edeline in Brooklyn, if she remembered anything when possessed.

'No,' she said, running her hand over Sasha's head to soothe him, 'because I'm not Edele. I am Gede or Ogou or someone.'

'So where are you – where is Edele – when Gede is possessing you?'

'I am in Ginen somewhere…'

'Fabrice,' I said, as we got into the car to leave, 'don't you worry about Edele? That she'll hurt herself or Sasha while her body is possessed?'

'I have never known this to happen,' he said. 'No one is ever hurt.'

'Does Gede make mistakes? He drinks…'

'I've never known him to make a mistake.'

So, a ringing endorsement for Vodou from Fabrice. However, before we departed for Plaine-du-Nord there was time to go back to Altesse, to see what harm he could come up with. This time I would be less restrained in my questioning. I felt easy about seeing him now. He seemed just like an ordinary – well, fairly ordinary – bloke.

As we got out of the car, brandishing the Johnny Walker he'd asked for, he was sitting outside the Rada temple, soaking up the early sunshine. He smiled on seeing the whisky – two bottles – and we moved to the shade to have a glass or two.

Three-quarters of a bottle later, he was more than happy to take me on a more extensive tour of his *lakou* – the courtyard that was for his family and immediate ancestors. And at last, still clutching the now-empty bottle, he took Chantal and me into the side room of the Kongo temple, the one with the picture of the Devil on.

First he knocked on the door three times. Then he opened the door, and entered backwards. I wasn't scared to follow a man of such notoriety into his den – I was following a drunk. But I was immensely intrigued.

I followed in backwards, and turned to see a damp, cave-like place. I could see that Altesse wasn't keen for us to linger here, but in the end he had to stumble over to open the shutters to let us see anything at all. My first glimpse was of rum bottles, which stood empty but with their stoppers in, and together surrounded a crucifix taking centre-stage in the room. It had three human skulls sitting at its base, a sword, rope, whip, silk sashes and many unlit candles. Further into the gloom I could make out two long boxes, which I realized were coffins, one full size, another for a child. There was a trap door, covered in glass – and I already knew we weren't going to be allowed there. Medicine men always preserve their mystery – it is theatre and in this lies their ability to convince their patient, and therefore their power to effect genuine change in him or her. If they open a box for you, you can be sure another box lies within.

Already, even after a few seconds, Altesse was trying to close the shutters to leave. However, my eyes were adjusting to the light, and I now saw two more coffins, these as small as shoe boxes and with leg and arm bones in a little heap on them. There were charms hanging from the cross – bead necklaces, a tress of blond human hair. And now I saw another coffin, and lying in this a model of Christ, nail holes in his hands and feet. I'd never seen a portrayal of Jesus after the crucifixion like this, even by the least reverent of modern artists: Jesus was meant to be rising from the dead and in this depiction he hadn't quite managed to pull it off.

'What are the bottles?' I asked, playing for time as Altesse stood holding the door open for my exit.

'They are the bottles drunk by the Devil,' Altesse said, getting cross with my dilly-dallying.

'And tell me again what you do here?'

'This is where I pray for people to die,' he said – and would not add a word more.

This inevitably left me feeling very frustrated. There were the bones to ask about, charms, the shoe-box coffins. And what – or who – was sacrificed here?

Previous page above: Near Gonaïves, an unusually fertile Haitian plain.

Previous page below: In Haiti, poverty is never far away. Opposite the main hospital in Port-au-Prince are shops selling the bandages and medicines you'll need before receiving treatment.

Right: A female pilgrim in denim and straw hat, dress of the agriculture spirit, Azaka, whom she serves.

Below: Aboudja, Emperor of the Kongo festival of Soukrie, contemplating near the temple altar.

Opposite above: Soon after, Aboudja astride the sacrificial bull while 'possessed' by the spirit Ganga.

Opposite below: Aboudja and a devotee, after the bull was sacrificed to feed Ganga.

Above: Altesse Paul, a sorcerer or *bòkò*, someone 'who deals with both hands', sitting with me in his inner temple chamber.

Right: Describing what it's like to be 'possessed', Vodou devotees talk of being 'ridden' by the spirit.

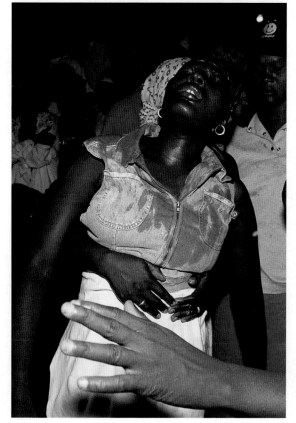

Opposite: Altesse Paul claimed to be able to create zombies, the 'living dead' so beloved of Hollywood movies.

Opposite: The festival at Saut d'Eau, where devotees immerse themselves in water to gain the blessing of spirits residing there such as Ezili Dantò, deity of love and procreation.

Left: Soukrie, where the Kongo spirit Mambo Inan manifests herself in the river.

Below: Taking part in rituals (such as this, at Soukrie) has always helped me empathize with customs that might other-wise seem impossibly alien.

Overleaf: Vodou initiate Edele in front of her altar, which is stacked with food, perfumes and other objects favoured by the spirits she serves. One of them, Ezili Dantò, is represented by the poster of a modern 'goddess'.

Coming out, I thought, I've scratched the surface. I want to scratch further.

I plied him with more of his favourite tipple – and more. But it did no good.

He couldn't have been at his sorcerous best that afternoon when a client turned up. It was an Italian woman in her late thirties, with purple hair and an amused air – a vacant, lost, whimsical face. A junkie, I thought. Got Aids sharing needles, and has come here for a miracle cure.

Altesse Paul had a constant stream of such foreigners, whom he evidently impressed because they kept coming back – or perhaps, like us, they left always feeling there was more. Sobered perhaps by the welcome thought of more incoming hard currency, Altesse moved into his role, conducting the Italian away for a consultation. He told his son Jackson to assemble his three drummers, and prepare the inner sanctum of the Kongo temple.

Altesse led his client off into the room, and soon a furious drumming could be heard from within. We stood outside, wondering what was going on. I could smell burning candlewax and a strange sweetness like incense. The door opened only once – to allow a reluctant sheep into the room. It was, at a guess, doomed.

We could learn little more, and decided to leave the Italian and the sheep to their fate. But as we were going, Altesse himself emerged. He looked dazed, and clutched the doorframe.

Drunk, I thought. But he wasn't. He was possessed. He staggered about outside the room, issuing a stuttering speech. 'Very characteristic of the Devil,' said Chantal, who knew about these things. Now he dropped to the floor, and was dragging himself backwards, ramming himself against the door as if wanting to take refuge in the place from where he had come. Jackson bent over him, trying to interpret his needs. Eventually water was splashed over his face, and he was just about Altesse again.

'I think we are going to need yet another visit,' I said, as he sat there, still confused. There was clearly more to Altesse Paul than we had seen, but how much more?

On 24 July, we arrived at Plaine-du-Nord. Many sights and sounds of the festival were already familiar to us from Saut d'Eau: the hawkers' stalls, the smells of their stews of crab and spinach. Pilgrims walked by with a score of hats on their heads, hoping for a few sales to pay for their pilgrimage. Others bristled with sunglasses, or with objects associated with Ogou himself: swords, red scarves, every trapping apart from his white horse. Here you could buy whatever you felt was appropriate to serve the great warrior spirit – indeed, given the money, you could buy what you needed to serve almost anything.

These people were not devotees, they were businessmen and that was fair enough. But what of the roadside priests who were also obstructing the way? Among the thousands of hawkers were hundreds of these *oungan* who had set up their seats and were giving blessings and prayers and counselling.

'How many are fakes?' I asked Chantal, shouting above the human traffic noise.

'Eighty per cent, maybe?'

This was shockingly high, but when we asked Verdieu, our minder, he put it at ninety. 'All this is rubbish,' he said, sweeping his great hands over the heated masses. 'All this selling, buying. This is all fake.'

Edele, determined to make a pilgrim of me, looked daggers at Verdieu, and adjusted the red scarf she'd already adorned me with. 'You are Ogou, don't forget,' she said. 'Coming here, you *become* him.'

She sploshed me copiously with Homme, a man's perfume, making my eyes sting. 'Ogou likes you to smell good. That pleases him.' It was my protection, she said, and she climbed on to a mule. Blessing passing pilgrims with Homme all the way, we began the hike up to the stone cliff called Porte-Saint-Jacques, where Ogou was more than once said to have manifested himself. Then we came back down to the church, where artificial red flowers framed the altar, and the back pews were being used as sleeping quarters. Finally, we headed through the crowds to what was a more frequented holy site than the church: the mud bath.

Springs and rivers were the home of *lwa*, and a bathe in these 'luck baths' enabled devotees to gain protection from them. Small luck baths were commonly found in the *djevo* temple chambers, and natural ones, such as at Saut d'Eau, were the subject of pilgrimages. Out here at Plaine-du-Nord, though, Ogou resided in a mud pool, Bassin-Saint-Jacques.

We squeezed through the bands of pilgrims, most sporting the silken scarlet sashes of Ogou, and caught glimpses of people emptying bottles of perfume over themselves on the edge of a huge grey sump. Edging forward to the front – and perilously close to the slippery edge – I saw before me a basin the size of a decent family swimming pool, but containing a metre's depth of ooze, and smelling like a fetid ditch.

Unlike me, the pilgrims standing on the edge were oblivious to the shoving crowd behind us, and were saluting Ogou, holding their candles aloft to him above the mud, not noticing even the hot wax as it dripped down, hardening on their hands. Others were rubbing herbs over themselves, others splashing rum about, others waved the heads of chickens or bulls, sacrificed to him nearby, others chucked whole chickens alive into the basin and some – though not many – launched themselves gloriously into the mud, rolling in it like seals. They wallowed, sinking themselves in Ogou, and though they went under, mesmerized, no one seemed to be drowning. With them out there, waist deep in the mud, were the only people here whose minds were alert to their surroundings. These were like the mudlarks, the children who used to patrol the Thames at low tide, scrounging what they could, but here in Haiti still in action, fishing for prayer candles, rum bottles and other offerings thrown in their direction.

Fabrice came up beside me. 'This is a place of judgement,' he said. 'A tribunal where you can ask for things, and your case will be assessed by Ogou.' Nearby, a worshipper was shouting at a mudlark for snatching his rum bottle before he had even done his prayer. Fabrice continued, 'You come with a bottle of rum, a candle. It is like you are paying.'

'What sort of things do people come for?' I asked.

'A house, a car. Or if he wants to kill someone.'

Odd, I thought, to hear such an advocate of Vodou as a modern religion talk easily about Vodou as an agent of death. Could I imagine a single parish priest in Christendom praying for someone to die? Or a single Christian pilgrim? Yet Fabrice had recently told me how misjudged Vodou was. 'I feel my place is to push, show what Vodou really is,' he'd said.

Standing with me now at Ogou's seat of judgement, Fabrice went on, 'But one thing: you must have a reason to ask for things. The first time I came here I find five people dead on the street. They didn't have a right to ask.'

Now there was a disturbance in the crowd as a bull appeared, around its neck a flag of red and blue. It had evidently smelt the water and come along for a drink, dragging its master with it. It looked around at the fleeing crowd, and yanked on its rope for more room till its owner had to let go. Freed, the bull walked happily along the edge of the mud bath, sweeping the crowd ahead of it. Following far behind was a temple group which was meant to be sacrificing it in some other place. They were now excited: the bull had come along of its own accord to present itself to Ogou. It finally moved down to the mud edge and drank from the ooze, before turning round – disappointed no doubt – and coming back.

Soon after, another bull's head thrust through the worshippers. However, this time it was only a head. It was tossed into the mud, for Ogou. Blood mixed with the grey slush, before the first mudlark got a hand to it and it was hoiked into the air. A brief fight sorted out who got the prize, big enough to feed a family.

We stood there for a while, and I couldn't help wondering what it was really like to be in that mud. Those few pilgrims who had taken the plunge were rarely fully aware of their actions. Most rolled off the bank, already possessed. Emerging from their union with Ogou in the mud, only their eyes not coated, they looked like Hollywood zombies – exactly the sort of image of the Living Dead that intellectual Haitians were berating the world for depicting.

So what was the sacred bath like? I was getting tired of myself judging Vodou on the sidelines, assessing this religion without feeling it. If my body couldn't be possessed by Ogou or the other spirits, then I might at least feel what it was like to be in a sacred bath, albeit one of mud and blood.

So I asked Fabrice what everyone would think if I went in. He laughed – amazed but pleased. 'They will think it is Ogou in that mud,' he said, yanking at my red scarf. 'They will be very happy.'

I edged around to the far side of the pool, and stepped in. The bath – or the mud at least – was exactly as one might expect it to feel like. Soft and embracing, the ooze pressed in on my skin, enveloping me and soothing me. The mudlarks flooded towards me, surprised to see a westerner for once down here among them. There was a band playing somewhere nearby, and we danced a little, gyrating in the mud. I passed through slowly, making my way towards the other side. More than anything I didn't want to slip and end up drinking this bacterial soup. Then I stopped. The toes of my right foot were being clung to by soft dead flesh. I pictured it down there like a jellyfish, engulfing my foot. A goat's intestines? A cow's stomach? I kept going. And a little further, borne along by the hot beat of a Kongo rhythm, I forgot about the slimy things lurking in the depths, and forgot myself. I found myself taking a possessed woman by the hand. Hitherto spinning in slow circles to her own trance, she now danced with me. It seemed the right thing for me to do; and only as I neared the other end of the basin, leading her out, did I realize what I had done. Meanwhile, all around me, up around the pool edge, were pilgrims gazing past their burning candles, down to the mud in which I'd made my lone trek through the heart of Ogou.

Finally, the mud was shallower, and I was out, the pilgrims backing away so as not to get smeared by my mud. I'd not been possessed by Ogou, but I had felt rather separated from every-one I had come here with – Chantal, the crew, everyone except Edele and Fabrice. The experience had felt like it didn't belong in my own time and place. It felt more than the sum of its parts – the parts being mud, blood and theatre. Standing on the lip of the bath, grey mud sliding off me, I wondered if I had perhaps gone closer to Ogou than I cared to admit to myself.

Edele took me quietly away and washed me in someone's yard, splashing water over me with a calabash. She treated me gently and lovingly, as if I was now made something slightly holy. 'Ogou has blessed you,' she said, as I unpeeled my shirt and shorts. She insisted I threw them away. 'You are renewed,' she said.

We retired to the hotel for the evening, and Edele confided her thoughts about Altesse, who was also at the festival and staying at our hotel. So far, she and Altesse didn't seem to be getting along very well.

'He is a *malfetèr*!' Edele hissed. 'A *malfetèr*!'

'You are afraid of him?' I asked.

'No, because I dress up so much, and spray myself with perfume – for Ogou, so he protects me.' She turned urgently to Chantal. 'Altesse deals with *magi*,' she said, using a word taken to mean something akin to black magic. 'He can change people into cats.'

'You know for sure what he does?'

'Altesse is not ashamed – I met him having rum on the veranda. He came straight out with it.'

She said it was very typical that Altesse was so open. 'These people speak because they know they are going to die. To be able to kill someone, you yourself have to be killed. He has sold his soul to the Devil, and when he is dead, he won't go to Ginen.'

Later, I found Edele on the veranda sitting with Altesse, who was still working through his bottle of rum. They sat there in the dusk light, relaxed in their cane chairs – or at least Altesse was. Edele was pouting like an adolescent, scorning and berating him. He was calmly deflating her, smiling goodnaturedly at her jibes. '*Vous êtes mort*,' she said in his face. 'You are dead.'

I sat writing my diary and occasionally looked up to watch Edele glare at Altesse, blocking him into the chair like a territorial animal. Seeing this go on, I wondered if Haiti would ever get off the ground. 'In this country,' I wrote, 'spiritual matters seem outside your direct control – there is always someone out there affecting you. When things go wrong, people don't look to themselves to see what they've done – whether they've sinned for example. They blame the world around them. And they don't say "why?" they say "who?" Whatever happens to you in your daily life, it's the action of a *lwa*, a sorcerer's action. It means there's no natural death – therefore it's almost impossible to defeat Aids – and it breeds suspicion. People around you may be dangerous, especially when you become rich, and your neighbours jealous. No, as I see it, far from unifying the country as Fabrice hopes, Vodou is actively involved in preventing it. It isn't a question of it being necessary for the "good side" now to take over, it is a problem with the whole thing – the way Vodou shifts responsibility away from yourself.'

However, these were only musings. We'd see.

CHAPTER NINE

'You are wrong to think I am bad. The powers I use come not from
me but the spirits. If someone asks my help, even to kill, I give it.
The spirits will decide if he is wrong to ask.'
Altesse Paul, bòkò *or sorcerer*

On 10 August I made my final trip to Altesse. This time I'll
get behind his mask, I thought, and I even went along to
the market and bought a black sacrificial goat that he'd
requested. He'd agreed to a ritual to demonstrate his power.
'I will scare Benedict shitless!' he had promised Chantal.

The market was situated uncomfortably close to Cité Soleil,
beside the sellers of charcoal and American second-hand clothes,
and beside a ditch filled with plastic bottles and sugar cane
junk; a pig was in difficulty trying to swim it. In Port-au-Prince
the rumour was that the hot Petwo *lwa* were gradually becoming
more popular than the earlier Rada ones, from Africa. That is,
Vodou practice was getting hotter, and potentially more aggressive. Looking around, I could understand why.

On the way to Altesse, we stopped at Edele's house – she'd
insisted on giving me 'protection' and perfumed me heavily. I was
instructed to wear my red Ogou scarf hidden in my back pocket.

We found Altesse sitting under the lean-to with Jackson,
and soon had opened up the Johnny Walker. The form of the
ritual was going to be up to Altesse – none of us had any idea
what was going to happen – and soon it became obvious that it
was time to talk about money. 'The spirits do not do things for
pleasure,' Altesse said with an apologetic smile.

Before long, the goat and I were more or less ready to get
under way – though both of us were now in an agitated state. I

suddenly realized, as Altesse led me to the inner sanctum which he used 'for killing people', that if he had asked me to write down the name of someone I wanted killed, I couldn't have done it.

The door to the inner sanctum was opened and we duly turned around and entered backwards. Candles had been lit all around, and though they illuminated coffins, skulls and crosses, actually the effect was to make the temple somewhat cosier than before. Perhaps I could now see too much. There was no place for my fears to hide.

A little white coffin had been placed in front of the cross, a human skull on it, and Altesse told me to draw up a seat, to face him in his chair the other side. Three drummers trooped in, and while they were tuning their skins I looked at the skull. It was meant to induce fear, or a certain trepidation, creating associations with the dead, the Other World. But it was a mere curiosity to me, not because I was particularly world-weary, but because all of us westerners are. Nowadays, there is little that alarms us spiritually; even regular churchgoers tend to dwell little on the possible horrors awaiting us on Judgement Day.

A large black-handled knife was also laid there beside a bowl. 'That's for the black goat's blood,' I thought to myself. 'Poor thing.' I sat in the chair – a little too comfortable, I felt – in front of the coffin opposite Altesse. The drummers began, behind me, the brisk, energetic beat of Kongo. Sometimes Altesse joined in, using his *ason* rattle. The drummers sang, their voices shaken by the pounding drum skins. Altesse orchestrated with his *ason*: 'Bon! Bon!' This was a classic witchdoctor scene of folklore – everything except the bone through the nose. And yet it could never be dismissed as mumbo-jumbo: you only had to remember how Vodou gave Haitians independence. You only had to remember that no religion is rational, that eating the body of Christ at Holy Communion is ritual cannibalism.

There was a lull and, as we sat, I asked a few questions. 'This skull, do you know the owner?'

'A friend, a good friend,' Altesse said, mopping his brow with his shirt sleeve.

I put it to him straight: 'If someone asks you to do something bad – you'll do it? If someone wants you to make a zombie, for example?'

'I have made two, but I can't do it at the moment, not for you now.' Because I hadn't paid enough, he meant. And I hadn't minded paying whatever we had paid. Vodou had been the power which saved the Haitians from the whites. Why should Haitians not expect a heavy price from them to have their power revealed?

Then a pause. We sat there. Was that it, the end of the session?

'D'accord?' he asked me. All right? 'D'accord,' I said, and thought to myself, 'so far as it goes…' Now Altesse said he'd show me something; he would now take blood from the goat. And he would do it *without even killing it*. The suggestion was that it would be an act to demonstrate his spiritual power. Let's hope this is more impressive than it sounds, I thought. The black goat, hitherto standing patiently in the shadows, was bundled forward.

There was more drumming, a really excited pounding. 'Bon! Bon!' called Altesse, stirring the drummers some more. They called in chorus, answering as Altesse sang out to them. A white sheet was spread over the coffin and, with Jackson's help, the goat was manoeuvred under it. Altesse disappeared under the sheet, with the knife and a bowl, and for a while there was an unruly struggle, first Jackson's head popping out, then the goat's. When the goat reappeared – looking in better shape than either Jackson or Altesse – some blood at least had been successfully extracted, a sprinkling of it lining the bowl. It wasn't exactly an impressive display of spiritual power – I think even I could have pulled it off with more panache.

Altesse made the most of the performance, playing his knife in the blood, mixing it with rum, lighting it up and spreading the flames in a blanket over the coffin. He sang to the drummers, they drummed and yelled back. Dust was rising, and the candlelit air became hazy.

No doubt much to his surprise, the goat found himself manhandled out of the door to freedom. Altesse announced that he would next go down 'into the house of the Devil'. He picked up a candle and walked portentously towards the glass trap door, which I'd totally forgotten about. 'You will hear voices,' he said, as the drums rang out. That'll be something at least, I thought.

Altesse thumped his foot on the trap door, announcing to the Devil he was paying a visit; he opened the door up. Altesse began the descent – taking it very slowly, one short step every second or two. It became quite a performance. I was moved – but not the slightest scared. This was like enjoying a piece of Wagner, the drumming in our ears like the flight of the Valkyries.

Finally he was down there – the steps leading to nowhere that I could see. I edged a little closer, and still could make nothing out. Altesse's voice to the drummers, '*Bon! Bon!*' was echoing, distant. Longer and longer periods of silence followed. I began to wonder what was going on. There was no voice of the Devil. There was no voice at all. And the next thing, Altesse was coming slowly up again. Something had gone wrong. He'd lost his nerve perhaps, performing like this for unbelievers. Soon, he was back in his chair.

Jackson sensed disappointment with the sacrifice – the truth was, it was disappointment with everything – and he told us that he'd now 'sacrifice himself'. This sounded better. There was drumming again and a waist-high hefty mortar was rolled in by two men. It must have weighed 200 kilos. Jackson then laid himself down, and carefully placed the skull between his feet. Next, with much huffing and puffing, the wooden mortar was rolled on to his chest. Jackson lay there, grimacing. However, all this was very circus-like – the exaggerated, drawn-out preparations prior to the death-defying act. Then, as the drums quickened, the two men began pounding pestles into the mortar – each pestle in itself heavy to lift. '*Marchez! Marchez!*' Altesse called, and the two men circled round and round, thumping down the pestles. He poured burning rum into the mortar, and blue flames licked the brim.

It was an attractive, rather than terrifying, sight. I wasn't the slightest worried that Jackson might be suffering. It was extremely dramatic, and with a bit of editing it might look good on the telly, but overall it was unimpressive. Maybe I'd just seen the act too many times before – it was the old hefty-object-on-your-chest trick. I didn't understand the physics, but exert a downward force and the pressure comes out not vertically but laterally. If Altesse was genuinely capable of anything more than circus tricks, he hadn't done any today. And oddly, that left me feeling not disappointed in him, but depressed about Haiti. He and his kind were surely feared by thousands, even millions, of Haitians; they were being kept back by these sorcerers – and, to judge by Altesse, for no reason. It was superstition.

It was about time I heard an anti-Vodou point of view again, and who better to give it than Wallace Turnbull, the veteran Baptist evangelical who ran a mission post up above Port-au-Prince. He was not one likely to be in favour of the government's push to celebrate the historic Vodou slave revolt at Bois Caïman. Indeed, he even had an anti-Vodou display, with a notice outside blaming Vodou for all Haiti's ills.

I walked around the mission, a spotless environment of classrooms, tended flowerbeds and groomed hedges. Here the Baptists were 'serving the whole person' a sign announced. They had programmes to teach people about irrigation, they had a dental clinic, they even had an eighty-bed hospital. And for visitors, the Mountain Maid tea terrace provided junk food and a disposable paper placemat with some propaganda on the back. I learned that the Baptist Haiti mission had 135 churches and 100,000 members – but even these figures were out of date, with the churches springing up every moment.

I met Wallace Turnbull in his garden, at the back of the mission. He wore a straw hat with a purple feather, and was a civil, likable man who you might have thought was pottering about in his retirement, interrupted while dead-heading the roses. We chatted a while. He told me that for ten Haitian dollars you could come to have your baby in the hospital here. 'They are grateful to us. They don't want children all their lives. They used to have ten or twelve. Two would die. Now for them if one dies it is a real tragedy.' His wife was running a family planning clinic – the first in Haiti, other than the one for prostitutes. And when he arrived in this country the Haitians knew nothing of terracing. 'They used to say the hills were giving birth – that is, the stones were rolling down out of the mother hill.'

As we talked, a youth went by, wheeling along a car tyre. 'Committed two murders, that kid,' Wally said, shaking his head. 'I said to him, "Why don't you get yourself baptized and join us? You benefit already by borrowing our facilities. Down in Cité Soleil you would have been shot by now."'

As it happened, downslope in Port-au-Prince a huge plume of smoke was rising from Cité Soleil. 'Just the usual,' Verdieu said, when I called over to ask what was going on. A street boy had been slashed to death with a machete, and other children had lit a heap of car tyres as a protest.

'People come here thinking how lucky I am, having ended up in this beautiful place,' Wallace went on. 'They don't realize I planted all this – the palms, the grass. Sometimes I just look at it and thank God.' He pointed to a honey bee, sucking at a white clover near my foot. 'That is one of my bees. They've helped make this a beautiful place, spreading the pollen.' He breathed deeply, drawing in God's sweet air. 'There is only one creature I can't abide, a type of woodpecker. They call it a sap-sucker, and it kills the trees. Otherwise it's a perfect place.'

I carried on listening to Wallace's case, now with an eye out for any sap-suckers I might see contentedly sucking on the trees behind him. 'Vodou doesn't build schools, hospitals, clinics. We do. Vodou is divisive. It sets people up against each other. Christianity unites.' The faith was rotten to the core. 'Take Danbala – St Patrick, the man who had control over the snakes. He is really a symbol of a type of evil. The word comes from Baal, a spirit from Palestine. And right across the world, the snake carries a message of evil. Here in Haiti they are harmless – yet Haitians stone them. And they are scared of the dead – even a mother that they loved, they get scared she'll attack them. So they sell all they have for the funeral. It's sick,' he said.

I tried to get Wallace to draw a picture of the Vodou he thought he knew. 'Some of the things vodou-ists get up to aren't fit to talk about,' was all he'd say. And what these things were, I couldn't imagine. I'd seen for myself that such a democratic religion lent itself to abuse by money-makers and sorcerers. True, so did a hierarchical one – was the power wielded by popes, mullahs and brahmins over the centuries always so godly? But in Haiti, anyone could be initiated, $300 should do it for a foreigner. And though *oungans* operated locally, for their *société*, and this helped make them accountable, their motivation was often financial. 'Financial and, for the men, sexual,' Verdieu corrected me when I suggested this. Whatever the truth about the nature of the benefits, that they got them in any quantity at all made them unlike most traditional medicine-man figures.

Wallace concluded our chat. 'The world is a battleground between the Devil and God,' he said, wishing me well. 'And Haiti is one of the battle sites.'

Before I left the mission station I stood for a while looking out down the hill at the mess that was Port-au-Prince – another fire under way in Cité Soleil. Down there cardboard boxes were recycled, stitched together with plastic binding; down there, Haitians often rubbed antibiotics into their infections, not knowing they should take them orally; others took AZT, a medicine to combat Aids, as a contraceptive.

'Vodou has been the cause of much of the tension in Haiti because of distrust,' Wallace had told me. 'Society has to have trust for progress.' By and large, I thought he was right there. And his argument overall was straightforward, even convincing: Haiti could be like his mission station. His world was a paradise, a paradise sponsored by America and disturbed only by that one sap-sucker, the Devil.

If only it was that simple.

It was 13 August, and preparations were now under way for the next major Vodou festival, Soukri. Edele and Fabrice again came

along with us; it was a Kongo celebration, and Edele was especially looking forward to it. 'I like to serve Jatibwa,' she said as
we trundled along through the plains. 'He is my special Kongo
spirit.'

Soukri was a quiet country village, not far beyond Gonaïves.
Far away stretched rice fields and mango trees, but here around
us were neat rectangular houses, made of mud and wattle and
thatch. The temple itself – a functional building of brick – was
positioned in the middle of the village and as we arrived the
peristil was being hastily given a new lick of paint.

Also important here were the 'houses' of the key *lwa*, Ganga
and Simbi-Ganga, two of the numerous offspring of the 'mother'
of Kongo, Manbo Inan. These houses were small blocks of
cement among the roots of two ailing trees on the little hill
above the temple. Later, they would serve as altars.

We were among the first pilgrims to arrive and, like the
others, milled around, getting to know our surroundings and
each other. A couple of stalls were already up and running,
chicken bubbling away in very old cooking oil. The drums were
being given fresh skins, the last hair being shaved off, and the
leather stretched into place. As the light faded, three drummers
sat side by side in the *peristil*, pattering their fingers, tuning their
instruments. And all the while, overseeing the preparations, was
Aboudja. Someone who had spent years working to bring *rasìn*,
roots, music to international attention, he was, like Fabrice, an
articulate advocate of Vodou. A wealthy man, he also had the
title of emperor of Soukri, which was not a religious post – it
would be the *oungan* and the *sèvitè*, the temple servants, who
guided the ritual – but one which gave him the honour of spon-
soring the festival. And tomorrow he would have the honour of
being possessed by Ganga himself when, at the climax of the
celebration, he would perform the feat of riding a live, and not
usually co-operative, bull.

Now, crowds were thickening around the *peristil*, and many
devotees like Edele had changed into white. Aboudja was beginning to raise his voice and use his not inconsiderable bodyweight
to direct them. The Kongo ceremony began in the way of all the

Haitian rituals – that is, with Catholic prayers, a litany of fast, mumbled words that hundreds of years ago the slaves had adopted from the mass as camouflage for their own traditions. Then, after the prayers, the drumming. This was where the African part began. Now the *lwa* were being called to be here, and though this was a Kongo rite, the Rada *lwa* were acknowledged first, beginning with Legba, the *lwa* who opened the gates to the spirit world, followed by Marasa, the twin spirits who balanced the elements of the worlds. We were moving through the pantheon from cooler to hotter *lwa*, Kongo spirits followed by the latest to emerge, the Petwo.

When this was done, the crowd erupted, launching into the electric, fiery Kongo rhythms. The *sèvitè* sang out the lines, and the block of ladies in white, in which Edele was swaying with the others, began responding in high, joyful strains, then dancing ferociously. Edele, heavily pregnant but seemingly unhampered, undiminished, lifted her skirt a little and bent forward with the others, her head down, elbows out and her buttocks projecting and shaking. This continued – a ripping, raw energy that charged the dancers, shifting their shoulders, stomachs, legs, hips – and then a man suddenly shrieked, as if stabbed. He was running in circles in the centre of the *peristil*, mad-eyed and yelling, 'Waah, waah, waah!' like a child gripped by a nightmare. Those around him guided him to a *sèvitè*, who gave him rum and made him greet the *lwa* in the proper manner. The man was turned in circles on the spot, as if steadying and settling the spirit into his body.

Now Edele herself was taken over by a *lwa*. It was Jatibwa, the brother of Ganga. 'He is tough,' Fabrice explained, watching her carefully to see if he could assist. He gave me a quick character sketch of Jatibwa. 'He lives in the country, the hills. He doesn't like perfume and he drinks.'

Edele settled again, and soon like the others had her head down, and skirt raised, ploughing forward, ploughing back. Like most of the pilgrims, I slipped away after a few hours, knowing there would be an early start tomorrow morning for the main ritual. We slept briefly on rush mats on the dark soil floor of the mud huts, the drums beating in our dreams, and then a young man with a straw hat and short dreadlocks walked around the village clanging a bell, and it was time to get up.

As the sun rose, the Kongo celebrations now shifted from the *peristil* to the temple altar in a room that became steadily more and more like a church, as the devotees sat and prayed towards the altar, heaped as it was with pictures of Catholic saints; candles lit the faces venerating them; incense drifted over them.

After a while, cakes, drinks and money were left at the altar for the *lwa* to enjoy and the worshippers became more boisterous; the women sang, drums thumped. Two ladies sat side by side with cassette recorders perched on their heads as they sang; a ruck of youths swayed in front; and a group of students for the first time noted proceedings of Soukri with their pencils – the academic establishment was at last ready to admit that Vodou was an acceptable study subject.

In waves, the crowd began coming and going from the church. Three goats, up until now staked out in the *peristil*, were raised up above the crowd, and their throats cut. The goats looked around confused, their blood spilling out over the white shirts and dresses. The devotees of Ganga processed, dazed themselves now, drunk on devotion as they rocked on their feet, walking around and around in a circle, the weakening goats travelling with them high on their shoulders, shedding their lives for Ganga, contributing to this spiralling life force.

Led by the drummers, the congregation left the temple and made its way gradually up the hill, towards the top, even the towering Aboudja almost lost from sight in the centre of them. There waited the altar of Ganga and beside it the young bull, tied to the tree.

As the crowd swept up the slope, like a slow but inevitably advancing tide, Aboudja was almost silent, a little less interested in policing the people. Because it was time for him to do his bit. Emperor of Soukri, he was now to ride the bull – in his embodiment of Ganga showing he was accepting the offering.

Aboudja was looking uncomfortable. The crowd of 400 was in the thrall of Ganga, and some devotees in the thrall of Jatibwa, but Aboudja wasn't in the thrall of anyone. He sidled towards the bull, three helpers shortening its rope to give it less room for manoeuvre. The crowd gathered around, like worker bees around their fat queen, and the helpers came back and shortened the bull's rope even more. Now its head was tight against the tree trunk: the animal had only a few centimetres of free range. This was getting ridiculous. At another festival, a donkey had collapsed under Aboudja's weight. And now the young bull's tail was being held down.

Finally, when I thought Aboudja was actually going to back out, he grabbed the bull's rope tight, and at last climbed aboard – and the bull didn't react, which was no surprise because it was already pinned down. Aboudja had got his balance now and for a second let go of the bull's neck rope and threw his arms briefly into the sky. The bull still didn't move. A second time he risked it, blowing out rum that he had swigged. And then he jumped off.

He was obviously relieved, and could now allow himself to be carried by the frenzy of the crowd. And carried by it he soon was. Blood was suddenly rippling from the throat of the bull into a bucket and Aboudja swigged heartily from it and began passing it to others to drink. He was in ecstasy, his eyes gone, his reddened tongue sticking out.

I was glad then that I knew Edele and Fabrice, and the other ordinary people that I'd met in Haiti. Otherwise if I'd chanced on this scene I might have thought I was seeing people who were barbaric, doing what Wallace Turnbull might have called supping with the Devil. I couldn't see Edele's face, only her reddened dress, but Aboudja was waving his tongue in the air, the blood flying from it.

My view of the spectacle was interrupted by a man who had his hand in my pocket. Then a lady took my camera and asked for money, and Fabrice had to rescue me. It wasn't an outbreak of thievery, he explained, it was Jatibwa – 'He loves taking things.'

The crowd was making its way across the maize and aubergine fields to a river. 'We go to where Manbo Inan lives,' Fabrice said, leading me. Edele, now lost to Jatibwa, plucked aubergines from the field as we walked, and stuffed them down her blouse.

The river was beyond the aubergine crop, beyond some millet and another field of maize. We walked single file to a small river now in flood. The crowd assembled on the bank, and waited for the drummers to catch up. Clearly, someone was going to end up in that water.

The drummers arrived – or maybe they didn't. By now all concerns were lost, as women suddenly began careering into the water, leaping to join Manbo Inan, the mother of Jatibwa and a hundred other children. And Edele was soon calling me into the water, and, even after my recent misgivings about the Ganga bull, I found myself in there with her. Together we splashed about, swimming hard to keep ourselves from being washed away, and revelling in the soapy-soft, very silty water. A friend of Edele's, clinging to a framework of tree roots, pulled off my shirt and rubbed me over with purifying leaves plucked from an overhanging bush. 'This is the *fin* of your journey,' Edele said in triumph, seeing how easy I had found it to join her in the water. 'It is all over. This is the end for you, until you come again.'

She was right, it was an ending. A cleansing after the turbulence. And even I, an often over-sceptical observer, felt very good. This Vodou I couldn't hope to understand, and some aspects I thought were dubious, unhelpful to Haitians. But it felt good to have taken part a little.

As I walked back, still dripping, I did feel like I was finishing here. I was already heading home. I came across a lady up a tree, paralysed with *sep*, that condition inflicted by a *lwa*. She was screeching and crowing like a bird, her friends unable to get her down. I heard her every now and again, her crowing coming at us through the dark.

I lay again on my mat in the mud hut, listening, wondering what to make of the traditions we call 'Vodou'. For one thing, medicine men all around the world talked about being special, being 'chosen'. But here in Haiti everyone was chosen. You couldn't voyage into the spirit world like a shaman, but anyone could have a conversation with a spirit who has possessed a friend or family member – it was like being on the Internet. Indeed, you could even marry a spirit.

Vodou had in some ways turned out to be very modern, democratic, liberating. But every now and then you got a glimpse, you felt, of darkness – the blood, something Stone Age we thought we'd left behind. 'Sometimes I feel good, feel a sense of creation of harmony at the ceremonies,' I remembered Chantal saying once, 'and sometimes I back away, feeling that this is what we have been trying to get away from for thousands of years.'

But are the vodou-ists any different from the rest of us? It was no good the Catholics coming along and stamping out 'superstitious' rites – their own rites included much the same formulas. And don't all religions have a dark side? Wallace Turnbull's did, as he showed in his fear of the Devil's works.

On the one hand, Vodou's rituals bind communities together – the intense communal celebrations could be likened to group therapy. And the ceremonies are only the tip of Vodou; the religion goes on twenty-four hours a day, encouraging, steering, reassuring people in their everyday tasks.

I had also sensed this religion was, just as Wally claimed, divisive; it bred suspicion. Vodou is, in essence, the externalization of evil. It blames outside influences, not your own sinful state, and that encourages a fatalistic approach, a lack of individual accountability – and the same could be levelled at shamanism and the other medicine-men religions in which sorcerers abound and spirits are responsible for anything and everything affecting our lives. Christianity, however, underlines the importance of self-improvement from an inherent state of weakness. But if Vodou has been holding back Haitians, how was it possible that Santería, a religion of similar origin in Cuba, is often practised by people who are now established in the middle class?

One way or another, Vodou is essential here in Haiti. You just can't ignore it as something that belongs in some backward or spiritual department. Some leaders have talked of trying to establish a hierarchy in Vodou, give it a pope and control those priests who exploit people's fear. But the attempts have come to nothing and anyway it would be the beginning of the end of Vodou as that rare thing: a religion not of a book, or a religious class, but of the people.

Vodou hasn't, in this anarchic and hitherto despotic society, really had a chance to work, nor speak for itself. To the Haitians, it's just something they do. Yes, you get the *malfetèrs*, and that seems to me a handicap. But their presence should be put in context: this is a place where people have been physically threatened at every step – by their health, by the authorities, or by the lack of authorities. The Haitians have a right to be fearful; like Europeans' fear of witches in medieval times, it has much to do with the cruelty of our physical, not spiritual, world. With no food, and only the Black Death out there, there was simply a lot of fear around.

So where did that thought leave me, as I lay on my rush mat in a Haitian hut? Oddly, to a positive conclusion. Because when I first came to Haiti, I had all the usual preconceptions of Vodou – of zombies and wickedness. But our perceptions of Vodou as a force of evil come in part from longstanding European myths of that Heart of Darkness, Africa.

Actually, of the traditions I have looked at so far, Vodou is the one I would bet on surviving. Others will disappear as their environments disappear, or as people leave for the cities and money. In contrast, Vodou continues to take hold wherever Haitian people have gone. It has proved a flexible, adaptable religion, not something stuck in the past as we imagine, but something of now and the future.

MEXICO
PILGRIMAGE TO THE DESERT GODS

CHAPTER TEN

'At the age of twenty I knew I had only this path – to be a *marakame*, a priest. In my dreams and when I ate peyote, Grandfather Fire taught me the formulas for obtaining rainfall, protection from sorcery, and health for my family.'
Jacinto, marakame

Whether in Siberut's forests, or in Tuva, or for that matter Haiti, I had found a belief in the interconnectedness of things. Cutting down a tree in this world may upset the balance of the spirit world; a sickness here may be a sign of a fault in the cosmos. Everything in the universe relates to and balances everything else. For those living close to the land, it is a belief that makes sense: even in Haiti, where the African religions have long been divorced from their ancient, hunter–gatherer origins, there is still an awareness that animals, plants and the weather can either nourish or destroy us. We modify them, they modify us. So the landscape is perceived to have its own consciousness; even pebbles might have souls. There is no gap between the physical or spiritual, the sacred and the profane. Every action becomes a prayer, a homage.

In cultures around the world this perfect balance is often upset by man's sinfulness; he has become separated from God or the gods. In all the Judeo-Christian cultures this becomes a 'fall' from Eden, and the Christian solution to the problem is Jesus, 'the second Adam', who unites people with God again. Likewise, among hunter–gatherer societies, the shaman can overcome this rift on his trance-journeys, travelling to the spirit world to bring back help and sustenance for his earthly people. I had witnessed medicine men engaging with the spirits – I had seen them sing, I had seen them drum – but I myself had so far been denied access to this Other Realm. Perhaps, coming as I do from an alien culture, a culture based around one of the major established religions, that was inevitable and everything I learned would have to remain second-hand. However, my fourth and final destination might provide the insight I was looking for.

I wanted to meet the Huichols, a remote people of northwest Mexico, who eke out a living in the barren Sierra Madre Occidental growing maize. Eight thousand of them still live in the sierras, their culture surviving in turn the Aztec empire, Spanish Catholicism and voracious farmers. The Huichols, having migrated from the desert, still show devotion to their gods, a temple group returning each year to the sacred lands they left. This is a gruelling pilgrimage, during which they try to acquire a pure state, and finally eat peyote, a hallucinogenic cactus, which they say enables them to be with their deities. So in this culture, ordinary people are, in essence, participating in the cosmic journey of the classic shaman, preparing themselves for an encounter with the supernatural beings that govern them.

I would try to join the Huichols on their pilgrimage – I say 'try' because already I had an idea of how suspicious they are of all outsiders. The Huichols are distantly related to the Aztecs – who had referred to their desert-dwelling cousins as 'northern barbarians' – but while the Spanish *conquistadores* were able to smash the huge and strident Aztec civilization, the semi-nomadic Huichols had survived for another 500 years by retreating further out of sight. We don't even know them by their name – called by us the Huichols, they traditionally know themselves as the Wixárika.

My interest focused on a community I shall call La Ocota, a pseudonym, to protect their privacy. Accessible only by foot, this is the most remote community of the Huichols, and also probably the most traditional. I began making enquiries about visiting there a full year ahead, explaining my project to Susana Valadez, director of the Huichol Center for Cultural Survival. An American who was married to a Huichol, she lived in the nearby lowland town of Huejuquilla, and dedicated herself to the Huichols, whose way of life was as threatened as that of all small peoples. She was developing a market for their beadwork and paintings, and hoping to give them a future that might incorporate their culture. Her devotion had earned her that rare thing, the trust of the Huichols. But she herself was suspicious – people rang every week, she said, asking her help to gain access. And she recommended to the Huichols that they didn't allow them in. Outsiders meant trouble – whether Jehovah's Witnesses handing out clothes for souls, Franciscan missionaries offering beans for church attendance, or further encroachment on the remaining Huichol lands by *mestizo* farmers, the mixed-blood descendants of Spanish and Indians. Not for years had anyone been allowed to film in La Ocota, and there was some tension: an American had died mysteriously on their land only a few years before.

'They have a tough enough time just being Huichol,' Susana told me. 'See, they do the pilgrimage because they believe it's their duty to the gods – their gods and ours.'

'Their duty to *our* gods?'

'They are keeping the eternal flame going for us,' she said.

Trying to understand this, I did some more research and learned that the pilgrimage is for the Huichols a journey back in time, not just to their forefathers, but right back to the earliest ancestors, who were gods. Their destination is Wirikúta, the Middle World, a vast, holy land where these gods performed deeds of creation at the beginning of time. The 'ancient ones' had undergone the journey themselves, and in so doing were believed to have knitted together the sacred elements of ocean, mountains and high desert plateau. The Huichol gods and goddesses personify natural phenomena: fire, air, earth and water. The greatest of the gods is Grandfather Fire, who existed even before Father Sun, another key deity.

On their journey, the pilgrims try to reach out to these gods, getting closer and closer to them by distancing themselves from the normal functions of mortals. In preparation, they have already foregone sexual relations, and on the pilgrimage itself they restrict their eating, drinking, washing and even the times they urinate. Furthermore, they conduct themselves by new rules, leaving their old world behind by renaming everything, and often subverting every concept they would have held true back home. Older pilgrims are called children, men are called women. Happiness becomes sadness, ugliness beautiful, the moon brighter, the sun darker. Thus they are released, able – if they are pure of heart – to join the ancestor gods in their sacred desert home.

And this is where the little hallucinogenic cactus, peyote, plays its part. If the pilgrim arrives in Wirikúta in a spiritually pure state, this sacred plant might allow a deeper level of access to the gods. Though peyote is also gathered for ceremonies back home during the year, the Huichols yearn for the experience of taking peyote at this time, for the chance of this ecstatic state, to be able to lose themselves in a fusion with the universe and their fellow humans, conversing with the gods and gaining their knowledge.

Gradually, over the months, Susana Valadez warmed to my project. She finally managed to arrange a meeting between me and a man called Matzuhua, a leader of the group that was to make the sacred trek into the desert, and in the first week of December I flew to Mexico. By now I was becoming anxious – the pilgrimage takes place a few months after the maize harvest in autumn. If I was going to get permission to join and also film the pilgrimage, I had better hurry.

John Hesling, my BBC producer, and I took a taxi from Zacatecas through a countryside of dry fields. Between parched grazing lands there were plots containing maize stubble, desperate -seeming apricot trees, and other crops too burnt by the Mexican sun to be identifiable. Nearer my destination I saw valleys without any crops at all, but studded with the prickly pear cactus – and all of them near dead from a severe winter a few years back.

It was a sobering thought that the Huichol pilgrims must come from the sierra through here on their way into the desert, their Eden, which was even drier than this. It was difficult to believe anyone ever lived out there, yet the Huichols' oral history points to their origin in the eastern deserts – and researchers have found them to be strikingly familiar with the region, though it was several hundred miles away. Furthermore, the archaeological evidence suggests that perhaps as little as seven centuries ago the Huichols were hunter–gatherers, only becoming maize cultivators just before they settled in their present location. Certainly, hunting themes remain in the Huichol world view and ceremony. The deer, a creature they used to depend on for food, is a sacred animal; he is Kauyumári, the messenger to the gods, he is companion of the deities and *marakate*, the Huichol priest-figures and their form of medicine men. He is always required at rituals, the blood used to bless maize, the bones regarded as a source of life. The Huichols might be maize growers now, but deep down they haven't quite stopped thinking as hunters.

So the journey to Wirikúta is not only an opportunity to pay tribute to and commune with the ancestral gods, but also helps the Huichols recall their past as hunting people. They talk about going to Wirikúta to 'hunt' peyote rather than 'find' it – the cactus and that other spiritual communicator, the deer, have become the same. Wherever peyote grows, there through the land of Wirikúta, the sacred deer has once trod. Indeed, peyote is seen as the actual flesh of the deer, and hung to dry back home just like venison, in strips.

Once settled in Susana's house, I waited around for Matzuhua. And waited. 'He'll be a powerful advocate of your case,' said Susana, 'but you'll have to get to know him.' And he evidently wasn't to be rushed. It wasn't that he had no influence in his community, just that it was an egalitarian society, one whose pace and priorities were different. 'They live on Planet Huichol,' Susana explained.

At least while I was waiting I could get my first glimpse of the people whose beliefs I had come to investigate. What struck me about the Huichols sitting around in the plaza was the brightness of their clothes – and that even the youths wore traditional dress in this day and age at all. Huichol girls and women wore vivid red, green, blue and white skirts and tops with ample sleeves but which were short and sometimes exposed the abdomen; cotton scarves sat carefully on their heads, hanging loose down the neck. Made out of whatever material was available, they were unwittingly advertising Budweiser, or displaying little-known flags of Caribbean nations. The men wore round, wide-brimmed hats with wool pom-poms and edged with a curtain of what looked like white leaves. Their trousers were as loose as pyjamas, their tops again voluminous, and across the white material, in bold primary colours, were deer, flowers and a round, segmented design that might have been a large flower bud, but was a stylized depiction of peyote.

Adorned in this way, the Huichols looked a more beautiful people than the other inhabitants, the *mestizos* – the men in white hats, propped in the shade and even the promenading *señoritas*. It wasn't a coincidence – the intention is to reflect the beauty of the gods. More than that: their ornate clothes were thought to give the gods pleasure, and in return they might be guided safely through life's difficulties. And I somehow felt they were confident in themselves. Why, I couldn't think. They had lost most of their land, and were still losing it. But instead of adopting T-shirts and jeans like everyone else, they wore their Huichol outfits. And they saw the fact that the Mexicans had adopted the ancient Aztec emblem of a double-headed eagle as a confirmation of their own superiority. When the Catholics crossed themselves it was an acknowledgement of the four corners of the Huichol sacred world, and the Virgin Mary they addressed as their goddess Grandmother Growth. Her statues had been placed where she had stopped on her own sacred journey to Wirikúta.

Not surprisingly, none of this impressed the local churchgoing citizens, for whom the Huichol religion was suspiciously like witchcraft. If children were naughty they were not told the Bogeyman would come for them, but the Huichols. Mainly, though, they tried to ignore these people, whose land they farmed and whose health they destroyed with pesticides, down in the coastal tobacco plantations where the Huichols were cheap labour. They regarded the Huichols as bad workers anyway – whatever chance you gave them, they would end up suddenly dropping their tools and leaving. The Huichols, conversely, saw themselves as conscientious – it was more important that the gods were served and, if the rest of the world chose not to serve them, the Huichols at least would do their duty.

Matzuhua finally arrived after about ten days, by which time John had had to return. He had a calm face, with bright eyes; he was tall and strong but fleshy. Seeing him, I was nervous about introducing myself. My hopes rested entirely on this one man and with my quite weak Spanish, and his very weak Spanish, it was difficult to imagine us striking up a rapport. I advanced towards him and he warmly offered me his hand. We talked about his complicated family – he had either three or four wives and also innumerable children – and then a little about how far La Ocota was, and how far Europe was, but we couldn't sustain it for long. It wasn't the language that was a problem, it was a reluctance on Matzuhua's part. I knew I was in the presence of a kindly man, and he smiled away at me as we stood there, but it was as if he wanted to know me more before committing even to a conversation.

Another Huichol, Jacinto, had arrived with Matzuhua, and though I wasn't able to get chatting to him either, again he smiled pleasantly, gently saying my name – 'Ah, Benito ... ' He was an unusually small man, a midget in fact, and I was not surprised to learn from Susana that he was a *marakame* – the singular form of the word *marakate*. As I'd seen now in so many cultures, his abnormality was seen as a sacred sign, not a fault. He had been marked out; he was one of the chosen.

Susana arranged for Miguel, an old Huichol friend of hers who looked after the communal pick-up – and was something of an interface between La Ocota and the outside world – to take all three of us to La Ocota the same day. Suddenly, we were getting in the car to leave.

I couldn't believe how my luck had changed. I was travelling not only with Matzuhua but also with a *marakame* – and there were probably fewer than forty of them in existence;

it would be a perfect chance to talk to him about his work. However, it didn't work out as smoothly as that. Whenever I asked Matzuhua something he would simply nod politely, and carry on looking out of the window, beyond the barbed-wire fencing to land populated by cacti and thin bushes. I kept on trying to think of ways into a conversation, all to no avail.

If Matzuhua wouldn't talk for now, what about Jacinto? I hardly knew where to begin with my questions for him. All Huichol prepare from childhood for the pilgrimage, but none more so than the *marakame*, responsible for the physical and spiritual safety of the pilgrims. But: silence.

Miguel must have felt sorry for me, and made more of an effort. He talked about the land around us, a description that became the story of Huichol retreat. 'A hundred years ago we lived here,' he said. Then, the old pick-up spluttering its way up the white, dusty road for another hour, up into the oak forests, and higher, into the pines: 'Fifty years ago we lived here.'

Though there was some Spanish presence in the sierra even in the mid-1600s, the Huichol region wasn't brought under colonial control until 1722, some 200 years after the conquest. Even then, the Spaniards were never able to force the Huichol off their *ranchos* and into the villages where they would be subject to sustained instruction in Catholicism. Instead, whenever pressures grew, they retreated into more inaccessible regions. Their exact line of retreat from the desert is impossible to reconstruct but the Huichols still know by name the key places along the way, and honour these on their trek back to the desert. They leave prayer offerings and talk of them not in terms of their ancestors' retreat, but of their ancestors having bravely ventured, in an age when they were gods, to their Holy Land, Wirikúta.

As we levelled out at the top of the plateau, we had a view back through the pines and Miguel slowed the pick-up so that I could appreciate the scale of the panorama. We looked out over the scrub, which far away, in the approximate location of the mystical place Wirikúta, became even drier. It was still beyond my comprehension that these people, who not infrequently were driven to begging when their maize crops failed, would still want to undergo the pilgrimage. Of all the indigenous peoples who use peyote, only the Huichols find it necessary to endure perhaps 500 kilometres of hunger, thirst, exhaustion and barbed-wire fences to gather a plant whose psychic effects they could easily duplicate back home with mushrooms and other more handy hallucinogens. Or of course they could pick the peyote nearer home.

'It looks so empty,' was all I could think of to say, looking at the barren plain. 'Are there even wild animals out there?'

Coyotes, Miguel said, some wolves still. And deer – 'He is our brother. He tells us about the world.'

Kauyumári, the Deer Person, I thought, the one who also manifests himself as the peyote cactus.

Reaching a plateau, we came to a fence, where the Huichols had finally stopped retreating. 'It's broken – right by the gate,' I pointed out.

'Farmers,' said Miguel, chopping twice with his hand. 'They let their cattle in, and when we chase them out, they tell the government that we are troublemakers.'

The climate was cool and pleasant up here. The grass, though still the colour of straw, grew longer. Donkeys and mules grazed in open pastures and we passed a few *ranchos*, clutches of flat-roofed mudbrick houses with Huichol boys flitting in the baked mud yard, and little girls lugging even smaller children on their hips.

We pulled up at Miguel's *rancho*, near the track end. La Ocota was somewhere down through the trees, an hour or so's walk with a mule. Matzuhua climbed out of the car and walked off over the fields. Jacinto gently squeezed my hand, and disappeared in another direction.

'Looks like you are sleeping with me, then,' Miguel said. But he pointed to an outhouse, beyond a washing line made from barbed wire, where I could lay out my sleeping bag. 'He'll come tomorrow morning maybe.'

I looked at Matzuhua disappearing without even a look back. The light was beginning to fade; there was a purple-fringed skyline dusk, the full moon rising large. Miguel went to see his wife and children. I was left alone with the turkeys and chickens. Soon even they left, stalking off for the night, up the plank bridges that led to their tree roosts.

The next day, after again waiting around, I managed to track down Matzuhua. He eventually announced we were off. 'To La Ocota?' I couldn't believe it was happening at last.

'No. We are going to a house where a god lives,' he said, leading me off across the fields.

It's hard to overemphasize the impact this announcement had on me. For ten days I had had nothing, and now I was about to be shown the house of a god.

'A type of wolf-god,' Matzuhua explained.

We crossed open grassland, through pine forest and down the edge of the escarpment to the start of the oak forest. I felt a surge of excitement. Even if Matzuhua was just doing this as a favour to Susana, he was devoting time to me, who was part of that ugly world down in the plains.

'You will be a *marakame* one day?' I asked.

'*No se,*' he said as usual. He didn't know. However, he added, 'I have been studying seven years – maybe another three and I will be ready.'

We walked on, descending through the grasses and small, large-leaved oaks.

'Can you tell me how you learn?'

He said it was through his *sueños*, his dreams. 'That is when the gods speak to me.' Hearing this, I was naturally reminded of the *kereis* of Siberut – how they believe that dreams are the journeys of your wandering soul. However, the *marakate*, who were nearly always male, were more along the lines of priest figures, officiating at the rituals of the Huichol calendar cycle as well as safeguarding their people's souls.

We came to a simple shelter of grass and branches, projecting from a cliff above us. The 'wolf's house' was in need of repair, collapsing back into the dust. Scrambling up the smooth cliff face, I could see offerings had been left – clay models of wolves, miniature arrows with coins attached to them, little clay discs patterned with pastry deer and cattle. There were deer antlers, which were obviously associated with the Deer Person Kauyumári, the messenger god who helps the *marakate* deliver prayers and whose role could be likened to that of the god Mercury, who served Zeus, in the Roman world. All the prayer arrows that lay here were somehow perceived by the Huichols to be antlers like these – for back in the time of perfection, when there were no divisions between gods, man, plants and animals and all entities were interchangeable, Tatewarí, Grandfather Fire, put his hunting arrows on the head of the deer, and these became his antlers.

However, this perplexing information I had gleaned from books, not from Matzuhua. I tried to encourage him to give me his explanation – for example about the wolf, said to have taught humans how to hunt.

'*No se*,' he said. Still, I could be grateful I had been brought to this site, at least. Half an hour ago I had nothing; now I was alone with a key figure in the survival of one of the least altered indigenous cultures in northern America.

Later that afternoon, we loaded two mules and with Cristina, one of Matzuhua's wives, and his nine-year-old son Celestino we walked down the steep slope to the community of La Ocota. A simple assembly of stone buildings, it was partitioned into family compounds, with an open communal area. No telephone wires, no roads, only spidery mule tracks joining it to the rest of humanity. We led our mules straight into Matzuhua's compound, consisting of about ten little houses hemmed by a small plot of maize, with a narrow yard occupied by the usual proudly strutting turkeys and pecking chickens.

I spent the night in an outhouse and the next day, Matzuhua took me on a walk with Celestino to a waterfall where children were taken at five years old to be 'presented to the gods'. As we returned home I was stopped in my tracks by the sound of what was, surely, a violin, singing through the silence. When La Ocota was at last visible below us I saw an old man playing as he walked by himself through Matzuhua's compound. It must be Matzuhua's father, the *marakame* Artemio, and he would be playing not only for himself but for the enjoyment of the gods around us. He was a magnificent sight. He had long hair and, though I knew he was about eighty years old, he walked with vigour and authority. For the first time I could see what the anthropologist Lumholtz meant when he wrote, 'The shamans, with their long flowing hair, their tobacco gourds, and their ability to cure and to sing, are thought to resemble the gods.'

It wasn't until nightfall that I had a further insight into the Huichol world – from two of Celestino's playmates, who sang a little song around the fire. Even to a westerner, there is something hypnotic about looking into flames, a sense of time and place lost – as if the fire, so important to our cave-dwelling ancestors, still holds a special significance, deep down. How much more so to a people whose ancestors lived as hunter–gatherers until recent times. Watching the boys sing into the flames, it made sense to me now why, though almost every unusually shaped rock or hill can be a god for the Huichols, their most cherished god is Tatewarí, Grandfather Fire. His flames provided warmth and protection during their desert past, and even now he seemed to stand for companionship and security. Conversely, though, the Huichols are no longer out in the desert, and depend on the sun to ripen their maize crops, Tayaupá, Father Sun, is feared as a desert-dweller would fear the sun, and his spirit allies include scorpions and poisonous snakes.

My progress with Matzuhua continued to be slow. It was only the following day that he admitted that there was a *xiriki*, or family temple, in the compound. Even then, he pretended suddenly not to be able to understand a word of my Spanish and I had to stand in front of it and point. It was a building much like the others, but above the door was an adobe brick moulded with deer and other animals. This, I happened to know, was a separate, sacred entrance for the gods. Somewhat hesitantly, Matzuhua went to the door and opened it up.

There was only the one room, bare except for an altar at the far end, supporting bowls of dried tortillas, offerings of maize, candles and prayer arrows laid out, and a small, symbolic bow, and other arrows wrapped in a deerskin quiver. The deer was present everywhere here – antlers on the wall, a deer's head made into a flat mask; below them crude red and blue drawings of deer, as if the etching of a cave man. These things confirmed the presence in the temple of the Deer Person god. To the side was a wicker chair, constructed from soft and hard woods – symbolizing, I'd read, the opposites that create the world. It was a balanced place where the *marakame* could sit and hear the gods. Here also, peyote would be stored, and I reminded myself that the Huichols even claimed to be able to mingle with the gods. It was the equivalent of being a Christian who was able not only to read the New Testament, but also to play a part in it, along with the disciples.

My questioning of Matzuhua about all these things met very little response. Later that day, though, I did make a little headway. We'd walked to the summit of a hill overlooking the valley, and sat and looked out on a splendid view. Thick layers of strata cut across the land. It was an old landscape that still gave life; it had sustained the Huichols and acted like a fort, as the world ate into their previous, lowland, home. On our way downhill, I asked Matzuhua, 'Can you describe the gods, just a little?'

'I'm too junior to see the gods,' he replied. 'The *marakate* can.'

It's an indication of how pitifully slow my progress was so far that I was excited even by this modest disclosure. I asked a second question. 'What would happen if you didn't go on the pilgrimage to Wirikúta?'

This time, Matzuhua's answer was full, if short. 'No rain, no food, no sun – everything will go wrong.'

'So it must happen.'

'It must.'

'And how do you know when to go?'

'We dream,' he said. 'And when we are told in our dreams we must always go.'

It seemed to me that all religions incorporate a belief in some sort of dark side, a devil or some fearful thing that helps us explain death and the miseries in life. For the first time I sensed

the darker side to the Huichol religion. I remembered
Matzuhua's temple, how it had seemed a quiet, tranquil, family
place. However, the deer antlers on the wall were there not only
to acknowledge the presence of Kauyumári, messenger to the
beloved god Tatewarí, Grandfather Fire, but because the deer
was the offering most valued by the sun god Tayaupá. And this
god could be a fearsome god. So the Huichols, though no longer
hunters, no longer needing the meat, offered up the animal that
had always meant the most to their ancestors; it was represented
at each and every ritual and, the essence of life, the Huichols
sprinkled its blood on every maize crop to ensure it grew. If they
didn't do this, their world would fall apart. And in this there
were echoes of the Aztecs, who in their fear made human sacri-
fices to the sun, to keep it rising each day.

The next day, up early, all ready to ask Matzuhua about the
dreams that instructed him, I found him apparently determined
to head back to town. He was more relaxed than I'd ever seen
him – I was a burden, and soon I'd be off his hands. However, I
took advantage of his buoyant mood to pass another question by
him: why had he committed himself to years of training to
become a *marakame*?

'My father, Artemio, said I should become one. I said I
wasn't so sure it was a good idea. I would never plant any maize
to eat – I would always be going here, going there. But he said
there would be no one to look after our family, after he died.
They would need someone to talk to Tatewarí.'

It was the longest answer Matzuhua had given to any of my
questions – and now I was about to say goodbye. 'And Artemio
saw you were different, special in some way?'

Matzuhua was hesitant again. He was a good man, agonizing
about not being able to tell me more during my stay – wanting
to, but in the end relieved, exhilarated even, at having got away
with saying almost nothing.

'We start eating peyote when we are young,' he said cheer-
ily, 'just a little piece. Even at the age of five. The older people
watch us carefully, to see how the peyote has affected us. I think
I knew at the age of eleven that I might be a *marakame* one day.'

In the event, I travelled back to town alone, Matzuhua having slipped quietly back down to La Ocota in the night. Despite my disappointment, Susana assured me I was doing well. 'You've travelled a long way with these people in just a few days. Just think how far you might get with them alone on their sacred journey!' Which was a wonderful thought, except there was still little sign that I was going to be allowed on the pilgrimage – or even that the pilgrimage was happening for a while.

I went back to England. And all the way I thought about the dreams that were instructing Matzuhua and the *marakate*, telling them when the time would be right – and whether I was coming along.

What do dreams do? They allow us to make order from chaos. Dreams, like art, struggle to express what is fundamental, making visible ideas that are invisible, making what's oldest in the human spirit contemporary. I could indeed see how, for hunter–gatherer societies, dreams might have been the earliest spiritual impulse. Early man must have had dreams long before he had language. After all, we share our ability to dream with other mammals, such as dogs that we see twitch in their sleep. Our ability to form sentences evolved perhaps only 100,000 years ago – and the dreams man had at the dawn of his self-awareness must have seemed like godly messages.

Back home, I had a chance to find out more about peyote. I learnt that man seems to have ingested plants for spiritual purposes right back in Palaeolithic times – even Neanderthal man seems to have used 'psycho-active' substances. And maybe it was the use of these plants that organized the spiritual wanderings apparently experienced in dreams into a cosmology, the beginning of a religion. Eating the hallucinogenic cactus, vine or mushroom, our ancestors were delivered into a separate reality where abnormal things occurred. Normally hidden, it was a world inextricably linked to our own reality.

Archaeological evidence points to the use of peyote in Mexico from 8500 BC, and by the time the Spanish arrived more than a hundred species were employed, whether to counter diseases caused by evil spirits, anaesthetize patients during surgery or to help along the souls of those chosen for human sacrifice on the Great Pyramid. Concluding that these mind-altering substances were 'pestiferous and wicked poisons' from the devil, the *conquistadores* began a systematic destruction of the Aztec's extensive ethno-botanical knowledge. In 1571 the Inquisition was introduced to Mexico and peyote officially outlawed.

Despite this onslaught, the Native Americans hung on to their peyote – it was too important to them to give up. A century on, the Catholic Church was beginning to find itself compromising, whether it liked it or not – just as, over in the Caribbean, it was adapting to Vodou. Missions sprung up with names such as El Santo de Jesus Peyotes. Elsewhere, Franciscans transferred the miraculous powers of the cactus to a saint called Santa Niña de Peyotes. Today, some priests have even incorporated the taking of the cactus into an all-night church ritual.

As for the Huichols, I would find out for myself what they said of the peyote cactus – or would if I was just given the chance.

After three weeks Susana sent a message saying that I should come back: the pilgrimage would happen soon, though no one knew whether I was joining it or not. 'You've just gotta hang out more here and see,' she said.

Back John and I came, arriving in the third week of January. I waited as patiently as I could, knowing that I might have the greatest reward imaginable: the chance of joining a pilgrimage to meet ancient gods, a journey that few outsiders had witnessed first hand. Or that I might be returning home tomorrow, or after a month, having seen nothing. And there was nothing I could do about it.

After a week, Matzuhua appeared and told Susana and me that no decision had yet been made, but he was here in town to talk to the most influential members of the temple group.

'He is worried,' Susana told me. 'It's already late January. Each year it's harder and harder to organize the pilgrimage – more and more distractions. Drink, jobs, Jehovah's Witnesses...'

By the close of day, I knew the verdict. Yes, I was indeed going to be allowed on the pilgrimage. It was quite difficult to believe at first: I was elated, almost stunned, that after so long waiting and hoping this was really going to happen. Susana explained for them that there was only one restriction: I would join them just after they'd set out, that is outside La Ocota – not all those in the community would take kindly to being filmed. The plan was to walk down from the sierra, and take a bus from Mesquitic. It would still be a month's round trip. We agreed that I'd take along Marciano, a young Huichol who worked with Susana and would be happy to interpret for me, and help me commit fewer blunders. But apart from him, although a film crew would join us for a few days, mostly I'd be alone with the *peyoteros*, these peyote-hunting pilgrims.

Matzuhua was visibly relieved that the pilgrimage was getting under way at last, stuffing his mouth with the special chocolates that John had brought for Susana.

'Don't expect too much of him on the journey itself,' Susana said. 'He'll be as focused on his duty as a neuro-surgeon.'

Another two weeks went by while the *peyoteros* prepared for their departure, making sure their families had enough provisions for their month's absence. The *marakate* organized a deer hunt so they might have fresh blood with which to anoint offerings and make them acceptable to the gods, and the deer bones were offered to Tatewarí, who would revive the deer, allowing it to be reborn. This sacred act done, a group of *marakate* left for another sacred place, Teakáta, where they paid homage and gathered a flint that would be used to start the first camp fire of the pilgrimage.

It was frustrating to know all this was going on while I was sitting around in town, but I did keep bumping into members of the temple group as they came to town and walked about in their sandals, busy stocking up with provisions for their families. I couldn't tell these Huichols from any of the others, but even if they wore western dress they were recognizably Huichols – stronger teeth than those of the *mestizos*, but worn down – and they all knew exactly who I was, and now even came up to say hello. One was a thickset youth, Marcelino. 'I'm a musician,' he said, flatly. 'A *peyotero* and very fine violinist. You will hear me.'

There was also Remigio, a short, strong man, who was working as a builder on the expanding Huichol Center. 'I have a wild past,' he said expansively, after John and I had invited him to join us for a meal. Looking at him, I felt he probably also had a wild present. His left eye was glass, his hair, brutally cropped along his fringe, carelessly curled down his neck and had embedded in it a pair of blue-rimmed sunglasses. Unlike any Huichol I had known he didn't listen but instead talked; he was the first Huichol I'd met who dominated the conversation. Not only was he fluent in Spanish, but he also enjoyed underlining his credentials as a man, as a father, as a lover, as a builder but presently as a true Huichol. 'I had women, drink, everything,' he said, his fingers miming an imaginary riff on a guitar. 'But I was missing balance – and that is what the journey to Wirikúta has given to me. My life consists of two parts – the life of a town man, and the life of a Huichol. I am balanced now, and I am free.'

The day came when the temple group members were gone from town – then we knew that the pilgrimage was about to begin. While John stayed to sort out the film crew, Miguel bundled Marciano and me into the community pick-up with our food and sleeping gear, and we were off back to the sierra and Miguel's house. He and Marciano walked off down the hill to La Ocota to find out when the pilgrimage was likely to come by. As it grew dark, I waited with Miguel's teenage son Joel around the fire. Joel, who attended school in Huejuquilla, was totally at ease with me, a foreigner, and it was from him that I heard my first description of the sacred land, Wirikúta.

'It is a beautiful place, such as you can hardly imagine. And there the *marakate* talk to the fire, and the fire can talk to them. They can speak to each other. Ordinary people cannot, so they take peyote, and they can hear all that the gods want to tell us.'

'When did you go there?' I asked.

'Oh, I haven't been. But I will go one day. And I will see the ancestor gods. You can see them in the rocks and the stones. It is so beautiful, you must wrap a scarf over your eyes the first time you go, so that you do not die.'

Up to this evening, I'd only ever seen Joel kicking around town with the *mestizo* adolescents, but now he was describing exactly what I'd read about the *primeros*, the first-timers, whose eyes were covered near the most sacred places, because they might be overcome by their wonder. Nor would someone even as young as Joel be talking entirely second-hand about the gods. Like all Huichols, he'd have been taking peyote throughout his childhood.

He remembered the first time he took it. 'The first piece was bitter,' he said. 'But after, I wanted more and more. It felt good in the stomach – though many of my friends just pretended to eat it and spat it out. I looked into the fire and then I saw wolves around me – but friendly. And deer walked right up to me. They were brushing against me.'

I asked if I might see these things.

'Yes, but you must make sure you have confessed – if you have slept with a girl. This has to be said aloud, even if the husband of the girl is standing beside you. Otherwise you will go mad when you take the peyote.'

I'd heard about this – men running into the night naked, others having to be held down. For the first time, it dawned on me that I would be taking peyote and might go berserk too.

'Most *primeros* vomit badly when they take it,' said Joel, and went on to describe the colourful scene.

Miguel, back from La Ocota, added to the unhappy picture. 'It's not so bad as the old days,' he said. 'In those times, if you vomited, you had to catch the vomit in your hat, and eat it again. You could not refuse – because you go to Wirikúta to be told something by the gods. They are waiting to speak to you through the peyote.'

We learnt from Miguel that the *peyoteros* were coming through here some time tomorrow. Right now they were walking around the fire, talking to Tatewarí. They were also making a calendar, tying knots in a long string, one for each of the key places en route. Wives were shaping maize dough into miniature animal offerings, others making pictures from yarn, these to act as visual prayers. Men were gathered around in the firelight decorating symbolic bows for the peyote hunt itself, others further into the darkness making firewood ready – food for Tatewarí to keep him going during the pilgrims' absence.

The next day I waited with Miguel, Marciano and Joel to hear the pilgrims and mules working their way through the pine trees. They would walk right by, Miguel said, and stop at the spring in the clearing next to his house.

The sound came in the late afternoon – a sound I'd been waiting to hear for a year. It wasn't the sound of feet and unwilling baggage animals but the strident, insistent sound of a violin calling the gods to join the journey and carry them to Wirikúta, and horns blown to announce to the world that the *peyoteros* were coming through on their mission. It was a sound made by people who were still resolute and strong, and about to do their duty to the gods. In their baskets they carried their sacred burden – dozens of prayer arrows, manufactured and blessed at the holy sites along the pilgrims' route last time and then used for conferring blessings back in the community throughout the year. Now, in return, they must be faithfully taken to Wirikúta to be laid before Father Sun at Cerro Quemato, the journey's end.

CHAPTER ELEVEN

'By doing this journey we are making the sun shine – because the very first pilgrimage of the gods, which happened at the beginning of time, enabled the sun to shine. And if one day we do not do the same, the sun will not rise, and you and I will die in the dark and cold.'

Xauleme, Huichol pilgrim

The *peyoteros* were setting out across their world – not ours, a globe with its lines of longitude and latitude, but theirs. It was held up by Brazil trees – one each in the north, south, east and west, and there was a fifth Brazil tree and this was in the centre, where Tatewarí was born, and which the Huichols saw as home. It was that same old symbol – the tree of life, the Axis Mundi, and channel to the gods.

Now through the trees I could see the line of men in white tunics, baskets on their backs. They wore little feather arrows in their hats, equating to the first antlers of Kauyumári, the magical arrows placed on his head by Tatewarí. I looked for familiar faces – Matzuhua walking second, behind the lead *marakame*, who must be representing Tatewarí; in his wicker basket the deer horns that would serve much like antennae, helping him communicate with the gods in Wirikúta and with home.

Behind Matzuhua came another old man, Felipe, the *marakame* who personified Tatutsí, principal assistant and female companion to the god Tatewarí, and behind him Jacinto and a fourth *marakame*. Men blew emphatically into their horns, and Marcelino was playing his violin. They all marched on, proud and certain, doing this job for their people and for all of us, walking faithfully behind Tatewarí in his authority, heading to Wirikúta.

It was a moving sight, the trek a triumph over the world at large; the Huichols, galvanized by their duty, were launching into the hostile territory of the lowlands, and all according to the dreams of their medicine men. The oppression of the animistic religions by Judaism, Islam, Hinduism, Christianity and even Buddhism has largely been to do with the threat to their control posed by individuals with such dreams and 'divine revelations'. The faithful are taught to dismiss those who have visions as the mad – even though founders of the great religions had themselves often been inspired by those who, like the *peyoteros*, had fasted in the wilderness, and found their revelation there. It is acceptable to pray, but not to hear a reply and converse.

This was why the sight of the *peyoteros* was a beautiful, valuable thing. 'A *marakame* is a radio,' Joel said, coming up behind me. 'The people can tune in and listen to the gods through him. They hear his transmission.'

The procession came to the spring beside Miguel's house. I counted twenty-four men, and only one woman. Among them were disorderly donkeys, which were led to the water, while two men ran forward to unload the baskets of Matzuhua and the four *marakate*. There was a buzz of activity, everyone checking their belongings, adjusting basket straps – all the business of the start of an expedition. Only the senior men stood still, the *marakate* silent, Matzuhua quietly issuing instructions. The next thing, the *peyoteros* were removing their right sandals, and hastily bringing them forward to be blessed. A gourd was filled from the spring and the *marakate* walked in a line, flicking water over them in turn, and saying their own prayers all at the same time. The *peyoteros* then briskly formed two facing lines, and the senior men walked along each, waving their feathered wands, summoning Kauyumári from the east end of the world, Wirikúta, to make the blessing from Tatewarí possible. Feathers, like everything else, were sensate and capable of speech and action on their own, and now were flying away to tickle him awake and persuade him to come.

When the praying was done, Matzuhua beckoned me over. Feeling very much an outsider, I walked up to the group and mumbled one of the few Huichol words I knew, '*Ke-ako*.' Hello. To my surprise, every single man answered back, together murmuring what must have been a sort of welcome. I hugged Matzuhua and shook a few hands. Marcelino the violinist nodded at me, Remigio strode up and gave me a slap on the back and Jacinto reached up to shake my hand. 'We are open,' he said, smiling up into my face. 'Ask me things if you do not understand.'

I hadn't previously thought of the *peyoteros* as open people, but before I had digested this novel idea they suddenly were leaving again, the *marakate* leading them off through the grasslands. Miguel drove us in the pick-up to a point in the road where we would intersect the procession, a glade where they would stop for the night. We said goodbye to Miguel, who shrank away hastily. It seemed that he felt he had no part here and later, as the *peyoteros* went about making camp, I could see why. I now was witness to a dazzling display of teamwork – one that I might have expected of an army platoon on manoeuvres, but not here, among a people who quietly worked the land with their digging sticks, each according to the needs of their separate, almost autonomous, family *ranchos*. Matzuhua and the four *marakate* stood in line facing west, the sun in their faces as it set through the pine trees. Every other pilgrim, however, was immediately off to do a chore – seeking water, grazing the donkeys, gathering kindling, while others hacked a tree down. When the wood was ready, the men brought it back in line like ants bringing resources to the nest; all was choreographed, even the stacking of the wood pile.

There would be two fires: one for Tatewarí, at the feet of the elders, the other, for Tatutsí, further away. Pancho, a grey-haired, stocky man with tearful, compassionate eyes, who was the *marakame* embodying Tatewarí, shuffled forward. A squad of men moved in with a sheet wind-break so that the flint gathered from the birthplace of fire could light the tinder. When this was done, the pilgrims took two pieces of kindling each and lined up to feed the two gods.

'Yours,' said Remigio, giving two each to Marciano and me. We tagged on at the end of the line, walking anti-clockwise around the fires, and laying on the sticks as we passed; I tried to copy the others, blessing the five points of the world while the *marakate* murmured their prayers. There was little that could go wrong, I thought – after all, I was only laying a stick on a fire.

Not so, it seems. I laid the first stick without a problem, but when I did the same with the second, disaster. The *peyoteros*, who, I now noticed, were carefully monitoring my every move, gave a collective grimace of horror. Remigio rushed in and laid the stick again. 'Its head was facing the wrong way,' he said.

'A stick has a head?'

Remigio frowned. The *peyoteros* saw me as his friend, and I was in danger of being an embarrassment. 'This is the head of the stick,' he said, crossly, picking up a twig and showing me the broader end, 'and this is the tail.' He let the twig fall, and he shook his head. The other *peyoteros* looked on sympathetically, like grown-ups around a sweet but dim-witted child who's getting a ticking-off for running into the road.

There was something rather depressing about having messed up my first Huichol ritual – here, even in the laying of sticks on the fire, there was precision. It was a little early to say, I thought to myself, but this sacred journey might turn out to be a nightmare.

The *peyoteros* had fed Tatewarí and Tatutsí with sticks, and they now moved on to the next duty, each shaping a wooden rod, called *itsuu*, which they would each carry all the way to Wirikúta, and bless at each sacred place along the way, bringing them back to La Ocota to feed the home fire.

I looked around me as they worked, the fires illuminating them, and the ceiling of oak leaves and stars. Now seated cross-legged in two lines extending from the *marakate* at the west end, along either side of the two fires, here was a whole system of government. *Peyoteros* came and went, consulting Matzuhua about this and that, or being despatched by others in a chain of command below. Marciano and I gingerly approached Jacinto, and with his help I jotted in my notebook everyone's duties.

Or rather tried to. Jacinto had said, 'We are open,' but this was too much openness at once. By torch and firelight I scribbled down page after page of notes, and only stopped in the end because Jacinto was getting a sore throat. The long and short of it was that there were three key people here. Pancho, the *marakame* representing Tatewarí, had the responsibility of walking at the head of the line. Matzuhua, who would walk behind, was the 'history teller' and instructor. He was the right hand of Pancho, and also the left hand of the other principal figure, Felipe, representing Tatutsí. Sitting on the outside of Pancho and Felipe, that is Tatewarí and Tatutsí, were the two other *marakate*, both known as 'Our Mothers', who did as they were directed by the female deities of the land and sea. One of these two *marakate* was Jacinto, the other Jose Candelario, a quiet man and one whom I was destined not to hear utter a single word on the entire pilgrimage.

Representing deities, the *marakate* didn't do duties around the camp or even, it seemed, lay sticks on the fires. This was a duty of the pilgrims, and they were split into equal halves, one for Tatewarí and one for Tatutsí, on either side of the two fires. The Tatewarí *peyoteros* were lined to the *marakate*'s left, the last in the row being a portly middle-aged man called Augustine, who was the 'judge' who oversaw them. Facing these pilgrims were the Tatutsí *peyoteros*. They were looked after by Xauleme, who had the pitted face of a drunkard who'd somehow survived a life in the gutter but who had an equivalent position of authority as Augustine.

There was more – and yet more. Committees who decided things, teachers, a policeman who wore a whip at his hip – this was the violinist, Marcelino – and even a Minister of Culture, who collected litter. But chief here was the great protector and guide Tatewarí – not only the god of the *marakate*, but also the *marakame* of the gods. However, though he was a great god, Jacinto referred to him gently and with diminutives, as you would a child.

'Tatewarí is a mirror,' he said with a tone that was a mix of gratitude, reverence and affection. 'You can see yourself in his flames. He is pure and so travelling with him cleans us, so that we are good enough to find peyote.'

Standing by the fire was Alexandro – a man whose custom was at all hours to wear a surgeon's mask to defeat the dust – and he explained why the *marakate* could not lay sticks on the fire. 'Long ago, there was no fire in the world. There was a star in the sky, and many times the gods would see it pass. They would say, "What's this? Let's stop it." So one day they shot it down with an arrow. They sent two *marakate* to see what it was, and bring it. And the *marakate* found that the star was actually an old man, Tatewari, who said, "Now you are my parents, because you found me, and I am yours." From that time the *marakate* have been privileged and don't put wood on the fire, only ordinary people do.'

Just then, a figure blocked the firelight. It was Matzuhua, standing up to warm himself nearer the flames. 'The fire is ours,' Matzuhua said. 'This is what we believe. That everyone else is borrowing him.'

Marciano and I went to bed, laying out our sleeping bags on the edge of the camp, between Augustine and the stack of spare firewood. I thought of the story of the origin of fire, and it reminded me of a Huichol painting I'd seen – the sun had been raining snakes, a wolf was transforming into a man, and a deer was rising from a fire. I could now see why I'd struggled so hard to understand the Huichols. These people conceived the world in terms of pictures, not our rational words – the Greek notion of *mythos* dominating *logos*, the logical or other way of interpreting the world. They were artists creating patterns to explain the cosmos.

I lay awake a little longer, wondering if I'd ever get close to the Huichols. Beside us burned the fires of Tatewari and Tatutsi, which were not allowed to die.

Dawn rose, and just as Marciano and I discovered our supplies had been plundered by Miguel's family and now consisted of two potatoes and a banana to eat over two days, the pilgrims moved into action. Donkeys were being loaded and Remigio was thrusting two sticks into my hand to lay on the fires as a farewell. I was waiting my turn and then I was nervously placing them – watched by some thirty pairs of eyes. Then we were off, the cow horns blowing. One *peyotero* started, the others followed up and down the line; and always, behind the raucous sound, Marcelino's violin calling out to the gods through the branches.

Above: 'La Ocota' settlement, as seen from the cliffs above. To the right is Matzuhua's family compound; the rounded, central building is the communal temple.

Right: *Peyoteros* walking through Wirikúta, the sacred land and home to the ancestors and gods.

Previous page: A Huichol, in typically colourful everyday attire, standing above 'La Ocota'.

Above: Augustine discussing with me the spiritual properties of peyote.

Left: Peyote is to westerners just an hallucinogenic cactus, but to the Huichols it's a form of the sacred deer messenger Kauyumári, who helps people communicate with the gods.

Above: The Huichol spiritual leaders stand facing west, waiting for the other *peyoteros* to prepare camp. Pancho, extreme left, is beside Matzuhua. Filipe is in the centre, and to his left Jacinto.

Right: Matzuhua, not yet a *marakame*, is leader of the temple group and was the key to my access.

Opposite above: The three *primeros*, or first-time pilgrims, at San Juan de Tuzal. Their eyes have been covered to protect them from the power of this sacred place.

Opposite below: A pilgrim gently placing the antlers of the *peyoteros'* guide, the sacred deer messenger Kauyumári, on a shrine.

Previous page left: Having taken peyote, Marcelino is entranced by Grandfather Fire, Tatewarí; Augustine, behind, also addresses a deity.

Previous page right: Pancho, senior *marakame*, prays on the *peyoteros'* behalf.

Above: The musician Marcelino, with *uxa* facepaint.

We trooped through the open woodland, dry leaves underfoot, and branches cracking as they gave way to the donkeys.
Antonio, an authoritative, slightly scary man, had the job of running the day-to-day non-spiritual practicalities of the pilgrimage,
and he walked alongside the *marakate*, but some distance to the
side, ready to assist them with any obstacles – and as we approached the farmlands, there'd surely be plenty of those. Marciano and I
marched halfway down the line, behind Marcelino.

Up and down ancient trails we went, Pancho ahead, the
Kauyumári's antlers in his basket guiding him, Matzuhua
behind, and Felipe behind him, bent from his load but beadily
looking up through his glasses. 'The line,' Remigio said, as we
passed through the fence marking the Huichol boundary. The
path began dipping, and soon after we were forced to a halt. It
was the first farmers' fence. Antonio battled with it a while,
pulling aside the poles blocking the path, and we were on our
way – only to be stopped ten minutes later by the next. Then we
were in the first pasture, and walking along a corridor of barbed
wire. And now Marcelino's violin seemed more like a gentle rallying cry; it was something to share that had been brought from
home and he had the heart-warming effect of a drummer boy
marching ahead of an army.

With the shortness of his stride, Jacinto was finding it
harder and harder to keep up, and I was also struggling. Every
peyotero was fasting, restricting themselves to tortillas and water,
but Marciano and I were looking at a starvation diet.

We stopped under a large oak at midday, and Antonio gave
the order for work. It was the second of the five years that this
temple group would make the journey to Wirikúta, and the
peyoteros knew exactly what must be done. Antonio stood in
the middle of them, evidently waiting to receive suggestions.

When I asked Matzuhua what was going on, he looked at
me blankly, not understanding a straightforward question. He'd
never been very expansive in his answers, but this was something quite different. It wasn't lack of trust, it was basic lack of
comprehension. When I repeated the question, in response he
looked around for Marciano to help translate. This was what

Susana had warned me about. He was now like a 'neuro-surgeon', as she had put it – unable to engage in anything other than his people and their operation.

'Everything will now be renamed,' Remigio said, explaining for me. 'The trees, the animals, our body parts, clothes, even the names of each of us.' He drew on his cigarette, and released an aroma remarkably like cannabis. 'It's like a fresh start. We are leaving behind our old world and preparing for the beauty of Wirikúta. It will be like this for days, building a new world which is beautiful.'

For an hour, Antonio stood among the *peyoteros* receiving new names from them, and every now and then making everyone go through the list. The sky would now be called the sea. The donkeys would be called pick-up trucks, horses would be lorries...

We walked on, the *peyoteros* now murmuring the new names, trying to memorize them and so facilitate the release from this world into a purer one. In a few days, when all around them had a new name, they would have released themselves from their old existence, and, once they had confessed their sins, be ready to embrace Wirikúta in a pure state.

On we went, filling our water containers at a spring that was evidently a favoured drinking spot of the cows – this particular *mestizo* obstacle the Huichol overcame with ease, simply popping a couple of iodine tablets each into their gourds – and began a steep climb, out of the plateau's last valley. Marcelino's violin sounded exhausted, buckled like us from the heat, and issued pained, screeching strains; the men's cow horns were not heard for whole hours on end.

The hardships of this journey were nothing compared to times gone by, of course. We would be in Wirikúta within ten days, if the plan worked and the bus was waiting for us in Mesquitic. The whole trip used to be done on foot, and the Huichol stories of the early pilgrimages hint at the need to travel at night to avoid the Spanish slavers. However, there were some new obstacles – the spoiled drinking holes, the fences. And this year's choice of route down into Mesquitic was secret, so that the farmers wouldn't be able to block their way.

We now had an horrendous climb; I kept myself going by thinking through the Huichol story of the origin of the pilgrimage.

One night Tatewarí called a meeting of the ancestors – characters that have now become gods – because they were sick with a variety of ailments. Tatewarí, their *marakame*, told them that they were sick because they hadn't gone to Wirikúta to hunt the divine cactus peyote, as their ancestors had done. 'Let us walk together to Wirikúta, there in the east, there where is the Burned Hill, there where there is Deer, and you will find life.' They prepared themselves by abstaining from salt, and their wives, and laid fires with wood, the favourite food of Tatewarí. These fires had to burn day and night, while they were gone. They headed east, behind Tatewarí, who played his bow string with his arrow. Behind walked his first assistant, Tatutsí, and all other animals and people – which, at this time, were one and the same. The journey was hard; there were many dangers and difficulties. They named the places where they camped, assembled and cooked tortillas, such as the place where the *uxa* bush grows, and today is cut and ground into face paint. One day they arrived at 'Where the Clouds Clash Together', which you must pass to approach the sacred places. Here Tatewarí asked Deer to hold back the dangerous clouds with his antlers to let them safely through. Finally, exhausted, they reached 'Where Our Mothers Lie'. There some Huichol women, all dressed in their finest clothes, were waiting for them. These ladies were Our Mothers – nowadays, the female deities of springs, waterholes, rain and fertility – and they gave the people water.

Grateful for the life-giving waters of Our Mothers, they left arrows and other offerings, and with the Mothers headed refreshed to where Deer was waiting. They perceived the Deer was the divine Hikuri, peyote; they pursued and killed him, and eating his flesh learned 'what it is to be Huichol'.

We made camp that night on the very edge of the plateau, on the edge of the precipice overlooking the own of Mesquitic. Through the evening, Antonio stood between the fires, drilling the *peyoteros* in the new words, loosening us from the labels that made up everyday life. Everything was undergoing change – we always walked within the camp circle with the fire to our left, the reverse of the procedure followed back home – and mock elections were held to reallocate the minor posts. To wild app-lause, a motley assortment of *peyoteros* dressed up as politicians, stuffing sleeping bags inside their coats in imitation of the fat *mestizos*, and repeatedly tested the microphone – '*Hola! Hola!*' – which was made from a torch tied to a length of string. They then launched into all-encompassing and fantastic election promises.

As the sun rose below us in the plain, we were descending the escarpment, winding down from the sierra to Mesquitic, which from here spread out from the dry river bed like a piece of dry lichen from a twig, radiating around it fences that looked like the lines of a spider's web. We were dropping as if to another dimension where different physical – and also spiritual – rules apply. The horns were blown, a glorious announcement to the world. The Huichols were unrepentant. The Huichols were unapologetic. They were coming down to the desert plains, as was right for them to do.

It was a beautiful feeling, being slowly drawn like this into the pilgrimage. Walking with them, I felt I was sharing in the common purpose, uniting with them. Doubtless a major func-tion of the pilgrimage was to unite the Huichol community as a whole, remind it of what it was to be Huichol. And the medi-cine man's entire purpose was to unify: even if no longer serving a hunting society, his use of animal spirit helpers and the way he 'becomes' animals while in a trance, remind us that his profes-sion originated in hunting societies, where he must unify the killer and killed, restoring the harmony of their souls. He also had a duty as unifier in his earthly society, resolving the tensions that exist in every community. And, I rather suspected, this would most dramatically be demonstrated in the confessions soon to be made, so that we would be able to take peyote with a positive, rather than negative, outcome. Transgressions would be brought out into the open, creating a unity, a uniform whole. Peyote was not just a communicator, it was a judge.

I asked Remigio what I had to confess to – everything? 'Just all the girls you've made love to!' he laughed. 'Twenty, thirty, forty!'

According to Remigio, up and down the line of pilgrims were individuals who were sweating away, thinking of what they had to own up to in front of their friends and family.

'They laugh it off now,' said Remigio. 'But inside…'

'And you?' I asked, as gently as I could.

'I am a good person. Before, no. Now, yes.' He shrugged, and smiled. 'No worries.'

We'd see – either at the time of the confession, or later, when he took peyote and might 'go mad' in the desert.

Down into the dust and heat of the lowlands. The first reaction of the outside world that we now hit – and it did seem like an impact – was from a herd of cows on their way for a drink. They panicked, seeing this relentless column, and couldn't retreat because a cowboy was riding up behind. The Huichols, who I'd only ever seen as passive, quietly accepting the turn of the world, surprised me by being entirely unsympathetic. They carried on marching at them. Several cows jumped through the barbed wire, ripping themselves. One charged through in pursuit of her calf, the fence spun aside. The *peyoteros* were not bothered; some gave the cows an unhelpful slap as they charged by. Perhaps the *peyoteros* were just tired, or perhaps an ancestor of the present farm owner had shot at the Huichols, killing them off until they gave up their land.

The cowhand didn't see this, and actually was extremely affable, saluting Pancho as he trudged through the billowing dust cloud. We walked on down the road, towards the outskirts of town. Tractors were parting the soil, water was being flicked over crops. Finally, we dropped to the river bed, where we would meet the bus tomorrow. Pancho stopped at where he divined would be the camp site, and turned to face the west. The other *marakate* lined up with him, and they stood, still bearing their baskets, while the *peyoteros* dropped their packs in their allocated positions on the left and right side, and ran around, gathering wood and fetching drinking-water, and cutting poles to construct a stand on which to place their hats and deerskin quivers.

Waiting my turn to lay my sticks, correctly I hoped, on the fires, I saw there was another level of complicated procedure going on here that I had entirely missed up until now. This was fire-making as I had never before seen it. First a white log was placed across the fire places – 'Each is a gila monster,' Alexandro said, speaking through his anti-dust mask. I knew this to be a type of large, slow lizard. We now placed our sticks across these wood chunks, the 'heads' of the sticks facing the east, the direction of our pilgrimage. Three white, sharpened sticks were placed around the Tatewarí fire place – which was always lit first – and one white stick either side of Tatutsí. These were the snakes that looked after the gila monster.

We drifted in twos and threes over the dry riverbed and into town to buy food and candles, then returned to our world. This was the first night in the lowlands and, as the dark gathered, we clustered around both fires. Matzuhua got up to warm himself, and we stood side by side. I had rather given up trying to communicate with him – the Spanish language seemed to have been pushed aside in his head to make more room for all things Huichol. But he looked down at the fires and said, fondly, 'Ah, Benito…'. Then, as if introducing me to a friend, 'This is Tatewarí, Benito.' I followed his eyes to the radiating, orange heart of the fire – friend to the Huichols, but also family, also life. It was a comfort in the darkness and all the more so because Augustine had just been stung by a scorpion that was in his bedding and we'd all been reminded of the hostility of this environment. There was silence again, but a comfortable one. Pancho, also warming himself there, said, 'Tatewarí gives us light and heat at night. The sun gives us light and heat in the day.' Neither man spoke any more, but they stood there for a while longer, lit by the flames.

At dawn, candles were handed out to all of us; I copied the *peyoteros*, standing with mine lit, facing the east as the *marakate* said prayers to greet Tayaupá, the sun – as yet behind a range of hills. It was a vigil as well as a welcome, a ritual to ensure the transition from night to day; as the sun rose from the horizon, giving us light to replace Tatewarí, we extinguished the candle flames over the embers.

The bus came into view, rocking along the river terrace. Leaving the donkeys in the hands of some young Huichols who had appeared somehow from somewhere, we filed out of the camp and on to the bus, the *peyoteros* taking their seats in reverse order so that Pancho, Matzuhua and Felipe could be in the front row and head the pilgrimage, albeit along the highway.

On a straight stretch of road, Pancho waved a hand and Matzuhua told the driver to pull up. 'I think it is time for the confessions,' Marciano said.

'Already?' I wasn't prepared.

However, it was a false alarm. 'Only the *primeros*,' Remigio said. 'We're later.' We let the senior men off the bus and then we all followed them along the highway verge. Cars streaked by, smothering us in pollution, and yet we were walking as if the combustion engine was yet to be invented and we were filing through empty, scrubby plain.

The *marakate* stopped us on the grass verge, and marched on ahead with a small group of *peyoteros*, including three 'policemen'. We waited with the *primeros*. It was the first time that they were distinguishable from anyone else. There were three of them: the woman, who tended to keep herself to herself but laughed at everyone's jokes, even mine; a skinny man who, to be frank, seemed a little half-witted, and a bit old to be a first-timer; and a man called David, who was also quiet – but possibly only because the *primeros* were not meant to engage in conversation. However, I had hopes of getting a word from David later.

All three of them put on headscarves, and pulled them down over their faces. The three policemen now came trotting back down the road to us and plucked out the *primeros* one at a time, to go and make their confessions. David was the first to be whisked off, and I was a little relieved to see that everyone was making fun of the moment – David pretending to hide, and the policemen running with him, howling like wolves and beating him lightly with a cotton belt. It looked like confessing wasn't going to be the ordeal I'd imagined – embarrassing, rather than traumatic, for anyone who had to own up to sleeping with another *peyotero*'s wife.

It was difficult to see what was going on up the road when each *primero* arrived. They were danced around, and thwacked lightly with the belt. Meanwhile, the *peyoteros* began reliving the best confessions of the *peyoteros* from last year.

'Juan Antonio, he had fourteen girls!'

'And one of them was Susi!'

'Ah, sweet little Susi...'

I now realized that the confession was not about faithfulness, but the act of sex itself. Marriage for the Huichol is not a state-documented thing – that is why in one of the world's most Catholic countries they can manage to have several wives. Once, when I'd asked Matzuhua how Huichols got married, he demonstrated by raising his hand and grasping at the air. 'Like snatching a chicken!'

I began running through the names of my former girlfriends, wondering if I'd forgotten anyone. Maybe the Huichols were doing the same, as time ticked away before tonight's confession.

We walked up the road, then stood in two lines, for Tatewarí and Tatutsí, and were blessed by the *marakate*, who waved their feather wands over us, giving us a blessing. We stopped for the rest of the day at the side of a track, sitting in the shade of the bus, and carried on renaming the world. Now the rocks, soil and pebbles were given new names, and Antonio, inexhaustible and exacting, made the whole class repeat and repeat after him. Some *peyoteros* scribbled the names in notebooks, others waved cassette recorders in the air.

The *peyoteros* carried on in this way, loosening their grip on their previous existence; soon the fasting would begin in earnest and at the most sacred times later, in Wirikúta, the outward signs of our mortality would be diminished further, when, at certain of the most holy times, no one would be allowed to urinate. With the help of many blessings and prayers, and by following the procedures of the ancestor gods, who first did this journey, we would regain the purity that was lost in the First Times.

The sun began steeply dropping and the sounds around us were the sounds of our landscape being shaped into firewood, food with which to nourish the sacred fires. Bushes, shrubs and trees were dismantled and brought to honour Tatewarí. This journey was a long prayer, and the devotional period would continue even after their return. I understood that it was some five months before they could sleep with their wives again. They would be faithful only to Tatewarí – 'We are married to him,' Jacinto told me, standing with the other *marakate*, while the *peyoteros* filed in with the wood.

The huge heap of firewood was a sign of a long night ahead – the night of the confessions.

After dark, Pancho began a long prayer, a slow chant that went on for over three hours, the *peyoteros* milling around all the while. Soon the confessions would begin, and some *peyoteros* were unusually silent. Some played at being nervous, some began teasing. 'You've left your torch on, you are so scared!'

Then the three policemen plucked the first *peyotero* out, to lead him up to the *marakate*. He made a performance of it, pretending to have fallen asleep. Everyone laughed as the policemen shepherded him forward, and he pretended to put up a struggle. He first mumbled a declaration to the fire, Tatewarí, to tell the truth, and then knelt in front of the *marakate*. Taking one of the prayer arrows that was laid before them, he dipped the tip in a bowl of deer blood, and blessed the five points of the Huichol world. The confessions weren't quite the loud public declarations that I'd expected, but even a whisper in this close community was enough. However, I'd already begun to understand that the confessions worked to heal divisions, not make them. There was no tension in the air and the *marakate* as well as the *peyoteros* listened eagerly for the next girl to be revealed. After each name, a policeman slapped the whip gently on the *peyotero*'s back, so even the furthest pilgrims could hear the number of girls he'd been with. '*Seis . . siete...*' And the nearest were listening in, giggling, then passing the names on, so that everyone else could also savour the latest sin.

By the time my turn came I was fairly relaxed. I started my list of former girlfriends with Patricia, who happened to be a Mexican. '*Una Mexicana muy bonita.*'

'A Mexican, hooray!' the policeman behind me exclaimed, thumping me with the cotton strap. A congratulatory cheer went around the camp. After completing my list, I washed my hands in the flames of both fires, purifying them as everyone else had done. We sat for a moment, and then the renaming of the world continued. Now it was the turn of our own names, and our renaming became an excuse to satirize the *mestizos*, just like the elections of a few days before.

A *peyotero* whom I didn't know was dressed up, a sleeping mat wrapped around his waist and secured with a cord. He wore a fur hat and dark glasses. He retreated into the darkness and was called on a telephone consisting of cow horns as receivers, separated by a long piece of string. '*Hola, Papa?*' said Antonio at one end. I gathered that this was a long-distance call to the Pope.

'*Sí, el papa aquí.*' Yes, the Pope here.

'Well, we have a favour to ask. We have lots of children here in Mexico that need baptizing.'

'Where?'

'Mexico.'

'You have good airports out there?'

'No, we have only airstrips, made of dust.'

'Then I'm not coming!'

'We pay well.'

'I'm coming straightaway.'

He steered a makeshift toy plane of kindling wood and silver foil through the air, a flashing torchlight held to it. It crash-landed with him on the plastic sacking runway.

The woman *primero* got on her hands and knees as a mule, and carried him into the camp, everyone clapping as he made his unsteady progress.

The pilgrimage was again performing a function of the medicine man – as well as doctor, psychotherapist and the multitude of other professions, he was the satirist, acting like the 'all-licensed fool' of a royal court to undermine divisions between the people and authority. And the divisions were there for all to see. Only the previous year, the government had prevented a Huichol community from expelling Franciscan missionaries because the Catholic Church supported their political party.

Each of us in turn was baptized, the procedure becoming more and more protracted because the Pope kept asking for more money. Each of us was crossed with water, dispensed on the end of a flower, and when my turn came Matzuhua whispered that I'd now be called Tutucruciara. 'In the name of the father, the virgin, and this soup' – he dipped the flower head into the water – 'raise many chickens and grow much taller.'

As I went to bed with my new name, 'Cross of Flowers', I watched the *peyoteros* breaking their fast, undoing their gourds as the southern cross became visible low in the sky. It was already nearly dawn, the coldest part of the night. My drinking water was frozen. The sleep deprivation and fasting are part of the whole process of detachment. Emotions run higher. You are closer to tears, anger and laughter. You are nearer to your soul, whatever its ingredients.

We continued in the direction of the rising sun, dodging the objects that had sprung up over the last few hundred years and now stood in the way. We wound in and out of sleepy villages – cowboys propped against walls in the shade – and jerked through the traffic of Zacatecas city. At dusk we stopped at a petrol station for water, and pulled up right by an electric plant, camping with it fizzing and droning beside us.

On we went the next day, Pancho directing the bus to the edge of a village, Villa de Ramos, that had a charming plaza with aromatic plants and cast-iron benches, but also, on the village outskirts, an ugly secret. I stepped from the bus to see, drifting unstoppably past us in the scrub, the village effluent; plastic litter bobbed on by, sometimes floating on a sickly black trickle, other times in a reeking gush. Well, we were obviously not going to camp exactly here, I thought.

But Pancho led the procession to within a few dozen paces of the oozing stream. He and the other *peyoteros* seemed unaware of it. Their minds were somehow focused not on their surroundings of today but on the surrounding of the First Times. It was the same as Matzuhua and his frequent inability to communicate with me. These things – the Spanish language, the fences, the cows, the effluent – belonged to the present day, which they had left behind. Bound together by the sacred duty they all shared, they had their own existence and in it were reaching back to a place and time that were cleaner than today. And if they failed in their journey, the sun would not weep tears of joy, the rain showering down in the form of serpents. There was no choice for them – this was a question not of cultural survival, but survival itself.

Through the evening, the *marakate* roasted a little pile of native tobacco, tending it gently by the fire. It was the first sign that we were approaching the time of the peyote hunt, for the Huichols believe that the tobacco is a companion of Kauyumári, the deer who is also peyote. Xauleme, the man with the battered-looking, not to say drunkard, face, wiped his nose on his sleeve and told me how this connection came to be.

'Benito, in the Old Times, long ago, when things were not like they are today, not at all, Deer was flying through the sky. He was out hunting, and his arrow fell to earth. And though he was forbidden to go down there, Deer decided there could be no harm in it, and swept down. There he was surprised to find two female deer. "Have you seen my arrow?" he asked them. "I have it," said the oldest doe. "But I will not give it to you unless you make love to me."

So, Deer made love to her – or began to, because he tricked her at the end, by pulling away just before he had finished. His semen didn't go in her, but scattered on the ground. Seizing the arrow, he disappeared into the sky.

'Some time went by, and he became curious about the female deer he had seen. He flew down and to his surprise saw tobacco growing where his semen had spilt. Then he saw a frog. "What's this?" he wondered, and kicked it. And then there appeared from the frog the seeds of the gourd plant. Later, he grew the seeds, and that is how he learnt about the gourd plant, and why we have gourds today. That is how it was, Benito.'

Xauleme proffered one of the little gourds that he and the other *peyoteros* wore and which dangled from strings over one shoulder. So far I had paid little attention to these, only noticing that the strings were forever getting tangled. 'The tobacco will be carried in these,' he said.

The *marakate* were going to have a hard night. The tobacco would be tended until dawn, and now Pancho began a three-hour prayer to a hill lying out to the west, a god that settled there.

It was already very obvious how much stamina the *marakame* was expected to possess – chants at the 'first fruit' festival were said to last three days and nights – and he fasted to a stricter regime than the ordinary *peyoteros*. His work also demanded social skills, dramatic and aesthetic gifts; he needed an understanding of psychology, current social tensions and, of course, herbal medicine. He had to be able to communicate with deities, defend his patients and interpret the supernatural. His memory had to be exceptional – he was expected to memorize his people's history, their songs, their myths. And as his job involved reaching and maintaining intense and abnormal psychological states he must, just like all the medicine men I had seen across the globe, have extraordinary self-control and mental balance. As I'd learned in Tuva, with Ai-chourek, any possible tendency to neurosis that may facilitate gaining access to Other Realities must be correctly channelled.

The pressure on the medicine man, therefore, is intense. Not only are all the people dependent on this pilgrimage, and the community as a whole dependent on that one person for their spiritual welfare, but he is doing this duty for the gods he has called as well. If he fails, his power would turn him to sorcery. He would have gained this power without the ability to control it. A deity might have sent a message to a young boy in a vision or dream that he must become a *marakame*, but success in fulfilling that call was not guaranteed and assumption of the office might not occur until middle age.

Pancho's prayer went on, through the evening. Some *peyoteros* were chatting and joking as usual, others were looking into the fire, the Great Transformer, the god that changes all he touches – wood into ashes, darkness into light, barren land into fertile land, cold into warmth, inedible flesh into food.

As Pancho finished his prayer, Marcelino struck up on his violin and the *peyoteros* gathered themselves, put their baskets on their backs and trooped out of the camp into the night.

I could get no explanation from anyone – they were all too pre-occupied. Off they went without a word to me, or even in Huichol to Marciano. They stopped eventually at a small tree, which they prayed at, laid offerings before, then hacked to pieces.

This was clearly more than just the cutting of firewood. Two pieces of wood were given to each *peyotero*, and then they stood around the tree stump, their baskets at their feet, saying prayers; there was a solemnity to the occasion, as if this was a funeral. The *peyoteros* walked back, approaching the camp slowly, padding along to the beat of the music, and laid their wood on the fires.

Later Xauleme told me that the cutting down of this tree was a ritual whose name translated as something like 'our Elder Brothers are breaking themselves'. The *peyoteros* are the fire-wood, I thought, suddenly. They have fed themselves to the fire. I looked around me at Remigio, Matzuhua and the others whose faces I could see in the flames. I felt alone. I had been left behind while the pilgrims travelled elsewhere.

At dawn, the preparations continued for Wirikúta. The *marakate* handed out a pinch each of the tobacco they had been roasting and more prayer arrows were made for blessing at the holy sites en route, ahead, for use back home through the year. Embers were raked out of the fire and their heat used to melt red, blue and green wax, which was wiped in decorative lines around the arrow stems.

According to my calculations it was now around the middle of February but, even for me, the passage of time was becoming less and less relevant. For the *peyoteros* themselves this must be far more so. Even bumping along in the bus there was a tangible sense that they were doing something they had always done; the bus, just like the fences and towns now stretched over their ancestral lands, was of no spiritual relevance. Our next stop would be 'Where Our Mothers Lie', Tatei Matinière, which had featured in the story of the first peyote hunt, led by Tatewarí – where the Huichols' forefathers had been washed and refreshed by the goddesses. On we went, through flatlands that became progressively drier and sparser. We had come 400 kilometres from the sierra now, maybe more. But this seemed a journey less and less about distance, and more and more about travelling back in time, or to another spiritual plane.

On the way we stopped in the middle of nowhere, an expanse of rock and sand desert, which any ordinary traveller would have concentrated on getting safely behind him. Not us. There in the dust we were lined up in two ranks, for Tatewarí and Tatutsí, and the *marakate* blessed us with their wands. Nearer and nearer, purer and purer, we went to Wirikúta.

We stopped just outside a little dusty village. I looked around excitedly. Somewhere here must be the holy site, the spring where the goddesses had washed the forefathers, and would wash the *peyoteros* in the same way. All I could see ahead was a patch of mud, carved by the feet of cows. Merging with it was an undistinguished-looking copse, around it a broken barbed-wire fence long since having failed to keep out the thirsty herds.

'Where Our Mothers Lie!' said Jacinto, marvelling at the wonder of it. I looked again – the fence, broken down, the mud. Cows wandered through; pigs wallowed. Not a pretty sight, I thought, yet the *peyoteros* were buzzing with anticipation and the *primeros* were now being blindfolded so as not to be over-awed by it.

Once again, I had that poignant feeling of having been left behind – I was far from the world these people were now inhab-iting. They were in what Susana had called 'Planet Huichol'. They saw splendour and purity around them, while I saw mud.

'We belong here,' said Jacinto. 'Our Mothers know every-thing about us. If we, the *marakate*, can't cure someone, he or she can go here, because it's where we belong.'

I still didn't get what all this meant, and nor, I suspected, did the local people who were rapidly assembling. Most were teenagers who leant on their bikes and straddled the fence, star-ing along with the cows. Marcelino played, the cow horns were sounded, and the *peyoteros* walked to the spring. There they laid out in the mud the prayer arrows and votive offerings brought all the way from La Ocota for mothers, sisters, fathers. Mainly, though, they placed little pictures, what might to the passer-by seem like children's artwork but were sacred messages, visual prayers understandable only to the artist and the gods they were to be seen by. Depicted on gourds, clay and cardboard, were deer, eagles, fire – innumerable gods, each constructed from beads, some from wool yarn or dough, some in crayon. On the back, in biro, were the names of who had made the prayer, and instructions as to where they should be placed.

The youths, fascinated by these strange goings-on, drew nearer and now hung from the fence only a few paces away. Some Huichols for the first time flicked irritated glances at the spectators, but their people had not survived these centuries by confrontation, and the *marakate* got on with their sacred business, blessing us each with a flick of the murky, cold water, and then our right sandals and feet.

The *primeros* were told to strip off their clothes at the spring source, a pool of clearer water right beside the fence, to be bathed in the holy water. They began doing just that, even the woman, with the *mestizos* goggling right beside them.

Remigio, who more than anyone here knew the ways of the *mestizos*, had had enough. 'If you want entertainment, go home and watch TV!' he yelled, and began moving over to them. The youths slunk away.

The *primeros* squatted down in their underpants, and a continuous stream of water was poured over them by a circle of men gathering it in their gourds from the spring.

We left the place to the gods and cows. For the *peyoteros* it had been a place of beauty, and they came away cleansed by the Mothers just as their ancestors had been. They hardly seemed to see the mud – like the fences, that belonged only to the present day. And as we boarded the bus no one bothered to look when I called out that the youths had come back and were ransacking the site. They'd parked their bikes and were presently prising off the coins from the offerings and stamping the prayer arrows and pictures into the mud.

CHAPTER TWELVE

'I ate peyote, who is my brother. And I felt lifted up like a small child to get a better view – and what I saw was the fabric of the universe. How the threads are connected, one to another – plants to animals, animals to man, man to the gods. I was part of that universe and, despite my sickness, there is no feeling more beautiful or complete.'
David, a first-time pilgrim

We drove on for a short while through open country to a hill, at sundown tumbling out of the bus into a desert thick with cacti. Though there were still cattle fences here, this place seemed untrampled by what is often called 'progress'. It was harsh but beautiful in its strangeness. Even I, whose soul lagged so far behind the *peyoteros* but was being carried along by their vision none the less, could believe gods lived here. For we were on the brink of Wirikúta, and this very spot was visited by Kauyumári in the First Times – an era which seemed increasingly to be where the Huichols were now. In the morning we would look for where the deer descended to earth back then – or, as the *peyoteros* seemed to see it, just now. He, or his prints, would be visible to us as his other manifestation, peyote.

For the third night in a row, Pancho prayed his lengthy prayer, and the next morning we rose early for the hunt. The deerskin quivers were laid out on the ground with the short bows, and blessed, and little patches of material embroidered with a deer and normally attached to the quivers were now placed on the hats of the *marakate*. Kauyumári would soon guide them to the peyote, where the deer trod.

Before they set out, the *peyoteros* fanned out to urinate, so that they would not do this function of mortals while engaged in this supernatural task, then placed in their mouths a ball of tobacco to help bring them to the sacred animal.

The *marakate* prayed again, both Matzuhua and Jacinto in tears as they implored the gods to look on them kindly; then they raised their drawn bows to the four cardinal points, and then the centre of their world, indicated as being at their feet, and set out to negotiate the first barbed-wire fence.

We spread out, walking slowly – as silent as any hunters, our eyes keenly searching. Hours went by, and still nothing. Peyote is a difficult quarry: it does not stand tall, protected by its spines. Its defences are its bitter alkaloids and its technique of hiding: a dark green colour, it lies level with the soil surface, its spongy face almost hidden, invisible apart from the pimples on its radiating segments.

We had been under the sun with no food or water for four hours now. It wasn't looking good, and I was beginning to see why. This desert wasn't as untouched as it seemed. Someone had been along busily making the prickly pears edible for their cows by pouring petrol over them, to burn off the spines. And there were little holes all over the place where small cacti had been removed, taken to town to be sold for middle-class gardens or, in the case of peyote, as an ointment for rheumatism.

Eventually, the decision was made to turn back. However, the *peyoteros* were as pragmatic as usual about this latest reverse in Huichol fortunes. The arrows were put back in their cases, the deer embroidery badges were replaced, and everyone scattered from the camp to urinate. It was only me that was left feeling despondent. It looked like the outsiders had defeated the gods at last.

Seemingly unthwarted, the *peyoteros* continued their journey. The next day we stopped at another of their springs, this in the region known to the *mestizos* as San Juan de Tuzal and to the Huichols as 'Where the Toi Flower Grows'. The *toi* flower, whatever it was, no longer seemed to be growing there, and this might have been to do with the cows that had mowed the turf to the edge of the various pools.

However, the desert laurel was to be found – the plant the Huichols know as *uxa*, the one whose roots could be ground to make yellow face paint. The ancestors had gathered it on the first pilgrimage, and the *peyoteros* did as they had done now, extracting it from the ground as they would peyote, to take back home for use on holy occasions through the year. Somehow the Huichols made what other people would call a desert into a storeroom, a depot for the body and soul.

We moved on, our prayer arrows blessed, feet and sandals purified once more, and the gourds filled with holy water to carry us through to our final destination, Wirikúta.

My experience of 'Where Our Mothers Lie' – but now also where the pigs and cows lie – had taught me that these holy sites existed for the Huichols not on the physical but the spiritual plane. Wirikúta was a place in the head or heart. However, as we came nearer the ancestral homelands I couldn't help searching the horizon for something special. Where it lay, the plain of San Luis Potosí, must consist of more than just the fine white dust now flooding into the bus.

Marcelino played the violin, but no one spoke. Everyone seemed to be waiting. The road cut through a steep, dark hill range, the Black Door, and here the bus was stopped by Pancho. We all got out and stood on the roadside for a final blessing with the feather wands before entering the home of the deities.

I was braced to be disappointed, and sure enough the view I saw, emerging through the Black Door, was of a desert like the others. However, behind, running right across the horizon, was a startling array of sober, arid mountains.

Jacinto, sitting next to my place in the aisle, tapped me on the shoulder and said, 'Unaxa.' He jabbed a finger at what looked from here to be the highest peak. On the map labelled Cerro Quemado, the Burnt Hill, it was the end point of our journey, the birthplace of the sun, where the last year's prayer arrows would be left and where their helper, Deer, first appeared. Sent down here by Tayaupá, Father Sun, it was then that he left his trail of peyote.

We bounced through a mudbrick hamlet. There were pigs, chickens, lone bulls behind spiky stick fences, and Sprite and Coca-Cola signs on the community shop which had been used for rifle practice. Our bus – coated thickly with dust and on its last legs now – pulled up with a heavy sigh at a grove of trees. An ageing hippie, here doubtless for his own, less legal, harvesting of peyote, quickly rolled up his sleeping mat, lobbed it into the back of his pick-up – decorated with paintings of daisies – and fled.

We went to sleep early. Tomorrow would be the day of the peyote hunt, the day we would all take peyote and, if pure, know the gods. Assuming, of course, there was still peyote to be found.

The following day we waited for sunrise as usual, standing with our candles facing east as the *marakate* prayed and the glow of dawn gathered ahead of us. Then the sun shed its first blast of light over the mountain crest, and we extinguished our candles over the fire, giving back to Tatewarí the light that he had given us.

The *peyoteros* walked out of the camp, and as before the bows and arrows were blessed, the deer badges moved from the quivers and placed on the *marakate*'s hats. We walked in a line out through high scrub, then through low cactus country, and there spread out, eyes to the ground.

This time, the peyote was present to be hunted. Within moments the *peyoteros* around me were kneeling on the desert floor, murmuring a quiet prayer. Those who did not have bows and arrows to shoot the peyote pulled an arrow from their hat, and placed it gently against the cactus. Thus 'killed', the peyote was swiftly severed from its root. The pilgrims swept the desert, bending, digging. Only the larger mother plants – and also one peyote that was within striking range of a rattlesnake – were left.

When the baskets were full we gathered around the *marakate*, who were clustered in the place where they'd decreed the 'deer had fallen'. The one arrow already shot into the ground grew into a thicket of arrows as the *peyoteros* each added their own. Offerings were laid and the peyote was stacked in the middle of our circle. We stood there, gathered together in the desert, while the *marakate* began to pray. What began as a gentle murmuring gathered in strength, rising into a tearful lament, a wringing of the heart. Matzuhua cried and wailed – to Tatewarí, imploring of him, or perhaps to Kauyumári, who had given himself to us.

The time was fast approaching when we would eat peyote, the substance that one researcher called Benítez, I distinctly recalled, had described as 'not a friendly drug'. How would it treat us? We were about to be judged – as the pure of heart, able to be with the gods, or as unworthy, unclean mortals. Remigio, standing next to me, I thought was unusually silent – even rather grim. Was there something he was now wishing he'd confessed? A girl he'd left out? I rapidly double-checked my own list.

Antonio prepared the peyote, cutting up the segments, plucking off its little tufts of cotton and picking out its little black seeds. 'The *primeros* will have to eat much more than everyone else,' Remigio said. 'Fifty, even eighty pieces!'

It did sound rather a lot. And I went over to the *primero* called David and managed to get my first word with him. 'Are you a little scared?' I asked. 'I know I would be.'

'No, because my heart is clean. I have confessed everything.' However, he didn't look all that content.

The three *primeros* were beckoned forward and told to kneel in the circle's centre. A huge pile of peyote segments was divided into three bowls and laid before them. Without any ceremony, they began, working through piece after piece of peyote, which, by the look of it, made an extremely rubbery as well as a bitter meal.

Antonio was meanwhile distributing six segments each to the rest of us. Better get this done with, I thought, and put a couple of pieces into my mouth together with an orange segment. I remembered Joel, Miguel's young son, talking of people vomiting up the peyote; however, after a few chews I decided that I'd be able to tolerate the bitterness – it was the quantity of spongy material that was a problem. You just couldn't swallow it down quickly, however great your inclination.

I stood with the others, and wondered when and if things were going to happen to the world around me. I was given another half-dozen pieces – though there was some discussion about whether this was wise, because they'd seen a foreign photographer take this much and in the end he'd gone all peculiar, unable to discern even the cameras hanging from his neck.

I watched Remigio pause a second before lobbing his peyote into his mouth. If I was having last-minute doubts about the purity of my heart, I'm sure I wasn't alone. Marciano went off to be by himself and I walked the other way. I sat on the desert floor, feeling nauseous and wishing that the film crew – already been and gone – were around to offer comfort.

Now the *primeros* began to vomit. The woman was the first to succumb, and this set off David and the other man. However, Matzuhua gestured at them to carry on eating. Looking greener and greener, they picked their way through the peyote, the ring of *peyoteros* around them, like a reassuring and protective fence.

I turned away, feeling a little drunk now. Remigio had said the peyote would take an hour to have an effect, and I was waiting, watching. Was it this forced concentration then that made me think that the sand, pebbles and shrubbery around me were more vivid than normal? They seemed to be projecting towards me, as if I was in a 3-D cinema. The colours seemed enhanced; I feasted on the tones – burnt umbers, siennas, cobalt yellows, jades, olives, in a place that had been only bleached greys and whites before. Now the ingredients of the desert reached to me; everything was in my face, as if my eyes were those of a bird of prey, and able to examine the minutest detail of the desert around me, even the texture of the dust.

As for the stones, they now seemed so bold as to be breathing, as vibrant as living things. I watched them for a moment, or it might have been an hour, or half a day, and only pulled myself away when I became aware of a feeling of increasing anxiety: the nearby *peyoteros* were a little too loud, and I wanted to be further away from them. I fought that feeling, making myself relax by breathing deeply. At last I regained control.

Looking over at the circle of *peyoteros*, I saw Remigio. He was bent over, retching. He looked terrible. Perhaps he also should have confessed about Susi.

Now a delicious feeling of energy and euphoria was overcoming me, and, it seemed, the others. They were now chuckling together or smiling at the world around them, their eyes red and glassy. I felt lifted in my spirit but also body – my limbs were weightless, as if borne by an invisible force.

It was time to get back to the camp. Antonio was lifting the baskets up for the *marakate*, and organizing bushes to be placed over the offerings, to hide them from the *mestizos*. There had been no ceremony, just this quiet time eating the peyote, flesh of the deer. The three *primeros* were quietly getting to their feet and were led off. No one had run off berserk into the desert or had to be held down. Veterans of peyote – they had, after all, been taking it since infancy – the pilgrims generally seemed well able to control when to let themselves journey. The file of *peyoteros* was disjointed but orderly. The *marakame* Felipe, the twinkly-eyed man who, up until now, had said very little to anyone, was now speeding along and singing. The *marakate* giggled to see him tear through the scrubland, scattering objects from his basket as he went.

Back around the campfires, the *peyoteros* sat quietly and let themselves be carried to wherever the peyote cared take them. As for myself, I wanted to explore my surroundings with my newly empowered eyes. And it wasn't the colours and textures alone that were enhanced; I was detached, wrapped in my own experience, and yet I was aware of each of the *peyoteros* around the camp, most of them with heads down, hats tilted forward. All senses were sharpened. Able to handle the world so easily, it seemed to me to slow. Even the click of my fingers was slow. It was as if the air had been replaced by water – I could still breathe it, but it was smoothing my movements. I felt the ease of a fish in the sea, the desert shrubbery around me like weeds swinging in the current. This comfort with everything might have been akin to drunkenness, except that whenever I chose I could focus my thoughts exactly. Nothing in the world that might appear before my eyes would surprise me – my senses were too powerful to be outmanoeuvred. And in this way I felt all barriers, all secrets had gone. Even though I was not a *peyotero*, I was surely feeling a little of what the peyote did for them; I could believe my soul was being carried to an Eden-like place where there were no divisions.

It was dark now, and I stood by the fire, staring into the embers. I found a biscuit in my pocket, and handed it to one of the *peyoteros*. He looked at me as if I was a strange, quite different, being. Then he began crying. He was taken away, sat down and wrapped in a blanket. No one was surprised. He'd talked to, or seen, a god.

Marcelino slumped against a tree, letting the peyote teach him a new refrain on his violin. A few men stood around the fire and talked; some stood before the *marakate* and made speeches. They talked about life – their own stories about how they came to be here. Some burst into tears and wailed. Most of the *peyoteros* just sat, watching or heads down.

Then Xauleme came up and stopped in front of me. With his floating eyes I had never seen him looking more like a tramp. However, he had something to say to me, and spoke clearly in what was normally appalling Spanish. He wanted me to understand each word. 'Benito, at the very first times, the gods were hunting for Elder Brother Deer. And when they had killed him, that's when all the gods were turned into mountains and stones and bushes. That's why everything is stationary – because Elder Brother Deer died.' It was a revelation, a vision, and I think he wanted someone to capture it. He'd known I'd be sure to write it down in my notebook.

I went to bed and watched the stars above. If I was feeling euphoric, a detachment from everyday reality and attachment to another one, how much more so the Huichols, whose preparation had been so much greater? Their whole lives led to participation in this pilgrimage. And now here they were, feeling, I guessed, a similar euphoria as I felt, but a greater sense of freedom. Hunter–gatherer societies were forever seeking harmony, and taking peyote and rising in a pure state to the gods they had a semblance of it. At last they were freed from the problem that shadows all mortals: the need to keep in balance with the spirits, plants and animals they affected each day, and whose souls they were forever causing distress.

More peyote was gathered the following morning to be boxed and taken back to La Ocota, but informally, the pilgrims coming and going as they chose. The camp was quiet, and, with my translator Marciano leaving tomorrow, I took the chance to talk to David, the *primero*, about his own experiences. He was lying on his back, not looking very well. He spoke of having seen something horrendous and black having come from the sky. 'It had bleeding sticks on it and it spread all over my body, and looked at my sins. It showed me what I had done wrong, me and my forefathers. There is a kind of net around me now that won't let me walk.' He clutched his stomach, digging his fingers into the muscle. 'It bites into me. And it will stay like this until I'm at the top of Unaxa tomorrow, and promise Tayaupá to make amends. If you think this is a game, it is not. It is a serious duty and once you eat peyote, as you must, you can be trapped by your wrongdoings.'

The following morning we climbed to the ridge of Unaxa, where the sun was born, and where the *peyoteros* would do their last prayers, thanking and begging and promising, as appropriate. We were heading towards a sacred spring where the *peyoteros* always drew water.

Not this year, though. The *mestizos* had got there first. We gathered around to look: where water had trickled, giving sustenance to gods and *peyoteros* since the beginning of time, now there were only sealed pipes. The spring had been cemented in.

It must have been a shock, but no one said anything. For a while Antonio tried bashing a rock at the cement, but most of the others just stared at it, or looked out over the land, which from here looked badly damaged, crudely carved up by fences, like a rich cake sliced for consumption. After a while Matzuhua made a suggestion. Everyone should bless themselves with the water leaking from one of the pipes. There was only a puddle of it, and it was polluted with goat urine, but it would do. Soon, without any sign of indignation, we were moving on.

Up to the summit ridge, where there was a further surprise. Well-meaning folk locally had made a rock and cement hut to protect any Huichol offerings from the usual rampages of other *mestizos*. Yet to have its thatch put on, it sat there dominating the scene like an army pillbox. Its architect, Humberto Fernandez, a local Mexican who was evidently sympathetic to the Huichols – in fact, by the look of him, he wanted to be one himself – was waiting for us. He stood at the top of the path, proud in his freshly bleached and ironed Huichol dress. He hugged the *peyoteros* in turn, and gestured to the provisions he'd brought them – a mule-load of firewood and four cases of beer. 'It's not just that

I value their culture,' Humberto told me, having explained that the hut was constructed so that it would survive even when the *mestizos* burnt the thatch off, 'it's because this is my religion too.' Did he believe the world would end if he didn't sacrifice to Tayaupá? Could the hunter–gatherer gods really become his?

No, was the correct answer, but before I could hear this from him the Huichols began assembling the prayer arrows which had served the community all year. Candles were lit, arrows spiked in the ground, and yarn paintings of wolves, maize, peyote and a score of other deities presented to Tayaupá. At last, the Huichols were fulfilling their duty, and as the *marakate* laid down the preserved head of a deer, as demanded by Tayaupá each year, Humberto took his own prayer arrow from his bag, and stabbed it in the soil next to a candle placed by David, who was sobbing quietly as he prayed for compassion.

The *peyoteros* swigged the beer, and danced for a short while in a circle. Humberto joined in. In some ways he did look the part; though well over six feet tall, he had a splendidly prominent Aztec nose. As if trying to convince himself he was Huichol he stamped his feet louder than the Huichols did, and when it was time to blow his horn, he blew harder than even Remigio. Only during the prayers was he silent, not knowing the words.

We went to bed early to avoid the cold wind that swept up over the slope. I was left to think, shivering in my sleeping bag, how a religion born out of a need to understand and survive the forces of the desert could be Humberto's, or indeed how anyone in the West could claim to be a shaman. So sheltered for generations from the rigours of the elements, we see in what we call 'nature' only beauty. Did Humberto fear certain of the *marakate*, as the Huichols did? Susana had once told me she wouldn't let some *marakate* into her house, they were so evil. Maybe I hadn't understood very much myself, but I had seen that to the Huichols these gods were not 'mystic' things, they were real. Nor was Tatewarí, Tatutsí or anyone else they worshipped supernatural; they were as utterly natural as people and trees.

In the morning, before we left Unaxa, we all assembled and two men lifted the firewood of both Tatewarí and Tatutsí and carefully revolved it to face west. We were heading home, west to where the sun set and away from where it was born. The *peyoteros* walked to a precipice and together blew their horns over Wirikúta, and then we descended the mountain.

In some Huichol traditions, the *peyoteros* hurry from Wirikúta, fearing their souls might resist leaving this paradise. We did not hurry – it was enough to trust to the protection of the *marakate*. With the experience and strength they'd acquired through years of preparation, they could safely lead the *peyoteros* from their ecstatic union with the gods. This done, the *peyoteros* climbed on board the bus, dusted down their seats, and began the long trip home, the first step towards recommencing their mortal lives.

Despite the fences, despite the cows that polluted the sacred water, despite the ancestral springs being cemented up, the Huichols had once more done what they had to do. I stayed with them another week, joining them on a hunt for Brother Deer, whose head is demanded by Tayaupá and must be brought on the next pilgrimage; and I watched them grind *uxa* and apply the yellow paint across their faces in spirals, stars and waves, as the ancestors had done. For their glorious return to La Ocota, the pilgrims scrubbed their white tunics on river boulders, sorted their hat feathers and re-embroidered designs where necessary, and Matzuhua walked into a dentist and had a bothersome tooth pulled out. The *peyoteros* would go home pristine in heart and body, in a state befitting people who had been with the gods.

My last night here was also my last night on this global odyssey meeting medicine men. I joined the Huichol in taking peyote again and lay on my back, watching the stars as I had for weeks now, and wondered what all that I had seen in Siberut, Tuva, Haiti and Mexico amounted to. These different peoples lived in such different habitats, and yet essentially they all used the same medicine man – the witchdoctor, the shaman.

I allowed myself to drift to wherever the cactus wanted to go. Again I felt the euphoria, the detachment. And as before, there were for me no gods, no visions of black clouds with bleeding sticks. However, some things I did see. From the clouds of my deep subconscious, geometric patterns appeared. There was a profusion of dots, parallel lines and squares, such as I had seen painted in yellow on the faces of the *peyoteros*. I wondered if they had simply been depicting what they'd seen on their own spiritual journeys, their own personal encounters with the sacred. I thought nothing more of the shapes, but just enjoyed them until they evaporated with the dawn.

It was only back in England, just a month ago as I write, that I saw those shapes again. I was flicking through a book on cave paintings and there they were, beside the Stone Age bison, the elk, the gazelle, the other mammals drawn in ochre over the cave chambers. They were the same dots and lines. They stood out to me as boldly as the stencil the artist had also left of his own hand. I wasn't the first with this idea – anthropologists have long speculated that the Palaeolithic animals and shapes were an expression of a shaman's experience of a trance-journey. But with the help of that innocuous-looking cacti I had discovered them for myself, and this was to me a confirmation of where I had gone in my mind: the cave paintings were expressing the infinite, the awe, the ecstatic journey that was normally limited to the classic shaman, but in the cave paintings were there for us, his people, to share.

That I was able to do something of the Stone Age man's journey thousands of years on tells me that we have not advanced far from those caves. We have only covered our desires and needs with a veneer of 'civilization'.

We are fond of calling the beliefs of those outside the mainstream religions as hidebound by fear and superstition. And the world faiths have encouraged this view – it's not long ago that we were depicting the devil as a man with horns, deer feet, a wolf's tail, a figure that resembled the shaman's animal costume. But if you are a hunter–gatherer it makes sense that there are gods, not a God – of course you honour a fire in the desert, the forest spirits in Siberut, a lone tree in Siberia. And if death is never far away – whether you live off the land, or in an Aids-riddled Haitian shanty-town – yes, fear will be well represented in your spiritual world. And are the medicine man's skills becoming less relevant? For the Huichols, the *marakate* are as crucial as ever. They have experience of crossing into other worlds, and handling the alien *mestizo* society that governs them requires similar skills. However, Tuva had shown me that the medicine man lived on, split into a dozen or more roles, even within our urban cultures.

Having a spiritual impulse seems to be a human characteristic. Perhaps it's our insecurity in the face of uncertainty, our inexplicable world. We have felt like children – we have felt the need to call God 'Our Father'. The ultimate aim, though, is to find a pattern in things, and above all, help us come to terms with our greatest trauma, our mortality. If we have a soul, it helps us overcome this trauma; it can survive the decay of our bodies.

Where does that leave those in the western world, the medicine man scattered into a multitude of pensionable occupations? In the 1960s intellectuals argued that religion was dying, that soon we wouldn't need it, because our lives were becoming more and more secure – that it was a case of security versus religion, not security as a result of religion. But for the time being we still have mortality to deal with and, even if we didn't, I suspect that we'd be casting around for something, anything, to believe in – the stars, a flag, an MTV idol.

It seems to me the number of westerners who feel that we've somewhere mislaid The Meaning of Life is increasing, not decreasing. So it looks like indigenous people will face a growing burden. As if the pressure on them isn't enough, more and more people from other cultures will, like Humberto in Wirikúta, rely on them to provide some answers, help them in their search for what we've left behind. But whether we find them in person or on the TV or in our heads, the truth is that we are shaped to a different world from theirs – we can never fathom ancient understandings born of a need to survive within the desert, steppe or forest. What we can do, however, is take comfort in the knowledge that, however we choose to describe the face, or faces, of God, the medicine man is nevertheless living on within our own society, in his different guises. He's still among us, guiding us in a thousand aspects of our twenty-first-century lives.

BIBLIOGRAPHY

Key references or sources for further reading:

GENERAL

Campbell, J., *The Hero with a Thousand Faces*, HarperCollins Publishers, 1988. A thought-inducing exploration of themes surrounding medicine men, and cultural heroes.
Castaneda, C., *The Teachings of Don Juan*, University of California Press, 1968. A tale of time spent with a New World sorcerer – whether or not Don Juan even existed, the book helped stoke awareness of Other Realities as perceived by shamans.
Eliade, M., *Shamanism: archaic techniques of ecstasy*, Penguin, 1989. The classic work.
Halifax, J., *Shaman: the wounded healer*, Crossroad, 1982. Something of a picture-book, but interesting cross-cultural references which build to a complete picture.
Nicholson, S., (ed.), *Shamanism: an expanded view of reality*. The Theosophical Publishing House, 1987. A sound overview, includes contributions by Hoppál, Eliade and Harner.
Vitebsky, P., *The Shaman*, Duncan Baird Publishers, 1995. An excellent little guide to this misunderstood character worldwide by a leading authority.

INDONESIA/SIBERUT

Schefold, R., *Function Follows Form: on the ritual efficacy of plants and textiles in Indonesia*, Indonesia Circle No 66, 1995. The properties, magical or otherwise, attributed to objects by the Mentawai.
Schefold, R., *The Siberut Project*, Survival International 5 (1) 4–12, 1980. The future of Siberut discussed realistically and sensitively.
Schefold, R., Schoorl, J.W. and Tennekes, J., (eds.), *Man, Meaning and History*, Verhand-elingen, 1980. Essays, notably by foremost Mentawai anthropologist Schefold, whose studies were based on the Sakkudei group.
Avé, W. and Satyawan, S., *Medicinal Plants of Siberut*, WWF International, 1990. Outlines the two Mentawai types of illness and medicine: the natural and supernatural.

SIBERIA/TUVA

Diószegi, V. and Hoppál, M., (eds.), *Folk Beliefs and Shamanistic Traditions in Siberia*, Akadémiai Kiadó, Budapest 1996. Very useful is the contribution of Vajnstejn, who discusses drum 'enlivening' and helped me understand the 'neo-shamans' of modern-day Tuva, who lack the soul-flight or orientation that essentially defines the shaman.

Hutton, R., *The Shamans of Siberia*, The Isle of Avalon Press, 1993. Concise general treatment, and easier to obtain than other sources.
Kenin-Lopsan, Mongush B., *Shamanic Songs and Myths of Tuva*, Akadémiai Kiadó, Budapest, 1997. A result of his quest to preserve fading traditions of Tuvan shamanism.
Van Alphen, J., (ed.), *Spellbound by the Shaman: shamanism in Tuva*, Etnografisch Museum, Antwerp, 1997. Thorough account for the general reader.

HAITI

Deren, M., *Divine Horsemen: the living gods of Haiti*, McPherson and Co, 1953. Essential reading, though given Vodou's amoebic nature, already seems a little archaic.
Doggett, S. and Gordon, L., *Dominican Republic and Haiti*, Lonely Planet Publications, 1999. Gordon's section is a much-needed, no-nonsense, thorough guide to Haiti.
Galembo, P., *Vodou: visions and voices of Haiti*, Ten Speed Press, 1998. Handsome photographic record, the static portraits and clear text cutting to the truth of the subject.
Hurbon, L., *Voodoo: truth and fantasy*, Thames and Hudson, 1995. Handy, simpli-fied round-up of Vodou past and present.
Rigaud, M., *Secrets of Voodoo*, City Lights Books, San Francisco, 1969. First published in 1953, but a solid, straight-forward account.

MEXICO

Benítez, F., *In the Magic Land of the Peyote*, University of Texas Press, 1975. By one of the few outsiders to access Huichol rituals.
Lumholtz, C., *Symbolism of the Huichol Indians: memoirs of the American Museum of Natural History*, vol. III, (1) 1–223, 1900. By the first anthropologist to document Huichols, now something of an historical document.
Myerhoff, B.G., *Peyote Hunt: the sacred journey of the Huichol Indians*, Cornell University Press, 1974. Eye-witness docu-mentation of one pilgrimage.
Schaefer, S. B. and Furst, P.T., (eds.), *People of the Peyote*, University of New Mexico Press, 1996. Essential reading for anyone interested in more than the superficial.
Valadez, S., *Huichol Indian Sacred Rituals*, Dharma Enterprises, 1992. The Huichol world-view explained through text, and also the vivid yarn paintings of Mariano Valadez.
Zingg, R.M., *The Huichols, Primitive Artists*, G.E. Stechert, 1938. One of the other rare, authoritative early accounts.

INDEX